Handbook of
road safety research

Geoffrey Grime O.B.E., D.Sc., C.I.Mech. E.

Butterworths
London Boston Durban Singapore Sydney Toronto Wellington

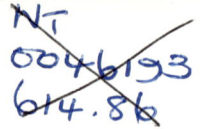

All rights reserved. No part of this publication may be reproduced or transmitted in any form or by any means, including photocopying and recording, without the written permission of the copyright holder, application for which should be addressed to the Publishers. Such written permission must also be obtained before any part of this publication is stored in a retrieval system of any nature.

This book is sold subject to the Standard Conditions of Sale of Net Books and may not be resold in the UK below the net price given by the Publishers in their current price list.

First published 1987

© Butterworth & Co (Publishers) Ltd 1987

British Library Cataloguing in Publication Data

Grime, G.
   Handbook of road safety research.
   1. Traffic accidents
   I. Title
   363.1'251   HE5614

ISBN 0-408-02780-0

Library of Congress Cataloging-in-Publication Data

Grime, G. (Geoffrey)
   Handbook of road safety research.

   Bibliography: p.
   Includes index.
   1. Traffic accidents–Great Britain.   2. Traffic safety–Great Britain.   I. Title.
   HE5614.5.G7G77   1987   363.1'25'0941   86-26427
   ISBN 0-408-02780-0

Photoset by Butterworths Litho Preparation Department
Printed and bound by Robert Hartnoll Ltd, Bodmin, Cornwall

Foreword

It is given to few of us to leave a record of our life's work which is likely to prove of permanent public value and importance, but in writing this book, Dr Grime has, without doubt, achieved this rare distinction. The pursuit of safety on our roads has been his preoccupation for virtually the whole of his long working life, whilst his professional role at the heart of the Road Safety Division of the Road Research Laboratory*, for a great part of that time in a period when the laboratory rightly became the most respected organisation of its kind in the world, has given him access to knowledge and insights which are unlikely to be surpassed by any other living person.

Road safety is understandably an emotive subject. It is therefore all the more important that all of us, whether professionally involved or not, should be able to stand back and look at the facts calmly and dispassionately, and make judgements and decisions which will truly bring us closer to the objective we all desire, which is that our roads should be made safer for everyone who uses them.

William Rees Jeffreys, who founded the Road Fund that bears his name, wrote 'Through many disappointments and a few achievements I have been sustained by a faith that the building and maintenance of roads – safe, adequate and pleasant – on sound financial bases is one of the surest ways to raise the standard of living, to advance civilisation and to promote the well-being of the people'. The Trustees of the Fund were therefore happy to support the publication of Dr Grime's work, which they believe will become an indispensable aid to the cause of road safety. They hope it will be studied by all those responsible for building and maintaining our roads and organising the traffic on them, by the designers of the vehicles which use them, the psychologists and doctors who have to deal with human behaviour on our roads and its consequences, the police and those responsible for making and enforcing traffic regulations, and by all those who seek to represent the public interest politically at all levels from parish to parliament.

But you, Reader, whoever you may be, you the road user, whose hand is in the child's or on the steering wheel, it is you to whom the book is ultimately addressed, because it is only by your own actions and those who represent you that our roads can be made safer. And if you believe that the truth is precious, then you will read the work of one who has lived his professional life in accordance with this precept, in an area that affects us all, with the respect and attention it commands.

K. Summerfield MSc, FICE
Chairman of Trustees, Rees Jeffreys Road Fund

* Now the Transport and Road Research Laboratory

Preface

This book is intended to be a reference manual for all whose work brings them into contact with the consequences of road accidents and who need to know of any research conclusions which may be relevant to the accidents they are concerned with. It is often impossible to obtain this information in the time available since the relevant material may be contained in research papers or books not readily available. An additional difficulty is that sometimes all aspects of a subject are presented, without reaching any definite conclusions. The results presented here are confined to those established by reputable research, and, as far as possible, controversial matter has been omitted. In many cases no evidence is given to support statements made, but in others references are supplied for the reader who wishes to pursue the subject in detail. A considerable amount of background material has been included where it was felt to be useful in providing an overall view of a subject. This book provides a quick summary of information required by an accident investigator, but its limitations should be considered. None of the subjects dealt with can be fully discussed, so if the circumstances of an accident cause controversy, as they may for example in court cases, the appropriate references should be consulted.

When investigating an accident or series of accidents, it is always important to examine the influence of the road, the vehicle and the road user, and to realise how they interact. This interaction is always present, even when one factor appears to predominate. Individual chapters are devoted to each of these three factors, and because interaction is so important it is discussed in Chapter 2.

In those parts of the book which discuss measures to increase safety, remember that a balance usually has to be struck between the probable savings and some opposing factor, generally directly or indirectly arising from cost, but which may be inconvenience or some other aspect of acceptability.

The contents of this book are mainly derived from research in Britain so the work by the Transport and Road Research Laboratory is mentioned a great deal in the text. Many valuable results of early research at the Laboratory were described in 'Research on Road Safety', published by HMSO in 1963, and few of the findings given in that study now need to be revised, but the results of much new work are now available in separate papers from the Laboratory. However, in a few cases it has been necessary to quote the early work as the most useful or only available reference.

References are given at the end of each chapter, and in some cases the same reference may be quoted at the end of more than one chapter. Since it has obviously been impossible to give references for all data, apologies are tendered in advance to authors who consider that their work should also have been mentioned. Publications quoted from the Transport and Road Research Laboratory are of three kinds, first, laboratory or supplementary reports (LRs or SRs), which are complete reports of investigations; second, digests, which give fairly complete summaries of these reports, and third, leaflets (LFs) usually giving the main conclusions of LRs or SRs, and sometimes including results not published elsewhere.

Chapter 1 outlines the main features of the road accident situation in Great Britain after a short description of the methods employed by the police in collecting the national accident statistics.

Chapter 2 draws attention to the importance of the part played in accidents by interaction between the vehicle, the road user and the road environment. Chapter 3 deals with road users as pedestrians, cyclists, motorcyclists or drivers. Their characteristics and capabilities and their involvement in accidents are described and discussed. Chapter 4 outlines the main features of roads which influence the risk of accidents, and is intended to assist accident investigators to give proper weight to the various components of the road environment.

Chapter 5 deals with matters which influence the course of the events preceding an accident, such as visibility by day and night, and the stability of vehicles at different speeds on dry and wet roads.

Secondary safety, that is, safety determined by factors which operate during and after the first contacts or impacts have occurred, is considered in Chapter 6. The main part of the chapter describes the characteristics of the most important types of car collision and the resulting damage, and this is followed by a brief consideration of motorcycle and commercial vehicle accidents.

The mechanisms of injury to the different classes of road user and the various kinds of protective device, of which the best known is the seat belt, are described in Chapter 7.

Chapter 8 lists the potential savings in accidents by the application of safety measures in Great Britain and Chapter 9 contains general advice and remarks on accident investigation. Two appendices on nomenclature and conversion tables and measurement and calculations complete the text.

Acknowledgements

This book is published with the financial support of the Rees Jeffreys Road Fund, a charitable body founded by the late W. Rees Jeffreys. The fund is dedicated to the general improvement of the public highways and surrounding lands and has contributed generously to research into road safety and to the wider understanding of the problems of road safety by the designer and manufacturer of road vehicles, the road engineer and the town planner.

I am indebted to Miss Barbara Sabey of the Transport and Road Research Laboratory and to Professor Allsop of the Transport Studies Group of University College London for invaluable assistance and criticism at all times during the writing of the book, and for many suggested references; to Ian Neilson and his staff at the Laboratory for help with those parts dealing with the vehicle; and to the Transport and Road Research Laboratory for financial assistance in the early stages.

Any views expressed in the book are those of the author.

I also have to thank the photographic division of the Laboratory for photographs and the Director of the Transport and Road Research Laboratory for permission to reproduce the photographs and Britax Excelsior Ltd for permission to reproduce Figures 7.1, 7.3 and 7.4.

Finally, I am much indebted to Mrs Saskia Fry of the Transport Studies Group for a great deal of work in typing the manuscript and uncomplainingly dealing with many alterations.

G.G.

Contents

Chapter 1 The main features of the road accident situation in Great Britain   1

Chapter 2 The interacting roles of road environment, vehicle and road user in accidents   14

Chapter 3 The road user   16

Chapter 4 Roads – features which may be related to accidents   31

Chapter 5 Movements of vehicles and road users before accidents   52

Chapter 6 What happens to vehicles during and after accidents   84

Chapter 7 Injuries to road users   120

Chapter 8 The potential for savings in accidents involving injury   134

Chapter 9 General remarks on accident investigation   136

Appendix 1 Nomenclature and conversion table   140

Appendix 2 Measurements and calculations   141

Index   145

Chapter 1
The main features of the road accident situation in Great Britain

In 1984, 5599 road users were killed, 73 059 were seriously injured, and 245 656 slightly injured. This chapter looks at the main features of accidents which contribute to the overall total.

At the outset it is necessary to understand what is recorded in the national accident statistics. These statistics are collected and recorded by the police and transmitted on standardised forms to the Department of Transport, who then analyse them in various ways, some of which are published annually by Her Majesty's Stationery Office (HMSO) in 'Road Accidents Great Britain. Recorded accidents consist of those in which someone was injured and which were reported to the police. By no means all of these accidents are investigated on site by the police. The police are not notified of all injury accidents. Hobbs, Grattan and Hobbs (1979) found that injuries to car occupants were likely to be under-reported by about 14 per cent, those to pedestrians by about 27 per cent, and those to pedal cyclists by about 60 per cent. Bull and Roberts (1972) found fewer instances of under-reporting in serious accidents, the deficits being least for pedestrians and drivers of cars and commercial vehicles. Deaths are fully reported.

Injuries are classified according to the following criteria:

(1) *Slight injury*. An injury of a minor character such as a sprain, bruise or a cut or laceration not judged to be severe.
(2) *Serious injury*. An injury for which a person is detained in hospital as an in-patient, or any of the following injuries regardless of whether he is detained in hospital: fractures, concussion, internal injuries, crushings, severe cuts and lacerations, severe general shock requiring medical treatment.
(3) *Death*. Death within 30 days.

Although not in general use for compiling national statistics, an alternative scale for classifying injury is used for research purposes, in which injuries are usually divided into seven levels. This is the Abbreviated Injury Scale (AIS scale) (Joint Committee on Injury Scaling, 1975 and 1980 revision) as follows:

   AIS 0: No injury
   AIS 1: Minor
   AIS 2: Moderate
   AIS 3: Severe, not life threatening

AIS 4: Serious, life threatening
AIS 5: Critical, survival uncertain
AIS 6: Death

Details of injuries falling into these categories for the different regions of the body are given in the reference paper. Alterations are made to these scales from time to time (Committee on Injury Scaling, 1980).

Since injury accidents are the only ones which are nationally recorded and analysed, these statistics underestimate the true numbers of accidents, because accidents which do not result in injury are not included (although a small proportion of these accidents are reported to the police). Intuitively it might be thought that all damage-only accidents were so trivial and occurred at such a low speed that they were not worth considering. That this is not so is perhaps best illustrated by an example.

Consider what happens when a car carrying a driver alone strikes a rigid wall head-on at a speed of, say 25 mile/h (40 km/h). Not every such accident results in injury. At any particular impact speed there is a probability of being uninjured, slightly injured, seriously injured or killed; and, of course, the probabilities of injury increase with impact speed and those of being uninjured decrease. When no injury results such accidents are not included in the national statistics, although other accidents at the same speed but in which the driver is injured are included. In similar circumstances, if there are two or more people in the car, the chances of an injury accident are, of course, greater than if there is only one occupant. In general, the greater the number of people involved in an accident of a given severity (in this case severity is measured by speed of impact with a wall), the greater the chance of it being an injury accident, and therefore of being included in the national statistics. Thus head-on collisions between cars are more likely to be recorded than accidents in which only one car is involved. Moreover, if the accident is of a kind in which the risk of injury is low, such as a rear-end collision between cars, the proportion of such accidents which appears in the national statistics is lower than for high risk accidents such as head-on collisions, or collisions with heavy commercial vehicles; and all types of accident in built-up areas where speeds are low are likely to have a lower proportion of injury accidents than those in rural areas, where speeds are higher.

These features of the national statistics should be remembered when making use of the accident data given in this book. The subject is discussed at greater length in Chapter 8.

1.1 International comparisons

Table 1.1 compares the road fatalities in Great Britain with those in seven other countries over the year 1983 and it will be seen that, whether judged by deaths per unit of population or by deaths per vehicle, Britain compares favourably with almost all others except Sweden.

Misleading conclusions may be drawn if only one of the rates, deaths per vehicle, or deaths per unit of population, is considered. For example, on the basis of deaths per 100 000 population both the Irish Republic and Spain have lower figures than the US, while on the basis of deaths per vehicle, the reverse is true. It was shown some years ago (Research on

Road Safety, 1963) that these contradictions arise because those countries with large numbers of vehicles per unit of population usually have large numbers of deaths per unit of population but small numbers of deaths per vehicle, perhaps because, as vehicles become more numerous, road users become more careful and road conscious. By comparing numbers of deaths from 1930 to 1950 in 18 countries, it was shown that there was an approximate relationship between deaths per annum per 100 000 population, D/p, and N/p the number of vehicles per 1000 population, represented mathematically by $D/p = 0.0003(N/p)^{1/3}$. Alternatively, the number of deaths per annum $D = 0.0003(NP^2)^{1/3}$. In later work, covering 70 countries, from 1960 to 1967, the same relationship was found to hold (Smeed, 1972).

Table 1.1 International road deaths and death rates (1983)

Country	Number of road deaths	Motor vehicles per 100 people	Road deaths per 100 000 people	Road deaths per 10 000 motor vehicles	Car user deaths per 100 million car km	Pedestrian deaths per 100 000 people
United Kingdom	5618	36[6]	10.0	2.7	1.0*	3.5
Federal Republic of Germany	11 732	46[6]	19.0	4.1	2.0	4.0
France	12 728	48[1]	23.4	5.3[1]	3.0	3.8
Irish Republic	535	24[6]	15.9	6.5	1.7[2]	5.2
Italy	8245[3]	43[1]	14.4	3.2[3]	1.7[3]	2.9[3]
Spain	6066	29[4]	16.0	5.2	5.9	3.7
Sweden	779	39[5]	9.4	2.3[4]	1.0	1.9
United States of America	42 584	71[6]	18.2	2.7[3]	1.2	3.0

* Great Britain only
[1] 1981; [2] 1980; [3] 1982; [4] Vehicle figures exclude mopeds; [5] Mopeds in use only; [6] 1983.

Figure 1.1 shows the first formula in graphical form, and we may regard points below the line as indicating better results in road safety than those above the line. However, the most important point to remember is that it may be misleading to quote just one of the two rates given in columns 5 and 6 of Table 1.1 as proof of the superiority of road safety measures in one country compared with those of another.

1.2 The trend in casualties in Great Britain over the years 1930 to 1984

The trends in casualties in Great Britain over the years 1930 to 1984 are graphed in Figure 1.2 together with corresponding figures for motor vehicles registered and traffic flow. A remarkable feature of these figures is that while up to the mid 1960s injuries have increased roughly in line with numbers of registered vehicles, the numbers of road deaths are now no higher than they were in the 1930s.

In the following figures and tables the main features of the accident situation will usually be given for the year 1984, which is the latest for which detailed data are available (Road Accidents Great Britain, 1984).

4 The main features of the road accident situation in Great Britain

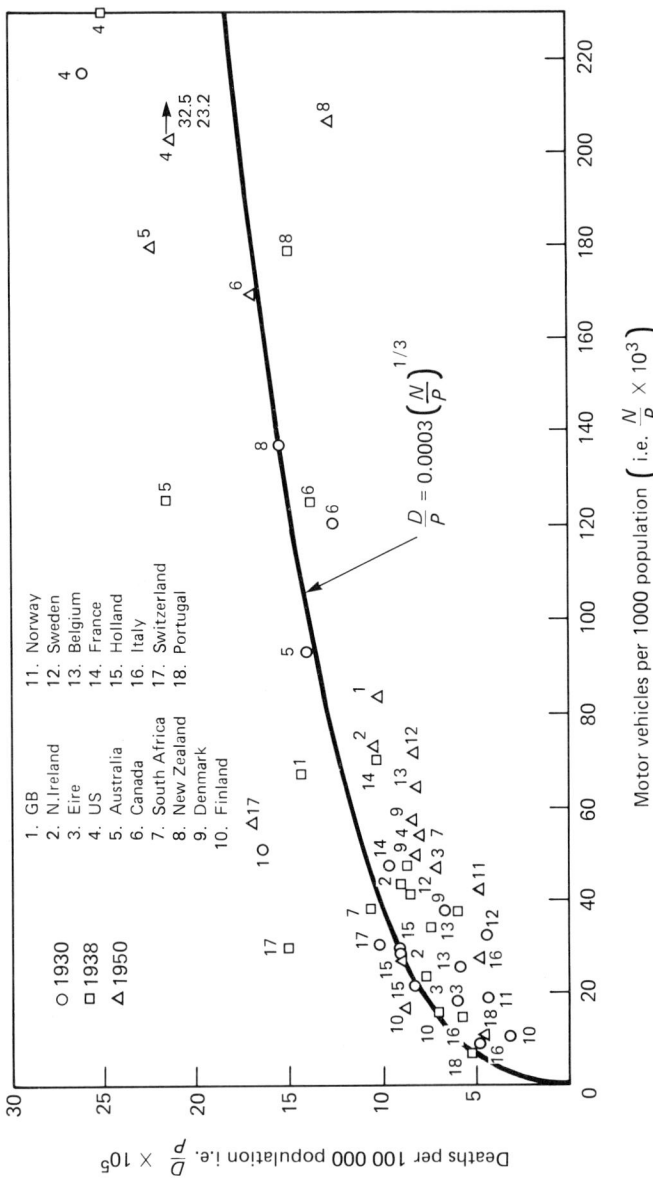

Figure 1.1 Relation between number of deaths per 100 000 population and number of registered vehicles per 1000 population

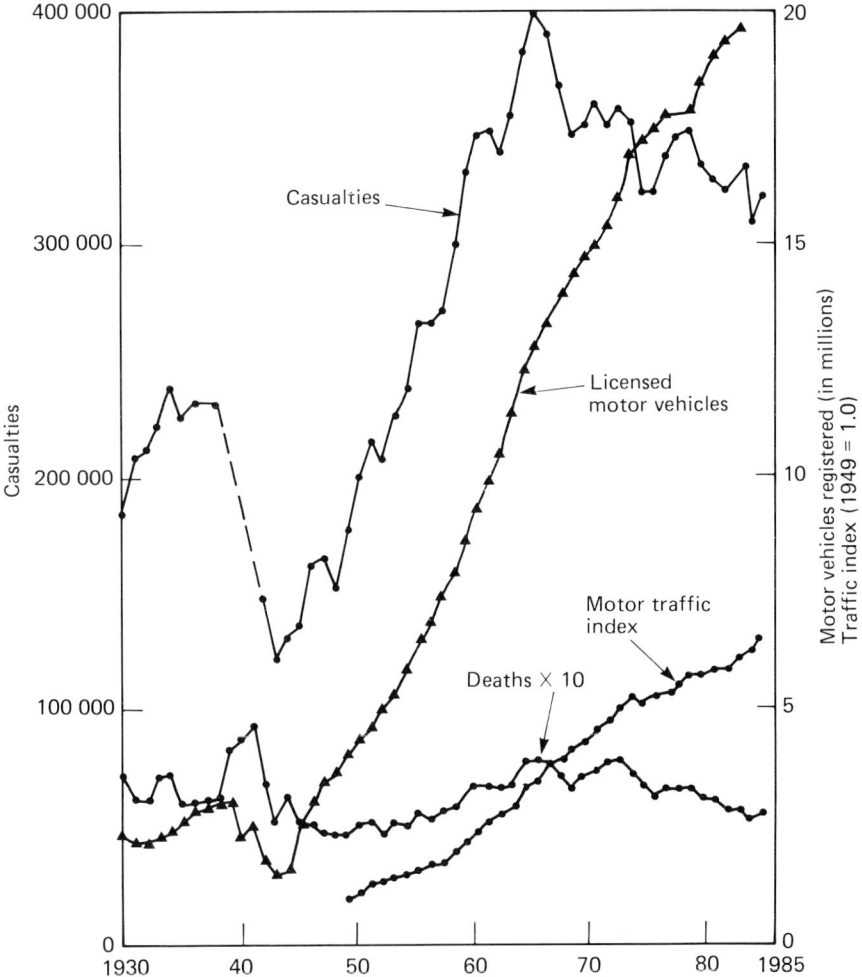

Figure 1.2 Licensed vehicles, motor traffic and casualties

Some general statistics

Although most of the accident data gathered from the national statistics are contained in the detailed tables and diagrams which follow, it is useful to outline some of the more important features of the accident situation:

- three-quarters of accidents are in urban areas
- one-half killed in urban areas are pedestrians;
- two-thirds of urban accidents are at junctions;
- nearly one-third of urban accidents involve a pedestrian and only one vehicle;
- three-fifths killed in rural areas are car occupants;
- one-third of rural accidents involve only one vehicle (only 6 per cent involve more than two vehicles);

6   The main features of the road accident situation in Great Britain

- in about one-half of rural single vehicle accidents overturning occurs;
- one-fifth of all casualties are pedestrians, one-quarter cyclists, and two-fifths car occupants;
- one-third of accidents occur in darkness;
- one-third of accidents occur on wet roads.

Types of accident

Table 1.2 gives the numbers of injury accidents to occupants and riders of vehicles in rural and urban areas by type of accident. Table 1.3 describes the relative involvement of different types of vehicle in these accidents. Over 90 per cent of all accidents to pedestrians occurred in built-up areas; most occurred near junctions, and in over 60 per cent of all such accidents the striking vehicle was a car.

Table 1.2 Numbers of injury accidents of different types to cars, commercial vehicles and two-wheel motor vehicles (MV) in rural and urban areas (1982)

Type of accident	Rural areas			Urban areas		
	Cars	Commercial vehicles	Two-wheel MV	Cars	Commercial vehicles	Two-wheel MV
Single vehicle	16 317	1793	5235	51 546	5535	14 336
Head-on collision*	7779	1772	1801	21 377	2601	8664
Intersection*	12 169	2551	4278	69 417	9465	30 650
Rear end*	6410	1972	1794	22 464	3905	7990

* Two vehicle accidents only

The accident pattern for pedal cyclists is similar. About 90 per cent occur in built-up areas and about two-thirds at or near junctions. Only about 5 per cent involved no other vehicle.

Casualty rates by age and sex

Figure 1.3 shows how casualties and fatalities vary with age and sex; female casualties vary in the same way as those for males but are always lower. Both the casualties and fatalities have a pronounced peak at about 20 years of age, but, while casualties decrease continuously with age from this peak, the fatalities rise after the age of 50 years. It should be noted that the age intervals are not equal so that the values shown for 17 to 19 are too low compared with those for other age intervals.

Casualties in built-up and non-built-up areas

Table 1.4 lists the casualties for the different classes of road user, separately for built-up and non-built-up areas, that is, for areas with 30 or 40 mile/h (48–64 km/h) speed limits, and for those with higher speed limits. Children under 15 years of age are listed separately from adults. The table shows the continuing dominant contribution of the built-up areas to the toll

Table 1.3 Combinations of vehicles involved in accidents and related user casualties (1984)

Accidents and casualties (First vehicle)	Single vehicle		Two vehicle accidents – second vehicle			Goods vehicle		All accidents with three or more vehicles
	No pedestrian	With pedestrian	Pedal cycle	Two-wheeled motor vehicle	Car	Not over 1.5 tons u.w.	Over 1.5 tons u.w.	
Pedal cycle								
Accidents involving User casualties[1]	769	35	94	302	4545	358	298	329
Pedestrians hit by cycles – casualties[1]	–	231	–	2	12	1	–	–
Two-wheeled motor vehicle								
Accidents involving User casualties[1]	4271	283	159	406	11259	117	445	1654
Pedestrians hit by TWMV – casualties[1]	–	1522	2	3	99	7	7	12
Car								
Accidents involving User casualties[1]	9661	73	28	318	11087	947	1715	4515
Pedestrians hit by cars – casualties[1]	–	13 955	14	24	579	83	63	158
Goods vehicle (not over 1.5 tons u.w.)								
Accidents involving User casualties[1]	537	3	4	16	480	106	146	222
Pedestrians hit by LGV – casualties[1]	–	1074	1	1	39	16	7	14
Goods vehicle (over 1.5 tons u.w.)								
Accidents involving User casualties[1]	286	4	2	4	108	22	165	630
Pedestrians hit by HGV – casualties[1]	–	445	1	–	14	2	8	15

[1] All user and pedestrian casualties are fatal and serious.
[2] Involving one or more vehicles of first type.

8 The main features of the road accident situation in Great Britain

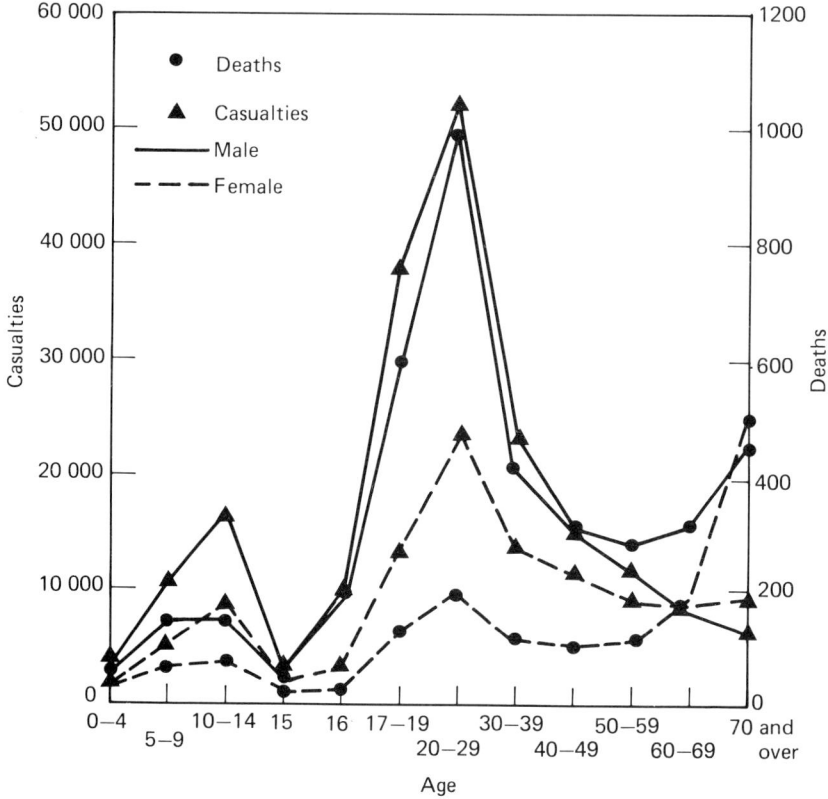

Figure 1.3 Casualties and fatalities for 1983 by age and sex

Table 1.4 Casualties by class of road user, type of area and severity (1984)

Class of road user		Casualties in built-up areas			Casualties in non-built-up areas		
		Killed	Seriously injured	All severities	Killed	Seriously injured	All severities
Pedestrian	Adults	1222	10061	35398	291	900	2322
	Children	266*	6179	23897	67	311	771
Pedal cycle	Adults	133	3242	17579	115	811	2451
	Children	55	1857	9615	41	316	929
Two-wheeled motor vehicle	Riders	459	12549	45994	392	4704	11907
	Passengers	64	1093	3975	52	696	1944
Car	Drivers	343	6482	47174	894	8810	33752
	Passengers	288	4984	34973	654	6541	27720
Public service vehicle	Drivers	1	33	310	3	22	150
	Passengers	27	711	9077	6	126	936
Goods vehicle (not over 1.5 tons u.w.)	Drivers	16	361	2496	48	517	2174
	Passengers	12	284	1518	35	287	1244
Goods vehicle (over 1.5 tons u.w.)	Drivers	9	141	795	57	453	1786
	Passengers	5	49	223	4	76	354

* Under 15 years of age

The trend in casualties in Great Britain over the years 1930 to 1984   9

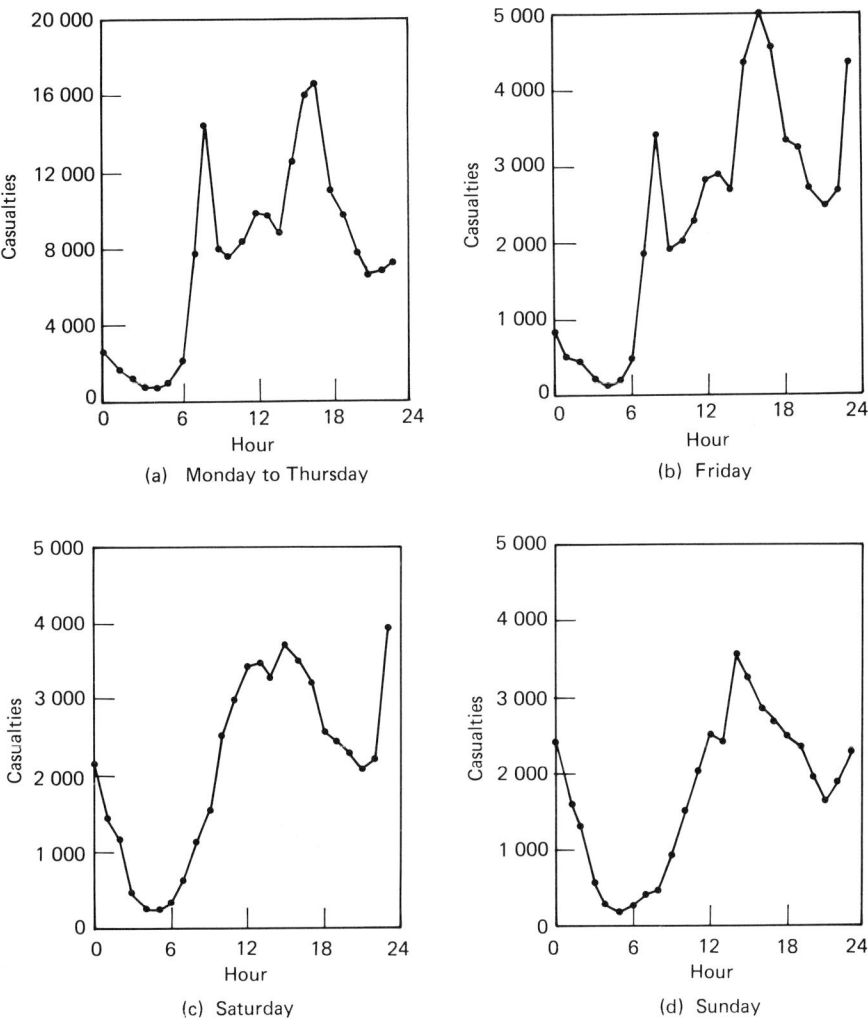

Figure 1.4 Casualties by hour of day and day of week (in 1984)

of deaths and injuries and the very high figures for deaths and injuries to motorcyclists, particularly in built-up areas.

Location of accidents

The places where accidents occur are given in Table 1.5. About 50 per cent occur on A-roads, both in built-up and non-built-up areas, and, in built-up areas, almost two-thirds take place at junctions.

Temporal variations in casualties

Figure 1.4 shows the temporal variations in all casualties in graphical form, the most notable feature being the late evening peaks on Friday, Saturday

Table 1.5 Accidents by type of area and junction detail (1984)

	Roundabout	T- or staggered junction	Y	Crossroads	Multiple junction	Other junction	Using private drive or entrance	All known junctions	Not at or within 20 m of junction
Built-up areas									
Fatal	54	1044	53	311	39	56	43	1600	1197
Serious	1450	17 068	858	5361	578	1720	774	27 809	16 020
All severities	9113	77 103	4027	27 638	2985	8297	3582	132 745	62 868
Non-built-up areas									
Fatal	16	286	78	120	10	61	22	593	1748
Serious	433	2652	626	923	67	907	154	5762	12 456
All severities	2477	8536	2121	2872	231	2906	571	19 714	37 848

Table 1.6 Casualties per hour by class of road user, day of week and time of day (1984)

Time	Pedestrians		Pedal cyclists		Two-wheel MV		Car users	
	(1)*	(2)	(1)	(2)	(1)	(2)	(1)	(2)
00.00–07.00	108	205	73	31	223	200	967	1310
07.00–09.00	2460	79	2051	113	3416	218	4862	813
09.00–12.00	2046	677	904	375	1470	698	4152	1896
12.00–14.00	2990	1186	1252	558	2529	1189	4529	2623
14.00–17.00	4482	1236	1956	595	2912	1364	5668	3178
17.00–19.00	4128	900	2589	446	4052	1167	6133	2768
19.00–22.00	1926	629	1014	238	2536	882	4799	2336
22.00–24.00	1562	843	377	112	2166	897	5925	3142

* (1) = weekdays; (2) = Saturdays and Sundays

and Sunday throughout the year. Table 1.6 gives similar information for all casualties to the different classes of road user.

Road condition and light

Table 1.7 gives figures showing the effect of road condition and light on accidents. The combination of wet roads and darkness is particularly

Table 1.7 Effect of road condition and light on accidents (1984)

Area	Daylight				Darkness			
	Dry	Wet or flood	Snow or ice	Fog	Dry	Wet or flood	Snow or ice	Fog
Built-up areas								
Fatal	1385	162	1	9	955	261	9	9
Serious	24 891	3285	89	104	11 692	3393	91	123
Slight	92 869	13 998	342	429	29 871	9697	312	403
Non-built-up areas								
Fatal	1150	173	5	14	797	163	4	23
Serious	9924	1620	88	169	5015	1124	56	171
Slight	21 004	3979	205	388	8381	2411	168	317

noticeable in increasing the number of fatal accidents and this is most marked in built-up areas. Snow and ice are factors in only a small proportion of accidents.

The vehicles involved in accidents

The numbers of different types of vehicle involved in accidents are given in Table 1.8 according to state of road surface and whether skidding occurred. Note that, although skidding is mainly a wet weather problem, skidding can also occur on dry roads; about two-thirds of accidents involve cars.

Table 1.8 Vehicles involved in accidents and the incidence of skidding (1984)

Vehicles	Road surface conditions						All conditions	
	Dry		Wet or flood		Snow and ice			
	Skidded	All	Skidded	All	Skidded	All	Skidded	All
Pedal cycles	516	24 175	301	7736	79	299	896	32 210
Two-wheel MV	6198	46 161	5048	18 100	707	1078	11 953	65 339
Cars	17 987	171 297	17 315	102 153	3656	6499	38 958	279 949
Buses and coaches	288	9522	278	3066	78	212	644	12 800
Goods vehicles								
Not over 1.5 tons u.w.	1191	12 900	1253	7471	270	540	2714	20 911
Over 1.5 tons u.w.	1111	8072	1217	5694	163	431	2491	14 197

Vehicle involvement rates in accidents

The involvement rates in terms of accidents per 100 million vehicle kilometres are tabulated in Table 1.9. On a mileage basis both motorcycles and pedal cycles have high rates compared with cars, but it seems likely that, on the basis of accidents per annum, the rates for pedal cycles would look more favourable, since pedal cyclists travel fewer miles per annum than cars; but the available data do not enable this comparison to be made.

Table 1.9 Vehicle involvement rates in different types of accident (1984) (Rate per 100 million vehicle kilometres)

	Pedal cycle	Two-wheel MV	Car	Bus or coach	Goods vehicle	
					Not over 1.5 tons u.w.	Over 1.5 tons u.w.
Built-up areas						
Fatal	5.3	17.9	2.3	7.7	2.1	5.4
Fatal or serious	148	399	42	92	33	36
All severities	737	1334	201	604	142	124
Non-built-up areas						
Fatal	15.0	23.4	2.8	7.2	2.1	4.9
Fatal or serious	121	268	24	37	18	25
All severities	306	594	71	109	55	63
Motorways						
Fatal	–	7.5	0.9	2.6	0.7	1.7
Fatal or serious	–	66	6.0	12.2	5.8	7.1
All severities	–	193	25	34	23	22

Table 1.10 Trends in deaths (1974–1984)

Road users	1974	1975	1976	1977	1978	1979	1980	1981	1982	1983	1984
Pedestrians	2642	2344	2335	2313	2427	2118	1941	1874	1869	1914	1868
Pedal cyclists	282	278	300	301	316	320	302	310	294	323	345
Motorcyclists											
riders	704	724	873	1031	1006	1027	1018	983	929	842	849
passengers	93	114	117	151	157	133	145	148	161	121	118
Car											
drivers	1553	1417	1441	1429	1525	1479	1339	1346	1472	1198	1237
passengers	1156	1027	1079	1012	1044	950	939	941	971	821	942
Bus and coach											
drivers	5	10	10	8	8	3	2	4	5	3	4
passengers	64	105	59	56	52	31	27	16	28	35	33
Goods vehicles not over 1.5 tons u.w.											
drivers	123	128	118	101	101	108	97	87	70	63	64
passengers	88	60	92	51	68	50	43	54	45	39	47
Goods vehicles over 1.5 tons u.w.											
drivers	94	96	79	83	78	85	57	50	58	44	66
passengers	31	27	19	26	14	23	13	12	9	15	9

Trends in deaths

Trends in deaths are given in Table 1.10 for the different classes of road user for the period 1974 to 1984.

Useful and detailed analyses of the accident data year by year are published annually by HMSO in 'Road Accidents Great Britain'.

References

BULL, J. P. and ROBERTS, B. J. (1972) 'Road accident statistics: a comparison of police and hospital information'. *Accid. Anal. and Prev.*, **5**, 45–53

COMMITTEE ON INJURY SCALING (1980) The Abbreviated Injury Scale 1980 revision. American Association for Automotive Medicine, Morton Grove 11, 60053, USA

JOINT COMMITTEE ON INJURY SCALING OF SOCIETY OF AUTOMOTIVE ENGINEERS, AMERICAN MEDICAL ASSOCIATION AND THE AMERICAN ASSOCIATION FOR AUTOMOTIVE MEDICINE (1975) The Abbreviated Injury Scale 1975 version. *Proc. 19th Conf. of the AAM*, San Diego, California 1975

HOBBS, V. A., GRATTAN, E. and HOBBS, J. A. (1979) Classification of injury severity by length of stay in hospital. *Transport and Road Research Laboratory Report* LR 871

RESEARCH ON ROAD SAFETY (1963) HMSO, London, Chapter 2

ROAD ACCIDENTS GREAT BRITAIN (1984). HMSO London

SMEED, R. J. (1972) The usefulness of formulae in traffic engineering and road safety. *Accid. Anal. and Prev.*, **4**, 303–312

Chapter 2

The interacting roles of road environment, vehicle and road user in accidents

The background and training of an accident investigator sometimes lead him to look for defects only in his own field of expertise, so he may neglect other important factors in accidents. Thus the police officer may tend to blame the road user, the road engineer to find defects in the road, and the vehicle engineer to find them in the vehicle. However, in most accidents many factors operate, which may be a combination of human errors and failings, poor road design or adverse weather conditions, and vehicle defects. It may therefore be wrong to concentrate on the contribution of only one of these factors and neglect the possible interaction of two or more factors. There is sometimes a temptation to do this, because it can be seen that, if one of them had been absent, the accident would not have happened.

Attempts have been made to estimate the percentages of road accidents which can be attributed to defects in or defective performance of the road environment, the vehicle, or the road user, and to study their interaction. The most thorough work on this subject is probably by the Transport and Road Research Laboratory (Sabey and Staughton, 1975), in which a four year 'on-the-spot' investigation was conducted in the area of South-East Berkshire between 1970 and 1974. During this period the accident investigation team attended 2130 accidents, representing 60 per cent of all injury accidents reported to the police, and 20 per cent of the reported damage accidents. Evidence was obtained 'by observations of roads, vehicles and road users and of weather conditions, by interview, and by assessing errors made by the road users, the part played by defects in vehicles, and by adverse features of the environment. The three types of evidence were in decreasing order of reliability, and it was particularly difficult to assess the relative importance of errors by road users compared with defective features of vehicle and road, since the answers depended upon opinions formed by members of the research team. Even so, the results of the study can be taken as giving useful indications of the relative importance of the three factors and of their interactions. The methods used were described by Staughton and Storie (TRL Report LR 762, 1977).

The results were shown in a diagram, of which Figure 2.1 is a shortened form. Human factors were judged to have been present in about 95 per cent of the accidents and to have been the sole contributor in about 65 per cent. The road environment was present as a factor in about 28 per cent, and the vehicle in about 9 per cent. In a small number of accidents, all three factors were present. Slightly different but generally similar results were recorded in a later but smaller investigation by the same team in the same area (Sabey, 1983). They are shown in parentheses in Figure 2.1.

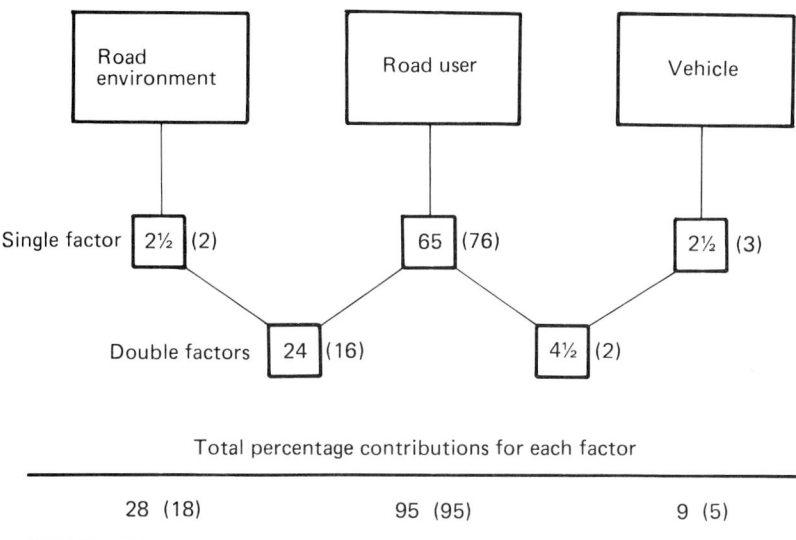

Figure 2.1 Percentage contributions to road accidents

Human factors were judged to be present in about 95 per cent of the accidents. This is perhaps not surprising since all accidents involve road users and it is almost always possible to think of some action which could have been taken by a road user to avoid the accident. However, when considering remedial measures, the most effective remedy is not necessarily related directly to the main factor, and may lie in a different area. Human behaviour may often be influenced more readily by engineering means than by education or the enforcement of legislation. Road engineering improvements can play a large part in reducing accidents where the road user fails to cope with the road environment (see Chapter 8).

References

SABEY, B. E. (1983) 'Recent developments and research in road safety remedial measures'. Road Safety in the 80s. Presented to Symposium, Salford, September 1983

SABEY, B. E. and STAUGHTON, G. C. (1975) 'Interacting roles of road environment, vehicle and road user in accidents'. Fifth International Conference of the International Association for Accident and Traffic Medicine, and the Third International Conference on Drug Abuse of the International Council on Alcohol and Addiction, London, September 1975

STAUGHTON, G. C. and STORIE, V. J. (1977) 'Methodology of an in-depth accident investigation survey'. Transport and Road Research Laboratory Report LR 762

Chapter 3
The road user

This chapter outlines the main characteristics of road users and the circumstances and factors which influence their liability to be involved in accidents. Much research has been carried out on this subject, but, when investigating human behaviour, it is always more difficult to express research findings quantitatively than when studying the role of the engineering factors which dominate any discussion of the influence of the road or vehicle in accidents. The results of research on human factors are most often expressed in terms of improvements in human behaviour. The assumption is made that improvements in safety are likely to result from improved human behaviour although the direct link is often difficult to establish. In many cases, therefore, simple conclusions in terms of safety cannot be stated from the research, and so it is particularly important to consult the references in the text for this chapter.

3.1 Characteristics common to all road users

Much of the material here relates to car drivers, since their behaviour is such an important factor in accidents.

Age and sex

Age certainly influences accident risk. Judged by the casualties per head of population, young people are more likely to be involved in accidents, whether as pedestrians, drivers or cyclists, than middle-aged people (Sabey, 1983) (Table 3.1). At least some part of the increased accident risk in young road users is due to lack of experience. The accident rate for newly qualified car drivers in their first year of driving has been found to be higher than for experienced drivers, particularly at night (Jenkins, 1979); young drivers did best in driving tests but also had the highest accident rates. Over 70 per cent of motorcyclists injured in one sample of accidents were found to be learners (TRRL Leaflet LF 620, issue 2, 1977).

The driving behaviour of men and women car drivers has been the subject of an investigation by the Transport and Road Research Laboratory. Storie (1977) found no significant difference between the sexes with regard to being at fault in accidents, but men and women were found to drive differently. Women failed to see hazards more frequently, were less skilful and less able to execute difficult manoeuvres, while men

Table 3.1 Casualty rates by age, road user type and severity: rate per 100 000 population (1984)

Age	Pedestrians	Pedal cyclists	Two-wheeled MV users	Car users	Bus and coach users	Goods vehicle users
0–4	2.0[1]	0.1[1]	–	1.0	–	–
	27[2]	1[2]	–	10	–	–
5–9	4.1	0.7	–	0.6	–	–
	80	17	–	11	1	1
10–14	3.4	1.8	–	0.9	–	–
	77	40	2	12	2	1
15	2.8	1.6	0.4	2.7	–	0.1
	55	44	14	27	2	2
16	2.4	1.0	5.7	4.4	0.1	0.3
	51	38	193	54	2	4
17–19	2.2	0.9	11.5	11.6	0.1	0.5
	40	21	256	156	1	9
20–29	1.9	0.4	4.8	7.1	–	0.5
	22	12	77	100	1	8
30–39	1.5	0.5	1.1	4.0	–	0.5
	14	7	21	53	1	6
40–49	1.7	0.5	0.6	3.1	–	0.6
	15	7	15	42	1	5
50–59	2.5	0.5	0.6	2.9	–	0.5
	18	6	11	36	1	4
60–69	3.8	0.6	0.4	3.4	0.1	0.3
	24	5	5	32	2	1
70 and over	11.5	0.6	0.2	4.3	0.3	0.1
	45	4	2	26	4	–

[1] Killed; [2] seriously injured.

were more likely to drive too fast, overtake improperly and be under the influence of alcohol.

The casualty rates for pedal cyclists, motorcyclists and car drivers, in terms of distance travelled, are given in Tables 3.2, 3.3 and 3.4, and are discussed in more detail under the appropriate headings.

Table 3.2 Casualty rates per 100 million km travelled, pedal cyclists[1]: Great Britain (1979)

	Killed	Killed or seriously injured	All severities
Both sexes[2]:			
Age 0–9	13	500	2300
10–14	11	190	880
15–19	4	110	540
20–29	5	96	490
30–39	2	58	310
40–49	4	63	270
50–59	7	67	240
60 and over	21	140	390
all ages[3]	7	120	540
Males[3]	8	120	550
Females[3]	6	100	480

Sources: *Road accident reports 1979; traffic estimates 1979; National Travel Survey 1978/9*
[1] Excludes passengers; [2] Includes unknown sex; [3] Includes unknown age

Table 3.3 Casualty rates per 100 million km travelled, two-wheeled motor vehicle riders: Great Britain (1979)

	Killed	Killed or seriously injured	All severities
Both sexes[2]:			
Age 16–17	15	360	1200
18–19	39	650	2000
20–29	14	230	700
30–39	9	190	610
40–49	4	100	330
50–59	6	110	320
60 and over	12	160	450
all ages	15	270	860
Males[2]	16	280	870
Females[2]	5	200	770

Sources: *as Table 3.2*
[1] Includes unknown sex; [2] Includes unknown age

Table 3.4 Casualty rates per 100 million km travelled, car drivers: Great Britain (1979)

	Killed	Killed or seriously injured	All severities
Males			
Age 17–18	2.8	44	160
19	2.3	35	130
20–24	1.2	18	68
25–29	0.7	10	39
30–39	0.4	6	25
40–49	0.4	5	21
50–59	0.6	5	21
60 and over	1.3	10	35
all ages	0.7	9	34
Females			
Age 17–18	0.7	30	160
19	0.7	21	100
20–24	0.6	16	81
25–29	0.5	11	61
30–39	0.3	8	46
40–49	0.3	7	41
50–59	0.7	9	44
60 and over	1.8	18	61
all ages[1]	0.5	11	55

Sources: *as Table 3.2*
[1] Includes unknown age

Medical factors

Medical factors have not been shown to play an important role in accidents, and all forms of sudden illness are probably responsible for about one or two accidents in 1000. Heart disease accounts for about one-sixth or one-seventh of these. Epilepsy is the major cause of sudden collapse, and any medical condition which can cause collapse when driving is regarded as a bar to obtaining a driving licence. A comprehensive review of medical conditions which are factors in accidents is given in 'Medical Aspects of Fitness to Drive' (1985).

Reaction times

The reaction times of road users to potential accident situations are often quoted. In this book, reaction time will be taken to mean the total time from the instant when the situation develops and its image falls on the retina of the eye to the time when action is taken by the road user. It is therefore made up of the perception time (the time taken to recognise a situation), the decision time (the time to decide on action), and the time taken to put that action into practice.

The time to react to an artificially produced signal such as a flashing light lies between 0.25 and 0.6 sec; it is least for young persons and increases with age. Since most accident situations develop over a period of seconds, reaction times thus measured are generally considered to be of minor importance compared with those in real accidents where perception and decision times are usually much longer and less dependent on age. They are dealt with in more detail in the sections on pedestrian and vehicular accidents.

Alcohol and drugs

Alcohol has a marked effect on accident risk in all road users; the role of drugs has not yet been quantified, and research on the subject continues.

Alcohol in the blood or urine is measured in milligrams (mg) of alcohol per 100 millilitres (ml) of blood or urine; alcohol in the breath is measured in micrograms (µg) per 100 ml. The Road Safety Act of 1967 imposed a legal limit of 80 mg/ml in blood or 107 mg/ml in urine; the Act of 1981 also specifies a limit of 35 µg/ml in breath. In May 1983, new legislation was introduced, aimed at increasing the effectiveness of the 1981 Act.

Equivalent amounts of popular drinks are approximately as follows: half a pint (284 ml) of beer or cider, a 125 ml glass of table wine, a 50 ml glass of port, sherry or vermouth, and a 25 ml glass of spirits. The less concentrated drinks such as beer or cider are absorbed more slowly than the more concentrated ones such as sherry or gin, and therefore give rise to a lower blood or breath alcohol concentration. Body weight, which governs the amount of water in the body to absorb the alcohol, is also important; a lighter person has less water in the body and will therefore reach a higher blood alcohol level for a given consumption than a heavier person.

After drinking, the blood alcohol level rises gradually to a maximum, while at the same time it is being eliminated. As a rough guide, an 11 stone man drinking one pint of beer (referred to as 2 units) quickly on an empty stomach will raise the alcohol content of his blood to a peak of 30 mg/100 ml after about an hour; it will then reduce at the rate of about 1 unit (half a pint of beer) per hour. It must be emphasised that this is only a rough indication of what is likely to happen. Rates of absorption vary so much with the type of drink, how long it takes to drink, whether food has been eaten, body weight and fatty tissue that the level at any time is uncertain.

20 The road user

The marked increase in accident risk with concentration of alcohol in the blood of car drivers is shown in Figure 3.1 (TRRL Leaflet LF 762, 1979)*. On average the risk of accident involvement increases sharply beyond the legal limit of 80 mg/ml, but it has also been found that marked differences exist between those most susceptible and those least susceptible to alcohol; nevertheless, the driving performance of all drivers is impaired by alcohol. (The facts about drinking and driving – TRRL Pamphlet, 1983.)

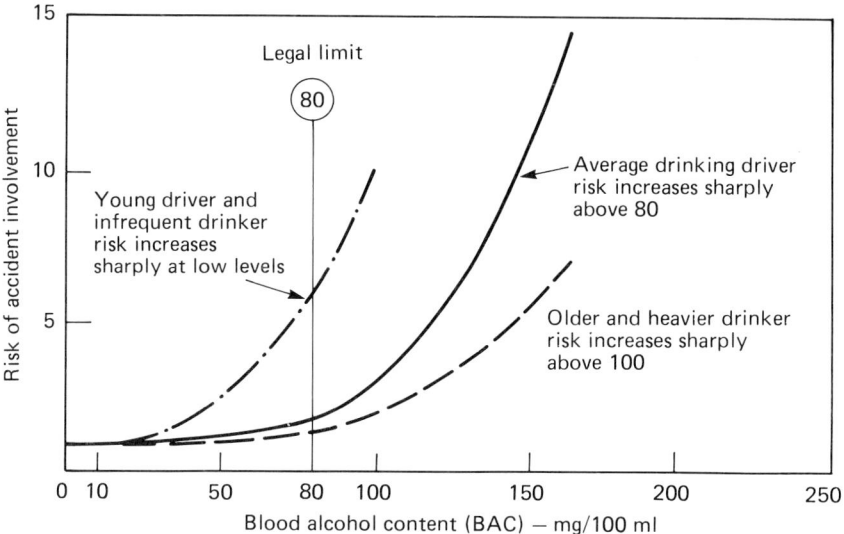

Figure 3.1 Accident risk and blood alcohol content in drivers

The 1967 Act had an immediate effect in reducing accidents and in reducing the percentage of fatally injured drivers with blood alcohol levels over 80 mg/100 ml; in 1967 it was 27 per cent, and in the following year it dropped to 17 per cent. In subsequent years the reduction declined, until in 1976 a new peak was reached above the pre-legislation level, followed by a downward trend reaching the pre-legislation level again in 1980. An analysis made in 1975 (Savey and Codling, 1975) of results up to 1973 revealed a marked difference between older and younger drivers. The older drivers (30 years and over) still seemed to respect the legislation, while the incidence of high drinking levels among younger drivers increased above pre-legislation levels, resulting in the observed overall increase in blood alcohol levels in fatalities. Similar effects of age were observed in 1980 (Sabey, 1982). The same investigation indicated that although the numbers of drivers killed and injured in 1973 had returned to the pre-legislative level the total number of casualties in Great Britain both killed and injured still showed a slight reduction of perhaps 2 or 3 per cent.

In spite of the declining effect of the legislation after an initial period, estimates made by the Transport and Road Research Laboratory (Beaumont and Newby, 1972) indicated that in the first four years (1967 to

---

* In this and later references TRRL and RRL signify respectively Transport and Road Research and the Road Research Laboratories.

1970) it had probably resulted in savings of about 4000 deaths and over 35 000 serious injuries.

The risk of a pedestrian being killed in a road accident also increases with blood alcohol concentration. In adult pedestrians of both sexes the risk of fatality has been found to increase rapidly above a blood alcohol concentration of 120 mg/100 ml (TRRL Digest SR 332, 1977). In a sample of 344 adults, 27 per cent of males and 7 per cent of the female fatalities were found to exceed this level. As would be expected, most of the alcohol-related accidents occurred in the late evening. In the hours 2300–0259, 51 per cent of the victims had blood alcohol levels of 150 mg/100 ml or more.

In 1980 the returns of the blood alcohol concentrations of adult fatalities dying within 12 hours of the accident gave the following figures for those with concentrations over 80 mg/100 ml: motor vehicle drivers, 32 per cent; motorcycle riders, 29 per cent; vehicle passengers, 27 per cent; pedestrians, 30 per cent; and pedal cyclists, 12 per cent; those with concentrations exceeding 150 mg/100 ml were respectively 21, 18, 11, 22 and 4 per cent (Sabey, 1982).

Attitudes

There is evidence to suggest that 'people drive as they live' (Tillman and Hobbs, 1949; Haviland and Wiseman, 1974). People who engage in anti-social activities in other areas of life (such as those with criminal convictions) are also more likely to be involved in traffic accidents. Some evidence (McMurry, 1970) suggests that fluctuations in personal adjustment, caused by events such as bereavement, or the stress of divorce proceedings, may temporarily change a person's likelihood of accident involvement. There are, however, at any one time, relatively few such people, so that prevention of these accidents – even if it were possible – will not change the accident picture substantially.

Accident proneness

A prevalent theory of accident proneness is that some individuals, because of certain reasonably stable characteristics, have a greater disposition than the average driver towards having accidents; statistical evidence indicates that some people are involved in more accidents than would be expected if accidents were distributed randomly. However, it has not yet been possible to identify attributes or characteristics in the driving population that can be used to distinguish between accident prone people and 'safe' drivers.

The term 'accident proneness' is also used to suggest that a small proportion of drivers – those who are accident prone – are responsible for a sizeable proportion of accidents, but it has been shown that the proportion of accidents in which accident repeaters are involved is relatively low and that the great majority of accidents occurring in any one year are first accidents (Stewart and Campbell, 1972). The cost effectiveness of introducing safety measures based on the methodology of accident proneness is therefore unlikely to be worthwhile compared with other

3.2 Pedestrian behaviour and accidents

Age and sex

The numbers of pedestrians killed or seriously injured in 1981 are given in Figure 3.2. The curves follow similar courses for males and females with peaks at younger and older ages. The large numbers of children under 10

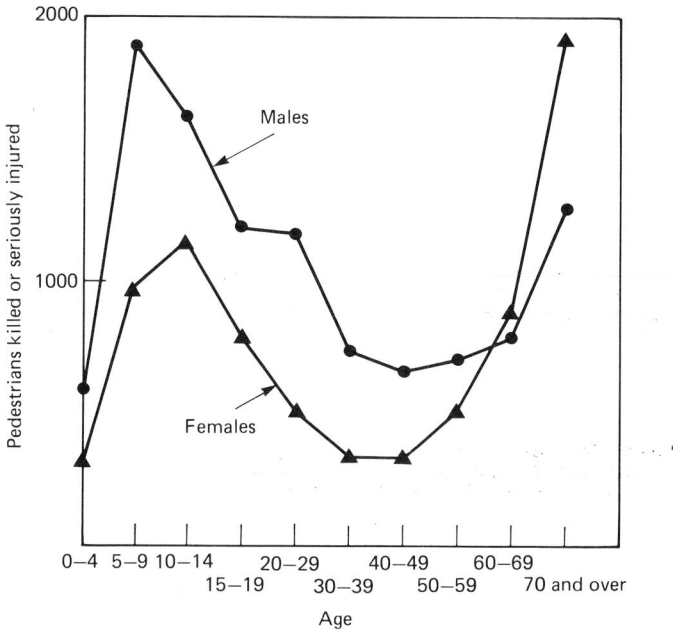

Figure 3.2 Pedestrians killed or seriously injured in 1981

years of age killed or seriously injured are noteworthy. Table 3.1 lists fatal or seriously injured casualties per 100 000 population in 1984 by age. Young and old pedestrians have the highest rates (Road Accidents Great Britain, 1984). A survey of pedestrian accidents and of pedestrian behaviour on the road has been given by Todd and Walker (1980).

Place

Over 90 per cent of pedestrian casualties occur in built-up areas. Most accidents to all age groups occur away from pedestrian crossings and near junctions. In about two-thirds of fatal and serious accidents the striking vehicle is a car, but, in proportion to distance travelled, motorcycles are three times as likely to be involved as cars. In about 20 per cent of accidents the pedestrian was hidden by a stationary vehicle; this proportion was rather higher for children than for adults.

When pedestrians cross the road they are more likely to be struck on the nearside of the road; for pedestrians over 60 years of age, there is a tendency, which increases with age, for them to be struck when on the farside (TRRL Leaflet LF 323, 1972).

Walking speed

The average speed of a pedestrian crossing the road is about 1.5 m/sec (5 ft/sec) and this changes little with age until the age of 60; over 60 the average speed is about 0.3 m/sec less (TRRL Leaflet LF 629, 1972).

Circumstances

Nearly 75 per cent of the pedestrians hit by vehicles do not see the vehicle which hits them; this proportion changes little with age. Most accidents to adult pedestrians occur in good weather, in daylight and on roads which the pedestrians are familiar with (TRRL Leaflets 323 and 324, 1972).

Although most pedestrian accidents (about 80 per cent) occur when the pedestrian is either crossing the road or stepping off the pavement or verge, a small proportion (about 5 per cent in all, but about 25 per cent in non-built-up areas) occur when he is walking in the road. These accidents are about 1.5 times more likely to happen when the pedestrian is walking on the nearside as on the off-side of the road.

Pedestrian crossings

How well someone sees a zebra crossing in daylight and dry weather depends upon seeing black patches side by side with white patches; they should always be laid down with the stripes parallel to the path of the oncoming traffic. To ensure contrast in wet weather the black stripes should have a rough texture and the white stripes a smooth texture. This also helps maintain contrast in street lighting. For best results at night the area of the crossing should be floodlit so that pedestrians can be seen.

Early research on pedestrian crossings concluded that the risk of injury to a pedestrian using a zebra crossing was less than that incurred when crossing elsewhere by a factor of about two, and that the risk was particularly great for pedestrians crossing close to but not on the crossing.

Zebra crossings are suitable for roads in urban areas where traffic is not very heavy. When both vehicular and pedestrian traffic is heavy, the crossings may cause considerable hindrance to the vehicular traffic so that light-controlled crossings are preferable. Such crossings, similar to traffic lights and operating on demand, were found to be safer than zebra crossings, but caused unnecessary delays to pedestrian and vehicular traffic when traffic was light (Research on Road Safety, 1963).

Pelican crossings were designed to combine the advantages of zebra and light-controlled crossings while causing less delay to traffic than the earlier light-controlled crossings. Inwood and Grayson published a report in 1979 of an investigation of the comparative safety of zebra and pelican crossings. They concluded that the pelican crossings were slightly safer and, because of this and the advantages in terms of traffic flow, pelican crossings are gradually replacing many of the zebra crossings. Probable sources of danger which remain are the small but appreciable proportion of drivers who cross either on the red or on the flashing amber signal when a pedestrian is on the crossing, and the large proportion of pedestrians (25 to 60 per cent) who cross against the signals (TRRL Leaflet LF 629, 1976).

Bridges and underpasses

Pedestrian bridges and underpasses give complete protection against vehicles, but pedestrians will only use them if crossing the road on the level takes at least as long a time as to use the bridge or subway. To ensure that this is so, whenever a bridge is built or a subway installed, a fence of an appropriate length on a central reservation or along the edges of the kerbs should be erected. This may not be necessary, if the bridge or underpass is integrated into a road improvement or town design which itself makes it difficult or impossible to cross any other way.

Accidents to very young children

A disturbing number of very young children, under 5 years of age, are killed or seriously injured in road accidents, almost all occurring in built-up areas. In 1981 there were 908 children seriously injured or killed in this age range. Many mothers allow children in this age group to play in the street and even to cross the road (Downing, 1982), so that the toll of casualties is not surprising.

3.3 Cyclists

Age and sex

Serious or fatal casualties by age and sex are shown in Figure 3.2, while casualty rates (in terms of distance travelled) by age for both sexes together are listed in Table 3.2. The greatest numbers of casualties are sustained by cyclists aged 10 to 14. They also have high casualty rates, which are, however, exceeded by younger riders, and for fatalities by those aged 60 and over. Taken as a whole, females have slightly lower rates for all severities of injury.

A considerable effort has been devoted to studying the manoeuvres of cyclists, particularly of child cyclists, in accidents, because of the substantial numbers of cyclists under the age of 14 killed and injured (about 30 per cent of the total) (Downing, 1981). The most important manoeuvres in terms of risk to cyclists of all ages were found to be:

(1) turning right into a side road;
(2) emerging from a footpath or driveway into the road;
(3) emerging from a side road;
(4) colliding with parked vehicles;
(5) watching out for vehicles emerging from side roads and turning into side roads across the cyclist's path.

3.4 Drivers of cars and riders of motorcycles

Age and sex

Serious or fatal casualties by age and sex are shown for motorcyclists in Figure 3.3, and in Figure 3.4 for car drivers, while casualty rates by age and sex are given in Tables 3.3 and 3.4. For motorcycle riders the numbers of casualties and casualty rates are highest for the youngest age groups. This is also true for car drivers, although the drop in casualties for ages 20 to 29, observed in the motorcycle data, is not shown in car driver casualties.

In Table 3.3, the casualty rates are shown separately for male and female drivers, and in general those for females are lower than those for males, markedly so below the age of 25 years.

Reaction times and other important times

The reaction time of a car driver depends upon the particular accident situation. The average time taken to apply the brake when the stop light of a vehicle ahead comes on is about 0.6 seconds. The time to take similar action when the vehicle ahead slows down without using a stoplight is 2 to 3 seconds. To respond to a turn signal, or to begin to overtake, about 1.5 seconds is an average time. To make a decision as to what to do when traffic signals turn amber, a driver has to anticipate conditions at least 3 seconds ahead; a driver must anticipate conditions 8 to 10 seconds ahead to judge when it is safe to overtake. To be on the safe side, it is advisable to regard the above times as minimum times (Research on Road Safety, 1963).

Overtaking

In the difficult manoeuvre of overtaking another vehicle in the face of oncoming traffic, car drivers make safer judgements at low speeds rather than at high ones. When the vehicle overtaken is travelling at 50 mile/h (80 km/h), the approximate distance required for overtaking is nearly 250 yds (234 m) (Research on Road Safety, 1963).

No similar tests have been conducted with motorcycles, but the conclusions on the reaction times of car drivers probably hold for motorcyclists. The most important types of accident for drivers and motorcyclists are described in Chapters 5 and 6.

Elderly drivers

The influence of age on the driving behaviour of car drivers, particularly at junctions, has been the subject of a study by Moore, Sedgley and Sabey (1982). Overall, the accident rate per kilometre driven for drivers of 65 years and over was found to be just below average, while the peak rate (for the 17 to 19 years age group) was more than three times the average. Elderly drivers had a higher than average risk of accident involvement for right turning movements at junctions and at rural junctions generally. For certain types of single vehicle accident, elderly drivers had a lower than average risk of involvement. The youngest drivers had a higher than average risk of involvement in all kinds of accident studied.

26   The road user

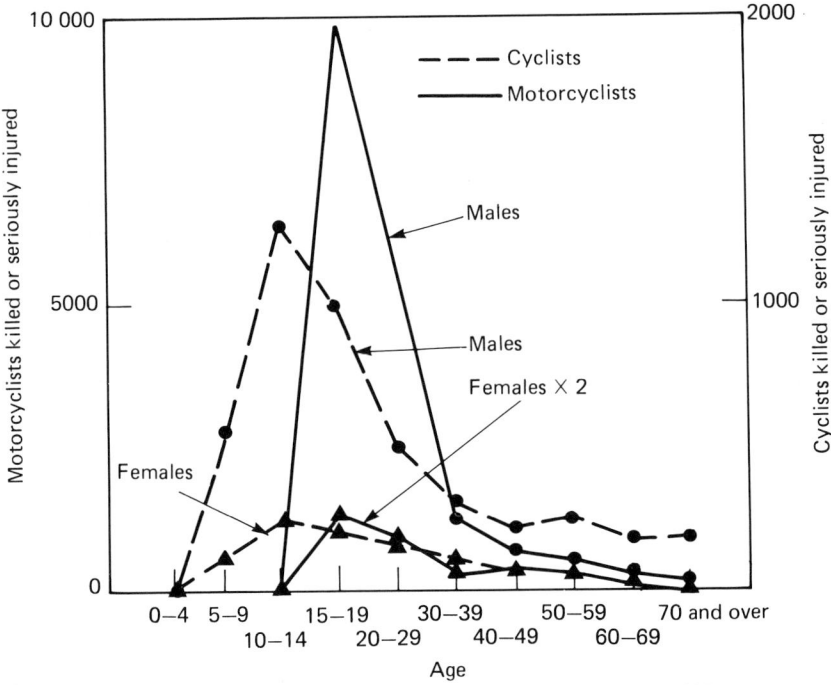

Figure 3.3 Riders of cycles and motorcycles killed or seriously injured in 1981

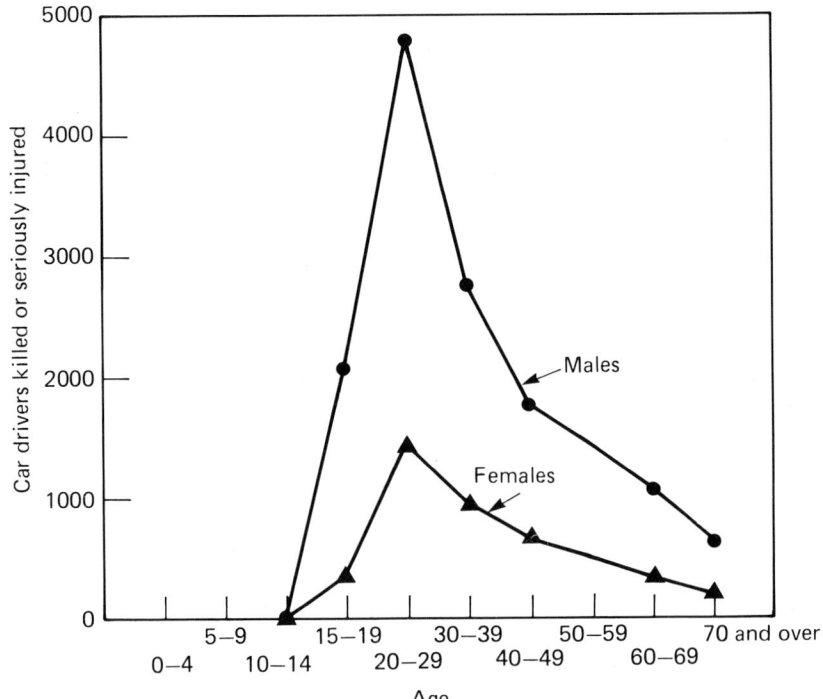

Figure 3.4 Car drivers killed or seriously injured in 1981

3.5 Ways of influencing road user behaviour

Road user behaviour can be influenced by education, training, propaganda, engineering and enforcement. To measure the effectiveness of these methods, whether separately or as a whole, is extremely difficult; but it seems certain that, taken as a whole, they can have a large effect. In Britain they have all been in operation in different degrees for many years, and have coincided with only a small increase in road deaths between the pre-war years and the present day, although total casualties have increased appreciably. In 1935 the number of deaths was 6502 and the total number of casualties was 228 000; in 1981 the corresponding figures were 5846 and 325 000. In the intervening years, the numbers of deaths changed little although casualties, after reaching a peak of 400 000 in 1963, decreased year by year.

Education, training and propaganda

Education, training and propaganda cannot easily be considered separately, since advice and training on road behaviour as pedestrians, cyclists, motorcyclists and drivers may be given in schools by various organisations, and by means of propaganda in all the mass media, while training is, of course, given in driving schools.

It is difficult to obtain evidence, in terms of accident reduction, of the effects of methods used to influence road user behaviour. Much is known about improvements in behaviour and it is reasonable to assume that improvements in behaviour lead to reductions in accidents. One of the main difficulties of confirming this assumption arises from the length of time required for the necessary investigations to be made. Injury accidents, the most reliable sources of data, are infrequent events (on average, for car drivers, about one in 60 years), so observations need to be carried out over several years with a large number of subjects; during that time many other circumstances may affect accident experience. It is also not unusual for improvements in behaviour resulting from education or training to decline with time. For these reasons, much more is known about changes in behaviour than about accident savings.

In a few cases, a link has been established between measures to influence behaviour and a reduction in accidents. The introduction of the Green Cross Code, which replaced 'kerb drill', by using television and the press was associated with a short-term 11 per cent drop in the accident rate to pedestrians mainly between the ages of 5 and 9.

Since 1959, considerable resources have been devoted to cycle training for child cyclists both by the Royal Society for the Prevention of Accidents (RoSPA) and by Local Authority Road Safety Officers, the basic aim being to teach children how to ride correctly and safely on public roads. Generally training has been found to result in large improvements in cycle behaviour, and to have had a less substantial effect in terms of accident reduction (Downing, 1981).

The Institute of Advanced Motorists is a private association whose membership is limited to drivers who pass the Institute's test. Hoinville, Berhoud and Mackie (1972) found that drivers who passed this test had about 25 per cent fewer accidents over the three-year period after taking the test than those who failed.

Behavioural studies, which have been concerned with car drivers, are mainly of two kinds: (1) observations of driver errors, and (2) devising and validation of training methods. Driver errors have been recorded by: (a) an in-car method, in which drivers are observed from inside their cars; (b) the observed-car method, when selected cars were followed and driver behaviour recorded, and (c) time-lapse photography, from the side of the road (TTRL Leaflet LF 538, 1975). The first method (a) was described by Quenault in 1966 (RRL Report No. 25, 1966). Driver training may include the use of simulators (TRRL Leaflet LF251, Issue 2, 1971) or lectures or both and test drives accompanied by observers (TRRL Digest LR 949, 1980), and, of course, the driving instruction given by driving school instructors who prepare students for driving tests.

Enforcement

Police enforcement is required to ensure compliance with speed limits and drink driving laws, and, with legislation in force on the wearing of helmets by motorcyclists and of seat belts by the occupants of motor vehicles, police activity is also necessary to ensure that safety requirements of all kinds are complied with. One may also include among enforceable safety requirements those coming under construction and use regulations for vehicles. The effect of imposing speed limits is described in Chapter 4, and the 1967 Road Safety Act, the drink driving law, in Section 3.1.

In January 1983 a law came into force making the wearing of seat belts by the occupants of the front seats of cars and light vans compulsory. Roadside counts made during the ensuing 12 months found that over 90 per cent of car occupants complied with the law. It appears that in the case of this law there was general acceptance of its usefulness, since wearing rates continued to be high; in other cases, such as complying with speed limits, the proportion of those obeying the law is much lower. The reasons for breaking traffic laws are not well understood and have been discussed by Sheppard (1981).

The results of the first two years of compulsion have been analysed, and reported in a publication issued by the Department of Transport (Compulsory Seat Belt Wearing, 1985). The results of the Transport and Road Research Laboratory were as follows:

- Wearing rates went up from about 40 per cent before to about 95 per cent after compulsion was introduced.
- The number of fatal and serious casualties in Great Britain among front-seat occupants of cars and light vans fell by approximately 7000 per annum (including about 470 fatalities per annum).
- The number of slight casualties fell by approximately 13 000 per annum.

There was a greater reduction in casualties among front-seat passengers than among car drivers and van occupants; for the former, reductions in fatal and serious casualties were approximately 30 per cent, and in slight casualties 20 per cent, while for the latter groups the reductions were about 20 per cent and 12 per cent respectively.

From figures given in the report it can be calculated that for front-seat occupants of cars and light vans the reductions of 470 deaths and 6520 serious injuries represent reductions of about 21 and 23 per cent respectively. The figures also allow approximate estimates to be made for the efficiency of seat belts, that is, the reduction to be expected from a 100 per cent wearing rate; for front-seat occupants of cars and light vans this was about 39 per cent; for front-seat passengers, considered separately, the efficiency expressed in this way was about 52 per cent. The figure of 39 per cent agrees favourably with that deduced from the Australian experience (Grime, 1979). These efficiencies all refer to deaths.

It is also worth noting that the total effect of seat belt wearing, that is, the sum of the effects of voluntary and compulsory wearing, was a reduction of about 37 per cent (assuming the efficiency to be the same in both cases).

References

'A controlled study of the role of alcohol in fatal adult pedestrian accidents'. *Transport and Road Research Laboratory Digest* SR 332, 1977

'Accident risk and blood alcohol levels'. *Transport and Road Research Laboratory Leaflet* LF 762. January 1979

'Accidents to elderly pedestrians'. *Transport and Road Research Laboratory Leaflet* LF 323, 1972

'Age differences in behaviour of pedestrians crossing the road'. *Transport and Road Research Laboratory Leaflet* LF 324, 1972

Alcohol and road accidents. *Transport and Road Research Laboratory Leaflet* LF 634. January 1977

CAMERON, C. (1975) 'Accident proneness'. *Accident Analysis and Prevention,* **7,** 49–53

Compulsory Seat Belt Wearing. Report by the Department of Transport October 1985

DOWNING, C. S. (1981) 'Pedal cycling accidents in Great Britain'. *Transport and Road Research Laboratory Report*

DOWNING, C. S. (1982) 'Sex differences in children's road accidents'. *Transport and Road Research Laboratory Report*

'Driver error'. *Transport and Road Research Laboratory Lefalet* LF 538, 1975

Evaluation of 'Better Driving' courses run by the police forces for the public. *Transport and Road Research Laboratory Digest* LR 949, 1980

GRATTAN, E. and JEFFCOAT, G. O. (1967) 'Medical factors and road accidents'. *Road Research Laboratory Report* LR 143

GRIME, G. (1979) 'The protection afforded by seat belts'. *Transport and Road Research Laboratory Supplementary Report* 449

HAVILLAND, C. V. and WISEMAN, H. A. B. (1974) 'Criminals who drive.' *Proc. 18th Annual Conference of American Association for Automotive Medicine, September 1974*

HOINVILLE, G., BERTHOUD, B. A. and MACKIE, A. M. (1972) 'A study of accident rates amongst motorists who passed or failed an advanced driving test'. *Transport and Road Research Laboratory Report* LR 499

INWOOD, J. and GRAYSON, G. B. (1979) 'The comparative safety of pedestrian crossings'. *Transport and Road Research Laboratory Report* LR 895

JENKINS, D. (1979) 'Car driving before and after passing the driving test'. *Transport and Road Research Laboratory Report* LR 499

McMURRY, L. (1970) 'Emotional stress and driving performance. The effects of divorce.' *Behavioral Research in Highway Safety,* **1,** 100–114

'Medical aspects of fitness to drive' (1985) – Medical Commission on Accident Prevention

MOORE, R. L., SEDGLEY, I. P. and SABEY, B. E. (1982) 'Ages of drivers involved in accidents, with special reference to junctions'. *Transport and Road Research Laboratory Supplementary Report* SR 718

'MOTORCYCLE ACCIDENT SURVEY 1974'. *Transport and Road Research Laboratory Leaflet* LF 620, Issue 2, 1977

'Pedestrian behaviour at Pelican Crossings'. *Transport and Road Research Laboratory Leaflet* LF 629, 1976

QUENAULT, S. W. (1966) 'Some methods of obtaining information on driver behaviour.' *Road Research Laboratory Report* LR 25

Research on Road Safety (1963) (Chapter 3), HMSO: London

Road Accidents Great Britain (1984) HMSO: London

SABEY, B. E. (1982) 'Recent experiences of drinking and driving in the United Kingdom'. *Conference on Alcohol and Traffic Safety. Cologne, October 1982*

SABEY, B. E. (1983) 'Road safety in the 80s'. *Symposium on Recent Developments and Research in Road Safety Remedial Measures, Salford, September*

SABEY, B. E. and CODLING, P. J. (1974) 'Alcohol and road accidents in Great Britain'. *Sixth International Conference on Alcohol, Drugs and Traffic Safety, Toronto*

SABEY, B. E. and STAUGHTON, G. C. (1980) 'The drinking road user in Great Britain'. *Transport and Road Research Laboratory Supplementary Report* SR 616

SHEPPARD, D. (1981) 'Why do drivers break traffic laws?' *Police Review*, 17 April 1981

'Simulators for driver training'. *Transport and Road Research Laboratory Leaflet* LF 251, Issue 2, 1971

STEWART, J. R. and CAMBELL, B. T. (1972) 'The statistical association between past and future accidents and violations'. Highway Safety Research Center, University of North Carolina, December

STORIE, V. J. (1977) 'Male and female drivers: differences observed in accidents'. *Transport and Road Research Laboratory Digest* LR 761

'THE FACTS ABOUT DRINKING AND DRIVING'. *Transport and Road Research Laboratory Pamphlet*, 1982

TILLMAN, W. A. and HOBBS, C. E. (1949) The accident-prone automotive driver. *American Journal of Psychiatry*, **106,** 321–331

TODD, J. E. and WALKER, A. (1980) 'People as pedestrians'. Social Survey Division, Office of Population Censuses and Surveys, HMSO

Chapter 4
Roads: features which may be related to accidents

This chapter outlines the main features of roads which influence the risk of accidents, and in many cases how hazardous features may be improved or eliminated. It is intended to provide information on aspects of road engineering which may be of assistance to those, other than road engineers, who investigate accidents. Road engineers, too, may be reminded of many safety principles, but this book is not a substitute for more comprehensive publications such as those produced by the Department of Transport and the Transport and Road Research Laboratory; the subject is so vast that reference must be made to more complete treatments if detailed information is required.

In the safety measures considered here particular attention has to be paid to the 'trade-off' between cost and benefit since the cost of changes to roads to enhance safety may be very high; and whereas in some cases the savings are well established from past experience, this may not be so in others. In general, low-cost engineering measures bring greatest short-term benefits.

4.1 Road geometry

The most general characteristics of roads are their widths in terms of numbers of lanes, whether opposing carriageways are separated, other cross-sectional characteristics, and their horizontal and vertical curvatures.

Road and lane widths

For two-lane roads, 12 foot (3.7 m) lanes have been found to be safer than 9 or 10 foot (2.7 or 3 m) lanes (Hazardous road locations, 1976). Research carried out in Britain some years ago (Research on Road Safety, 1963) indicated that at low traffic volumes three-lane roads had lower accident rates per mile travelled than two-lane roads, but that their accident rates increased as traffic flow increased above about 10 000 vehicles per day. However, later investigations have not confirmed this and the relative merits of two- versus three-lane roads are still uncertain. At high flows four-lane roads have lower accident rates, but, if they are designed as dual carriageways, special attention has to be paid to junction design, since without such attention the overall accident rate may even be greater than on an undivided four-lane road (Research on Road Safety, 1963).

Shoulders and medians

Other cross-sectional characteristics are shoulder and median widths and design. Very narrow shoulders, where these are provided, less than 6 feet (1.8 m) wide, have been found to be associated with higher accident rates than wider shoulders, and although the evidence is not very strong it is in accordance with expectation. These observations refer to shoulders with flush kerbs, which are considered preferable to upstanding kerbs with vertical edges.

The width of median, however narrow, is probably better than none at all, since it segregates opposing traffic. There is evidence that, as may be expected, the frequency of cross-median accidents decreases as the width of the median increases. To reduce this frequency to negligible proportions, however, on high speed roads, a width of 50 feet (15 m) or more is required (Research on Road Traffic, 1965).

The cross section of a median may be either raised, depressed or level. If crash barriers are provided, the median should always be level so that cars which strike the barrier do so at the correct height. There is little conclusive evidence to show that one contour is better than another if no barriers are present.

Horizontal and vertical curves

In rural areas accidents tend to cluster on bends and accidents have generally been shown to increase in frequency with degree of horizontal curvature. There are a number of possible reasons for this. Chapter 5 shows that there are limiting speeds on bends above which a vehicle may skid and lose control, particularly when the road is wet; the road layout may also convey a misleading impression of the curvature of the bend, or sight distances may be inadequate. Realignment of isolated bends has resulted in reductions in injury accidents of 60 per cent or more. Nevertheless, alterations which result in higher speeds without realignment, such as superelevation, sometimes increase accidents. It has also been found that roads with long straights and few bends, particularly if they are sharp bends, may have higher accident rates than roads with more bends (Research on Road Traffic, 1965).

Vertical alignment

Accidents tend to occur at crests and near the bottom of downgrades. This is probably due not only to restricted sight distances but also to speed differentials induced by gradients. The usual remedy is to provide an extra lane so that slow moving traffic can be safely overtaken on the upgrades with double-line lane markings to safeguard overtaking near the crest.

Combinations of vertical and horizontal curves sometimes produce visually deceptive conditions which constitute hazards. There is evidence that accident rates are higher when horizontal curvature coincides with vertical crests or sags or when access points are sited on sharp curves (Department of Transport Notes TD 9/81 and TA 28/82; and Layout of roads in rural areas, Ministry of Transport, 1968, HMSO).

The layout of junctions

About 31 per cent of serious and fatal injury accidents in non-built-up areas in 1984 occurred at junctions. Just under 60 per cent of these were at three-way or staggered junctions (this figure includes Y-junctions; without these the figure is 46 per cent). At most types of rural junction nearly 80 per cent of accidents involve two or more vehicles. In built-up areas about 63 per cent of fatal and serious accidents occurred at junctions and 65 per cent of these were at three-way junctions.

Most accidents at rural three-way junctions involve one vehicle turning (usually right) and one going straight on, both along the major road (Research on Road Traffic, 1965). On rural dual carriageway roads, too, the most common type of junction accident is one in which a vehicle turning right is hit by another vehicle travelling straight along the major road – usually the turning vehicle is struck by a following or overtaking vehicle.

Much can be done to lessen the risk of accidents at junctions by altering the layout of roads and the geometrical designs of the junctions. It was found some years ago (Research on Road Traffic, 1965) that the numbers of accidents at rural three-way junctions are approximately proportional to the square root of the product of the traffic flows on the two roads. This relationship, which has recently been found to be true for urban junctions, provides theoretical justification for restricting access to main roads, by combining the flows on minor roads before they enter the main road at a single junction.

Right-hand splay junctions are safer than squared junctions which are safer than left-hand splay junctions (see Figure 4.1). Thus squaring of left-hand splay junctions has been found to decrease accidents, while squaring right-hand splay junctions increased accidents dramatically.

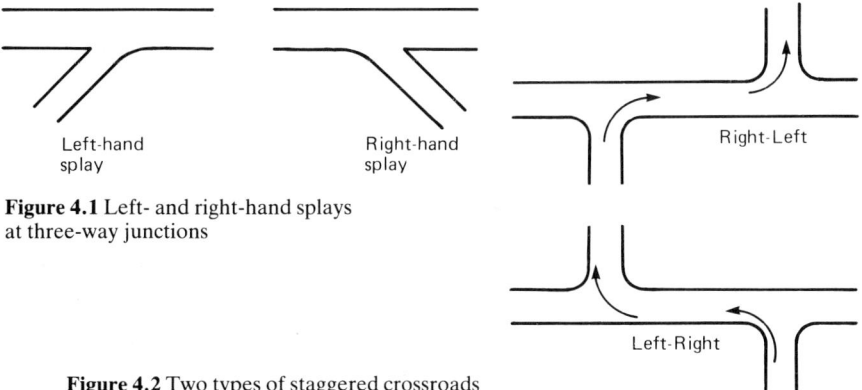

Figure 4.1 Left- and right-hand splays at three-way junctions

Figure 4.2 Two types of staggered crossroads

Straight crossover roads are less safe than staggered junctions (the offset should be about 120 feet (36 m)) and on undivided roads a right-left staggered junction is safer than a left-right stagger (see Figure 4.1).

However, slightly offset crossroads as shown in Figure 4.3 are less safe than the straight crossover type (but see also Figure 4.4, an intersection with offset island).

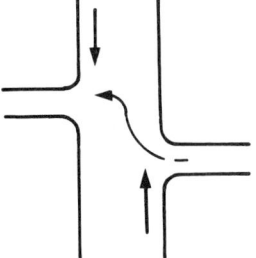

Figure 4.3 Slightly offset crossroads

Figure 4.4 Junction layout with offset islands

The layout of intersections as roundabouts with priority rules also reduces accidents, and the introduction of mini-roundabouts has greatly increased the number of intersections at which this change is possible, particularly in urban areas. In both urban and rural areas, the installation of mini-roundabouts at a number of priority controlled and light-controlled junctions resulted in significant accident reductions (Green, 1977).

The safest layout for junctions with heavy traffic flows is, of course, that in which there is complete grade separation.

The previous paragraphs have dealt with the overall geometric features of intersections. Some more detailed considerations follow. It should be emphasised, however, that it is not possible, in this book, to do more than state general principles; for much fuller treatments, references at the end

(1) The radius of curvature of both the entry to and exit from the major road for left turning vehicles should be adequate, so that vehicles are not compelled to slow down excessively, although the resulting angle at which a vehicle enters the main road should not be great enough to make it difficult for the driver to see vehicles with which he is merging on the main road. Guide islands either raised or marked on the carriageway may be used to channel cars to the turns.
(2) Visibility, mainly from the minor road, at junctions can be improved:
   (a) hedges can be trimmed or removed to enable vehicles on the minor roads to see those on the major roads;
   (b) warning of the presence of an intersection may be provided by a central island with white indicator lamp; if this is offset it will also reduce entry speeds into the intersection (see Figure 4.3) (Faulkner and Eaton, 1977);
   (c) the stop lines at the entry to the major road should be placed as far forward as possible to improve the view along the major road;
   (d) the view along the major road may be restricted by a crest or a bend in the road or by a combination of the two. How far these defects can be remedied by engineering measures depends upon the cost involved.
(3) The reduction of conflicts. Conflicts arise when one stream of traffic crosses or merges with another, and within a single traffic stream when a vehicle suddenly slows down and may be struck by a following vehicle (Russam and Sabey, 1972).

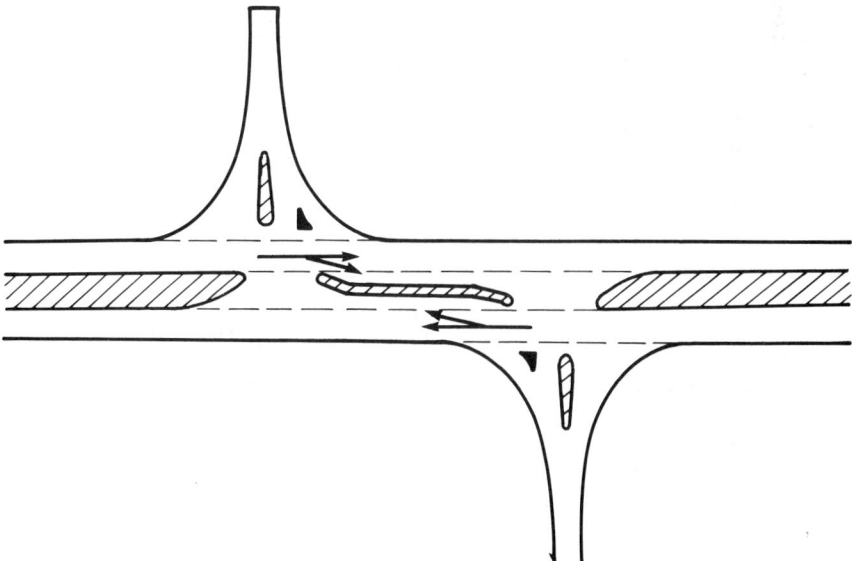

Figure 4.5 Methods of reducing conflicts at staggered crossroads

Many of these principles are illustrated by Figure 4.4, based on diagrams in the Department of Transport Technical Memorandum TA/20/81 (1981). Central islands provide deceleration lanes and extra road space for traffic turning right into the opposite minor road, and so reduce the risk of head to tail collisions. At the lower junction of a minor with a major road, exit from the major road is on a curve of large radius to reduce the risk of head to tail collisions here also.

To minimise the time during which conflicts can arise when one traffic stream crosses another, the islands at the exit from the minor road are arranged so that vehicles emerging and either crossing to the central island or turning right along the major road do so at right angles to the path of the main road traffic.

Figure 4.5 shows a solution for a dual carriageway road. If junctions on single carriageway roads are treated on the basis of similar principles, it is advantageous to widen the road at the junction to allow islands with deceleration lanes to be installed (Figure 4.6). T-junctions may obviously be treated in a similar way to that shown in Figure 4.5, the only differences

Figure 4.6 Widening at junction to provide space for central islands

Road geometry 37

being that the island at the centre of the diagram then provides only one deceleration lane, and that there is only one central lane for vehicles emerging from the minor road.

Roundabouts

Although, taken as a whole, roundabouts are safer than junctions of other types, those with require sharp turns to be made present special hazards to commercial vehicles with high centres of gravity by inducing overturning if the speeds at which they are negotiated are too high; for example, overturning can occur at about 15 mile/h (24 km/h) on a curve with a radius of 60 feet (18.5 m). Articulated vehicles are particularly prone to this type of accident (Figure 4.7).

Figure 4.7 Test showing articulated vehicle roll when sideways acceleration exceeds 0.2 g

In some cases, the shape of the entry curve may be deceptive, particularly at night. The entrances to large roundabouts are, or have been in the past, designed, by using sharp curves, to discourage entry at speed and as a result many night accidents occur when vehicles run on to the central island. It is usual therefore to place conspicuous direction signs on the islands. There is some justification for discouraging high entry speeds, but none for making the exit difficult; nevertheless, the exits from roundabouts are more often of similar design to their entrances so that vehicles accelerating rapidly out of the junction are unable to take the exit curve and are forced into the opposite carriageway, or, if there is a central reservation with lamp standards, they may collide with a lamp standard.

The detailed design of roundabouts is described in a publication of the Department of the Environment (Technical Memorandum on Roundabout Design, 1975; and Department of Transport Note TA 23/81); see also the Accident Investigation and Prevention Manual published by the Department of Transport, 1974.

4.2 Road delineation and marking

Road delineation and marking is effected by paints which may be reflectorised, by raised reflecting studs in rubber mounts for self-cleansing, by reflecting prisms or by surfaces of contrasting colour and texture.

The chief uses of the various methods of marking and delineation are:

(1) as lane markers and delineators of the edges of roads;
(2) the channelisation of traffic and indication of priority at junctions;
(3) the control of traffic at bends, crests, and sites at which roads become narrower;
(4) the warning of the approaches to pedestrian crossings, and the marking of the crossing itself;
(5) the marking of the entrances to and the exits from motorways by different coloured delineators;
(6) prohibitions of various degrees of severity on stopping and waiting on carriageways.

At night in rural areas, and especially in wet weather or fog, the absence of adequate delineation constitutes a hazard, although no estimate of the extent can be made. The hazard arises from the lack of contrast between

Figure 4.8 Hard shoulder with colour and texture contrast with road

the carriageway and the verge or central reservation, and the inadequacy of road markings. Some reflectorised lane markings containing glass beads, which give very good results in dry weather, may not show up when flooded by heavy rain.

Several methods have been shown to give improved conspicuity in adverse conditions. Catseyes and upstanding reflectorised prisms actually produce better contrast when the road is wet than when it is dry, and are used to advantage as lane markings and to outline the edge of the carriageway, particularly where there is a flush kerb. On roads with hard shoulders, it is good practice to furnish the hard shoulder with a coarse-textured surface constructed with a light coloured aggregate. There is then a contrast between shoulder and carriageway in both dry and wet weather (Figure 4.8).

4.3 Traffic signs and traffic signals

Traffic signs may be of three types: direction signs, warning signs and mandatory signs. The siting of signs is particularly important at the approaches to priority controlled junctions, where drivers may sometimes fail to recognise that they are approaching a junction and therefore fail to stop.

For many years traffic signals have been a recognised method of controlling traffic and reducing accidents at junctions where the volume of traffic warrants their use. The installation of signals has been shown to result in a significant reduction in injury accidents (Research on Road Traffic, 1965, Chapter 16).

4.4 Road surfaces

Surfaces slippery in wet weather

The surfaces of carriageways may be slippery if the surface is wet or icy. When wet, the surface may be slippery to vehicle tyres even if it looks coarse-textured. The slipperiness of surfaces is a complicated subject involving interactions between characteristics of both tyres and surfaces and these aspects are discussed in detail in Chapter 5.

Tyres do not slip on dry surfaces, because they have high coefficients of friction, but even on dry surfaces skidding and subsequent loss of control can occur.

It is well established that substantial reductions in accidents can be made by changing surfaces to improve wet road skidding resistance. A skid resistant surface should have sufficient macro-texture (rough texture), with easily visible surface particles, and a fine texture (micro-texture) with sharp edges resistant to polishing by tyres. Figure 4.9 illustrates these terms and their combinations (Sabey, Williams and Lupton, 1970).

The importance of the type of surface texture in influencing the skid resistance of a carriageway surface is shown in Figure 4.10, which gives changes in the coefficient of longitudinal friction of a treaded tyre as a function of speed. Surfaces A and C, harsh at the microscopic scale, both

40 Roads – features which may be related to accidents

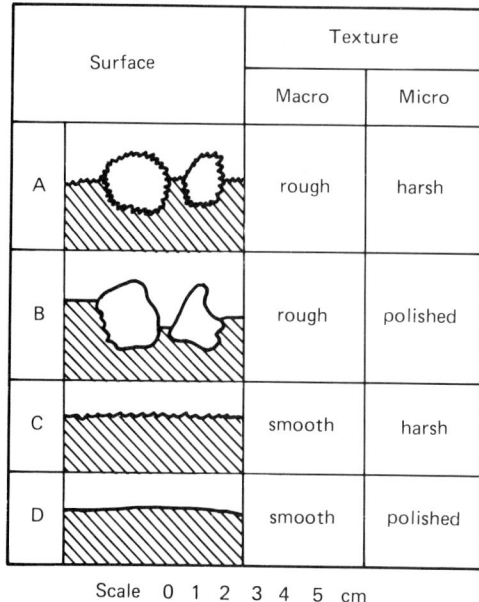

Figure 4.9 Illustration of terms used to describe the road surface texture

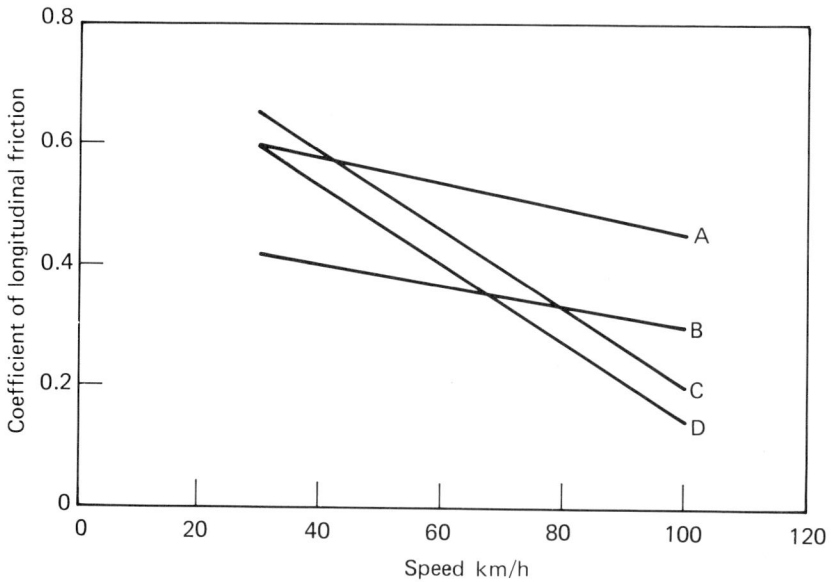

Figure 4.10 Locked wheel skid resistance on wet surfacings illustrated in Figure 4.9 (new treaded tyre)

show a high coefficient at low speeds, 31 mile/h (50 km/h) as does the smooth surface D, probably because the tread pattern provides adequate drainage; the polished surface B has a lower coefficient at the same speed. The fall in the coefficient of friction with increase in speed depends on the absence of sufficient macro-texture: with surfaces C and D there is a

Table 4.1 Minimum values of skidding resistance for different sites

Site	Definition	SFC (at 50 km/h) Risk rating*									
		1	2	3	4	5	6	7	8	9	10
A1 (v difficult)	Approaches to traffic signals on roads with a speed limit greater than 40 mile/h (64 km/h). Approaches to traffic signals, pedestrian crossings and similar hazards on main urban roads.						0.55	0.60	0.65	0.70	0.75
A2 (difficult)	Approaches to major junctions on roads carrying more than 250 commercial vehicles per lane per day. Roundabouts and their approaches. Bends with radius less than 150 m on roads with a speed limit greater than 40 mile/h (64 km/h). Gradients of 5 per cent or steeper, longer than 100 m.				0.45	0.50	0.55	0.60	0.65		
B (average)	General straight sections of and large radius curves on: Motorways Trunk and principal roads Other roads carrying more than 250 commercial vehicles per lane per day.	0.30	0.35	0.40	0.45	0.50	0.55				
C (easy)	Generally straight sections of lightly trafficked roads. Other roads where wet accidents are unlikely to be a problem.	0.30	0.35	0.40	0.45						

* The risk rating is a measure of the risk of skidding at the sites described.

marked decrease, while the coefficients decrease less for A and B. However, to maintain a surface with characteristics similar to A on a road with heavy traffic is extremely difficult (see Chapter 5).

A rough macro-texture is therefore particularly desirable for high speed traffic; consequently this criterion should be verified, especially if skid resistance or frictional coefficient measurements can only be carried out at a moderate standard speed of, for example, 31 to 37 mile/h (50 to 60 km/h). Texture depths should be measured using the sandpatch method (RRL Road Note 27 (1969)) to ensure satisfactory skid resistances at speeds up to 56 mile/h (90 km/h). Minimum values should be 1.0 mm for bituminous surfacings and 0.5 mm for textured cement concrete surfacings.

The degree of harshness of the micro-texture usually depends on the properties of the aggregate employed and is a function of the micro-texture of the particles, their shape and sharpness. A good skid resistance can be maintained under heavy traffic only by using stone material which is highly resistant to polishing and wear, and it is vital that a stringent selection be made. The main criterion is resistance to polishing assessed on the basis of results of laboratory testing of accelerated polishing, using the British Standards BS 812 method.

The coefficient required for a particular road section depends on the accident risk the surfacing presents for the road user, and this depends on factors such as the type of road or site (junction or non-junction), traffic density, speed of traffic, etc. Table 4.1 gives recommended minimum values of skid resistance obtained with the SCRIM machine (see Figure 5.13) at 31 mile/h (50 km/h) for a number of road conditions.

The techniques available for treating slippery road surfaces are the roughening of the surface by mechanical methods such as grooving or hammering, which is useful only for concrete, or the addition of surface layers.

Spray

In wet weather the texture of the road surface influences the amount of spray which is thrown up by fast moving vehicles; the smoother the road surface, the greater the amount of spray thrown up. Spray is greatly dependent on two factors: the heavier the vehicle, the greater the amount of spray, and for all vehicles the amount of spray increases very rapidly with speed. Simple mudflaps, such as those usually fitted to all types of vehicle, are of little value, their main function being to act as stoneguards; commercial vehicles, which are the most important generators of spray, require complex mudguards (TRRL Leaflet LF 602, 1975) if a worthwhile reduction in spray is to be achieved (Figures 4.11 and 4.12).

There are difficulties about translating these findings into practice, and in November 1984 a regulation was introduced which goes some way towards achieving the desired result. This requires that certain heavy goods vehicles and trailers shall be fitted with spray reducing devices satisfying British Standards Specifications BS AU 200, 1984.

Treatment of the road surface to produce a surface with very pronounced macro-roughness (sandpatch 1.0 to 1.5 mm) reduces the amount of spray considerably, and surfaces which also provide internal

Road surfaces 43

Figure 4.11 Spray from a heavy commercial vehicle with conventional mudguards

Figure 4.12 Improved mudguard for heavy commercial vehicle

drainage are almost completely effective, but the problem of maintaining such surfaces has not yet been solved.

Surfaces of verges, shoulders and central reservations

Verges, shoulders, and central reservations of dual carriageways present hazards to motor vehicles, particularly to cars and motorcycles if the surfaces are uneven, or contain drains, ditches, concrete channels, steep slopes or banks, or if they are soft. All such features are likely to induce loss of control in vehicles which leave the carriageway, and such hazards should never be built into roads, particularly where speeds are high.

4.5 Lighting

Street lighting

The aim of the road lighting engineer is to throw light on the road surface in such a way as to produce maximum brightness and uniformity with minimum glare from the light sources. Objects are then almost invariably seen as dark silhouettes against a light background (Figure 4.13). To achieve this there are three requirements.

(1) To promote uniformity the light must be well distributed across the road, and the street lamps placed as close together as is economically possible.
(2) The light sources should be screened to reduce glare.
(3) The road surface should have a pronounced macro-texture, that is, it should look rough and have a great enough texture depth, thus broadening the bright areas of road surface (Figure 4.14). This is particularly important when the road surface is wet.

Figure 4.13 Seeing in street lighting: dark object; light background

Economic considerations largely determine how closely the light sources can be spaced and how well they can be screened to reduce glare, since the greater the amount of screening, the shorter the length of road that can be illuminated by a single lamp, and therefore the closer the spacing has to be to coalesce the patches of light on the road; the closer the spacing the greater the cost of the installation. The type of installation now favoured in Britain is that of semi-cut-off low pressure sodium lighting, which is a compromise between the more heavily cut-off lighting developed on the

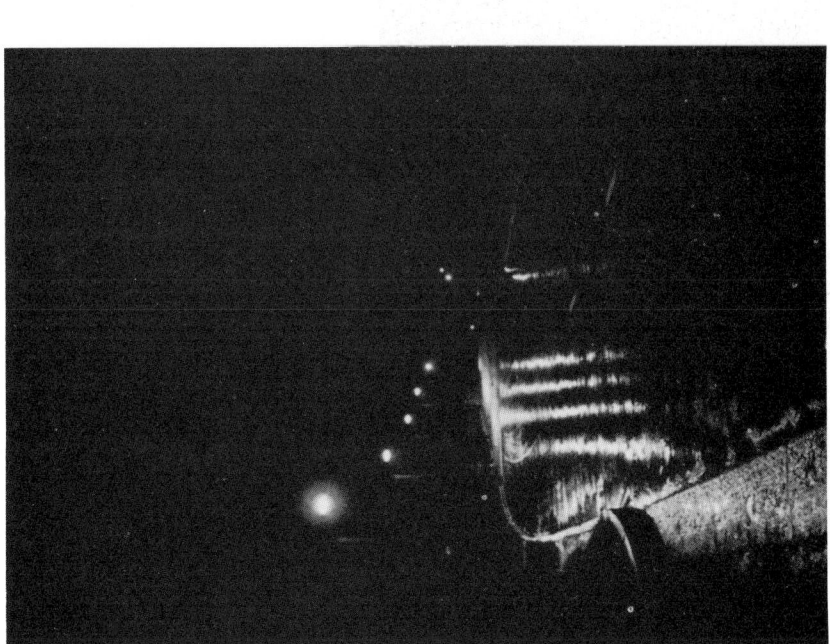

Figure 4.14 Effect of texture depth on appearance of wet roads at night. (a) Texture depth = 0.007 inches. (b) Texture depth = 0.04 inches

Continent and the old non-cut-off high angle lighting which used to be common here.

Lamp columns on main roads and motorways are usually at least 25 ft (7.6 m) in height and may be as high as 50 ft (15.2 m) in special cases. On certain motorways catenary lighting has been installed with high columns on the central reservation, spaced well apart, and connected by cables, from which are suspended a number of closely spaced lamps throwing light on the carriageway. The illumination of the road surface thus provided is very bright and uniform.

On residential roads, where lighting is mainly for the pedestrian, the height of lamp columns is less, usually about 12 to 15 ft (3.7 to 4.6 m). For further details of lighting practice, the Code of Practice for Road Lighting, published by the British Standards Institution, should be consulted.

Anti-dazzle screens

At bends on unlit dual carriageway roads, including motorways, glare from opposing headlights may reduce visibility and cause annoyance to drivers on the outside of the bends. Anti-dazzle screens, sited on the central reservation, largely remove this hazard. Such screens consist of a succession of vertical strips of metal or other opaque material, set at right angles to the road, and so spaced that, while there is little obstruction to the view at right angles through them, when they are viewed at angles of up to say, 30 degrees from the direction of travel, they overlap and cut out glare from opposing headlights.

4.6 Obstructions on and off the carriageways

Street furniture

Street furniture of all kinds presents serious hazards to motor vehicle occupants or riders, both in urban and rural environments. In 1982, nearly 5 per cent of all road deaths occurred in collisions with lighting columns alone. Other roadside equipment or obstructions, such as trees, telegraph poles, traffic signs, walls, fences and bollards also present hazards, so that a total of approximately 20 per cent of deaths involved collisions with these items. Obviously, the nearer the equipment is sited to the carriageway the greater the danger that it can be struck, but there is no universal rule for a safe distance. On motorways, or other dual carriageways, where speeds are highest, vehicles which are out of control may even cross the central reservation, the opposite carriageway and the opposite verge, so that no harmful obstacle should be sited near the limits of a motorway.

Obstacles in the form of motorway bridges and signs must often be sited in hazardous positions. When this occurs bridges are always protected by crash barriers – a measure which has been shown to reduce injuries. More attention needs to be paid to signs, however, since a collision with even a comparatively weak metal post may result in injury to car occupants.

Lamp columns of light metal construction have been developed which overcome this hazard because they are easily detached from their bases when struck. The resulting damage to the striking car and its velocity change are then such as to minimise the risk of injury to the occupants of a

Road surfaces 47

Figure 4.15 A breakaway lamp column struck by a car at 60 mile/h (97 km/h)

Figure 4.16 An early test damage to a concrete lamp column struck by a light car at 20 mile/h (32 km/h)

striking car (Figure 4.15). The breakaway columns can usually be fitted with new base components and replaced. Even heavy concrete columns often have to be replaced after comparatively minor impacts as was shown in early tests (see Figure 4.16).

Field experience of breakaway columns in five public installations was reported by Walker (1974). As expected, the severity of accidents involving lighting columns was considerably reduced. It was estimated that the reduced cost of the breakaway column accidents more than compensated for the higher capital cost of the columns.

Crash barriers

Crash barriers sometimes may be regarded as obstructions. The main function of a crash barrier, when sited on the central reservation of a motorway, is to prevent out of control vehicles from crossing on to the opposite carriageway. When motorway traffic is very light, however, the chance of a collision with an opposing vehicle is small, and the barrier may be more harmful as an obstruction than beneficial in preventing encroachment on the opposite carriageway. When motorway traffic is heavy, the benefits outweigh the drawbacks. There are no clear-cut rules to determine the changeover point. For further information reference should be made to original papers (TRRL Leaflet LF 400, 1974). Crash barriers on medians cannot be expected to prevent heavy commercial vehicles from encroaching on the opposite carriageway.

Kerbs

Vertical kerbs and even those with a 45 degree face can also cause the loss of control in cars and motorcycles, and probably even in heavy commercial vehicles. They do not prevent vehicles from leaving the carriageway except when speeds are low and the angle of approach is small.

On the central reservations of dual carriageways kerbs are sometimes sited in front of crash barriers. This is bad practice since a crash barrier can only be expected to operate efficiently when a car strikes it in an undisturbed condition. Thus the surface in front of a crash barrier should always be level and hard. On rural roads flush kerbs are less of a hazard than upstanding ones, but they are required to be made conspicuous at night as described on p. 38.

Obstructions in the road

Obstructions in the road, mainly road works, generate a small proportion of vehicle accidents. They should be indicated by road signs in accordance with the recommendations of the Department of Transport.

Parked vehicles

In 1981 parked vehicles were involved in about 8 per cent of vehicle accidents in urban areas and 4.4 per cent in rural areas. Laybys are therefore an essential provision for rural roads. In urban areas 'clearways', where stopping on the carriageway is prohibited, have been shown to reduce accidents on heavily trafficked approaches to towns. It is particularly important to prevent parking at the approaches to intersections. In all cases it is in the interests of safety to do so. In urban areas the presence of a single parked vehicle also seriously restricts traffic flow at intersections carrying heavy traffic flows.

4.7 Speed limits and speed control measures

The first effective review of the effect of speed limits on speeds and accidents was made by Smeed (Smeed, 1960). His study covered the results of the imposition of speed limits in a number of European countries as well as in New Zealand and the US. He found that, although many motorists still exceeded the limits, speeds at the top end of the range were reduced in most cases and when this had happened casualties fell, the reduction in deaths being particularly marked. Speed limits made their greatest impact in urban areas, but had an effect even on motorways.

Similar results were found in two later studies (Sabey, 1975 and Scott, 1977), which also showed that the amount of the reduction in accidents and casualties depended on many factors such as type of road, urban or rural environment, traffic flow and composition and time of day. There were indications that the effect of limits tended to decrease with time.

Table 4.2 Speed survey: Great Britain (1983)

	Cars	Two-wheeled motor vehicles	Buses and coaches	Vans	Heavy goods vehicles
Single carriageway roads					
Speed limit (mile/h)*	60 (96)	60 (96)	50 (80)	50 (80)	40 (64)
Percentage over limit	5	8	17	17	56
Dual carriageway roads					
Speed limit (mile/h)*	70 (112)	70 (112)	50 (80)	50 (80)	40 (64)
Percentage over limit	12	13	64	61	89
Motorways					
Speed limit (mile/h)*	70 (112)	70 (112)	70 (112)	70 (112)	60 (96)
Percentage over limit	40	47	31	19	39

* (km/h values in parentheses)

In 1983 a survey of speeds on British roads was carried out, for single and double carriageway roads and motorways. Table 4.2 shows the percentages of vehicles of the five main classes exceeding the relevant speed limits. In all classes of road, buses and heavy commercial vehicles exceeded the limits by large margins, although on motorways cars and motorcycles exceeded their limits by similar margins.

In addition to normal methods of speed control by speed limits and traffic police and radar, engineering measures can also play a part in appropriate situations. On town outskirts traffic signals linked in such a way as to control speeds to a safe value can reduce accidents, particularly at night (Road Safety: The Slough Experiment, 1957). At roundabout approaches a series of yellow bars across the carriageway with decreasing spacing have been found to reduce the speeds of vehicles entering the roundabout, and to reduce accidents. Road humps can effectively restrict vehicle speeds on residential roads. They must be carefully designed, however, to avoid causing vehicle damage (Watts, 1973; TRRL Leaflet LF 665, 1977; Baguley, 1981).

4.8 The application of safety measures to whole areas in towns

In medium-sized towns with a traditional layout (i.e. other than new towns) up to one-third of the accidents occur in town centres, while the rest are almost equally divided between the main traffic routes and the residential areas. Within the town centre accidents are heavily clustered. Outside the centre, clusters of accidents are less evident, accounting for about one-third of the accidents on the arterial road network, and virtually none of those on the roads and streets of the residential areas. Thus in the typical urban area more than one-half of the road accidents are scattered diffusely. Among these scattered accidents there is a markedly higher proportion of pedestrian and cycle accidents (specially involving children) than is found in the clusters of accidents. A major urban safety project has, therefore, been initiated by the Transport and Road Research Laboratory and is now in progress (1985) to develop a management system for improving safety in existing towns (outside central areas) and to demonstrate the benefits in terms of accident reduction. Five towns are being studied with the cooperation of local authorities and police. The main aims of this study are to estimate the numbers, severities and distribution of accidents over the road network, and to monitor traffic and the effects on access and on pedestrian movement. A report is expected in 1987, when the data has been analysed and measures for improving safety have been devised (Ward and Allsop, 1982).

References

Accident Investigation and Prevention Manual (1974) Department of Transport Road Safety Directorate

BAGULEY, C. (1981) 'Speed control humps – further public road trials'. Transport and Road Research Laboratory Digest LR 1017

British Standard Specification B.S. Au 200: Part 1 (1984) and Part 2 (1984)

DALBY, E. (1979) 'Area-wide measures in urban road safety'. *Transport and Road Research Laboratory Digest*, SR 517

FAULKENER, C. R. and EATON, J. E. (1977) 'Accident investigation and prevention by applying the location sampling technique to rural crossroads'. *Transport and Road Research Laboratory Digest*, LR 780

General principles of control by traffic signals. *Department of Transport Technical Memorandum*, TA 16/81, 1981

GREEN, H. (1977) 'Accidents at off-side priority roundabouts with mini- or small islands'. *Transport and Road Research Laboratory Digest*, LR 774

'Hazardous road locations: Identification and countermeasures' (1976). Organisation for Economic Cooperation and Development, Paris (Chapter 4)

'Instructions for using the portable skid-resistance tester' (1979) *Road Research Laboratory Note* 27. HMSO: London

'Junction layout for control by traffic signals'. (1981) *Department of Transport, Roads and Transportation Directorate Advice Note*, TA 18/81

'Junctions and accesses: Determination of size of roundabouts and major/minor junctions'. (1981) *Department of Transport, Roads and Local Transport Directorate Advice Note* TA 23/81

'Layout of roads in rural areas' (1968) Ministry of Transport, HMSO

'Layout of roads in rural areas – a guide to revisions' (1982) *Department of Transport, Roads and Local Transport Directorate, Departmental Advice Note* TA 28/82

NEWBY, R. F. (1962) 'The central reservation and direction of travel as factors in accidents on the London-Birmingham motorway' *Road Research Laboratory Note*, LN/154/RFN

Research on Road Traffic (1965) HMSO, (Chapter 13)

'Road layout and geometry: highway link design' (1981) *Department of Transport, Roads and Local Transport Directorate, Department Standard* TD 9/81

'Road safety: The Slough Experiment 1955–57' (1957) Ministry of Transport and Civil Aviation. HMSO: London

RUSSAM, K. and SABEY, B. E. (1972) 'Accidents and traffic conflicts at junctions'. *Transport and Road Research Laboratory Report*, LR 514

SAVEY, B. E. (1975) 'Experience of speed limits in Great Britain'. Int. Symposium on Traffic Speed and Casualties, Denmark, April

SABEY, B. E. and STAUGHTON, G. C. (1975) Interacting roles of road environment, vehicle and road user in accidents'. *Fifth Int. Conf. of International Association for Accident and Traffic Medicine, London, September*

SABEY, B. E., WILLIAMS, T. and LUPTON, G. N. (1980) 'Factors affecting the friction of tyres on wet roads'. *Proc. of the Society of Automotive Engineers, June*

'Safety fences on motorway central reserves'. *Transport and Road Research Laboratory Leaflet*, LF 400, 1974

SCOTT, P. P. (1977) 'Speed limits and road accidents'. *Proc. Traffex 77, Traffic Engineering and Road Safety Conference, Stonleigh, Warks, April*

SMEED, R. J. (1960) 'The influence of speed and speed regulations on traffic flow and accidents'. *Fifth Int. Study Week in Traffic Engineering, Nive, 1960*

'Speed control humps in Abbotsbury Road, Kensington, London' (1977) *Transport and Road Research Laboratory Leaflet*, LF 665

'Technical memorandum on roundabout design'. (1975) Highways Directorate, Department of the Environment, H 2/75

'Water spray from heavy vehicles' (1975) *Transport and Road Research Laboratory Leaflet* LF 602

WATTS, G. R. (1973) 'Road humps for the control of vehicle speeds'. *Transport and Road Research Laboratory Report*, LR 597

Chapter 5

Movements of vehicles and road users before accidents

This chapter deals with matters which influence primary safety, that is, with factors which affect the occurrence of accidents. Secondary safety, dealing with factors which influence the injuries sustained when an accident has occurred, is discussed in Chapter 6.

5.1 Visibility from vehicles by day and night

The driver's view to front and rear

For an average medium-sized car the driver's angle of view through a windscreen is about 30° to the right and about 55° to the left (nearside). The angle of view through the rear window is about 30°. The windscreen pillar on the driver's side may be wide enough to hide a pedestrian who is about 30 ft (9.5 m) or more away.

The bodywork of the car on the offside rear may produce a hidden area when viewed through the windscreen mirror about 10° wide, which can hide a motorcycle about 7 ft (2.2 m) behind the car on the offside.

The road surface in front of the car may be obscured by the bonnet of a car for an average driver for a distance of 40 to 50 ft (12 to 16 m). To the rear of the car, the distance depends very much on the placement of the rear-view mirror, and in this instance it is more important to place the mirror to provide a horizontal view to detect vehicles at a distance than to see the road surface near the car (Grime, 1960).

In commercial vehicles, the angle of view through the windscreen is more variable but obscuration by the windscreen pillar can be similar to that in cars. There is a view directly behind the vehicle only if the cab is fitted with rear windows and an internal mirror.

Mirrors

Flat mirrors are best for internal rear-view mirrors since they allow the speeds and distances of following vehicles to be estimated. They should be wide enough to allow the whole of the rear window to be seen. All rear-view mirrors (including outside mirrors) should be placed as near as possible to the line of sight of the driver (Grime, 1960). They should provide an angle of view of not less than 15° (1 in 4) to the rear, i.e. a flat mirror at a distance of 2 ft (0.6 m) from the driver should be at least 6 in

(16 cm) wide. Thus flat mirrors on wings are of little value and flat mirrors on doors suffer from the double disadvantage of being far removed from the driver's line of sight and needing to be large and clumsy to provide the required angle of view without frequent critical readjustment.

Car colour

In normal daylight car colours are not very important in determining whether or not the car is seen. In poor visibility no one colour is always best. Using sidelights or dipped headlights is much more effective than colour alone. In daylight in thick fog there is a view that full headlights should be used since maximum intensity is required to pierce the fog and dazzle is not a problem. In thinner fog or haze, dipped headlights are enough to make sure the car is seen.

Headlights

A driver using headlights at night on an unlit road sees bright objects against a dark background, in contrast to street lighting, in which the objects are dark and the background is light (Figures 4.13 and 5.1). Upper beams (full headlights) concentrate almost all their light into relatively narrow beams since they are required to detect objects and reveal the road at considerable distances. Dipped or meeting beams are much wider since they are required to throw light on the road near to the car so that the

Figure 5.1 Seeing with headlights: bright object, dark background

driver can see where he is placed in relation to the kerb. Even with dipped headlights the visible area is much narrower than it is by day.

Estimates made some years ago, and still approximately correct, of the distances at which grey objects, placed at different positions across a 20 ft (6.2 m) wide road, are first detected in the presence of opposing headlights, are shown in Figure 5.2; both cars had well-aimed headlights. These are maximum distances, and if the headlights of one car are mis-aimed upwards and those of the other correctly aimed or mis-aimed downwards, the driver of the more glaring car will see further than the other, whose 'seeing' distance will be even less than expected from Figure 5.2.

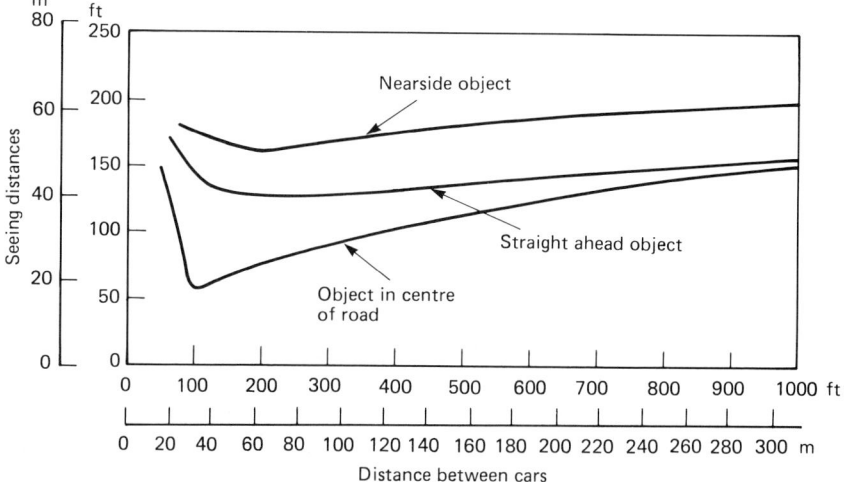

Figure 5.2 Direct seeing distances for grey objects (luminance factor 7 per cent and 18 in (46 cm) high) on a road 20 ft (6.2 m) wide

Figure 5.2 was obtained by combining the results of practical tests with lighting theory. The calculations were made for the so called 'Anglo-American meeting beams' at that time almost universally used in Britain (Jehu, 1955). Continental type headlights, which have different distribution of light, with less glare to oncoming drivers, are now more usual on new cars. The light distribution curves for the two types of meeting beam are shown in Figure 5.3. Field trials of the two types in the meeting situation were made in 1968 and 1969 and the results are summarised in Table 5.1 (Yerrell, 1976). Neither beam was found to have an overall advantage, although as already mentioned the continental meeting beam is less glaring (Yerrell, 1971). Seeing distances in the most unfavourable conditions similar to those shown in Figure 5.5 and Table 5.1 may be less than the possible stopping distances (Yerrell, 1976); (see Figure 5.14 for the braking distances of motor vehicles).

Seeing distances with full headlights (intensities greater than 20 000 candles) and no opposing glare are much greater (Figure 5.5) (Jehu, 1955). The colour of light makes no detectable difference to seeing distance

Visibility from vehicles by day and night 55

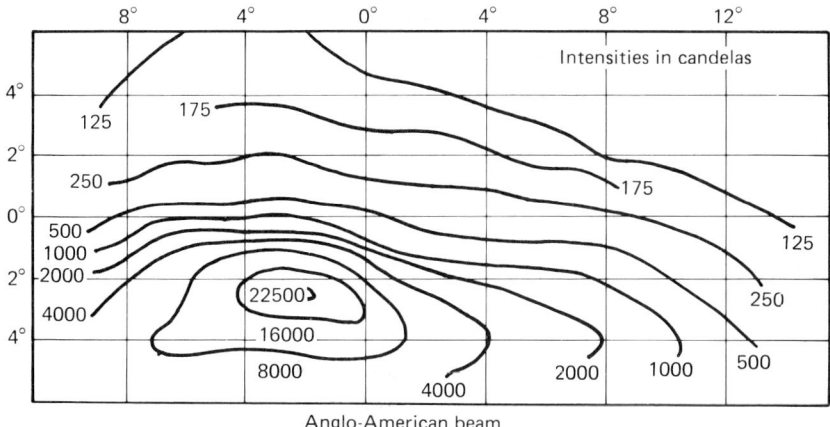

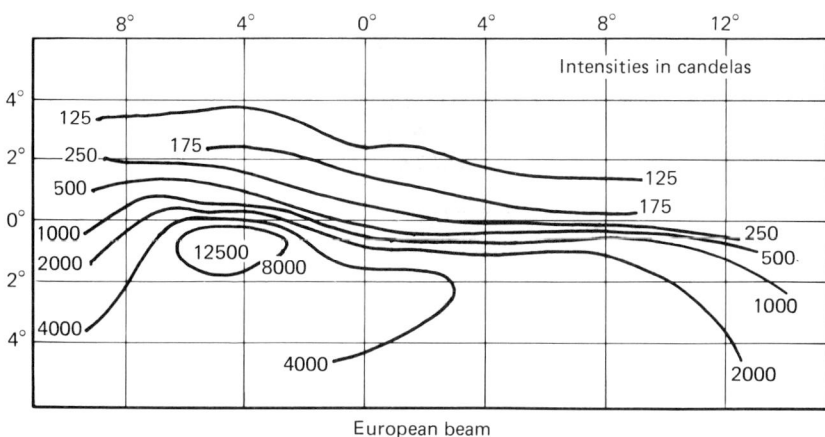

Figure 5.3 ISO candela diagrams

Table 5.1 Recognition distances found in trials of Anglo-American and European dipped headlights – mean recognition distances for a target with 10 per cent reflection factor

	Nearside object		Offside object	
	AA beam (m)	European beam (m)	AA beam (m)	European beam (m)
Straight road	51.4	50.4	22.1	24.8
Left-hand curve	37.5	32.6	40.9	40.9
Right-hand curve	25.8	27.6	15.6	21.8
Bottom of hill	26.5	26.8	16.8	16.7
Top of hill	48.5	42.3	23.7	24.6

56 Movements of vehicles and road users before accidents

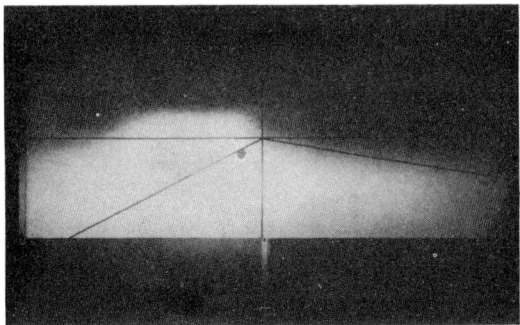

Anglo-American headlight

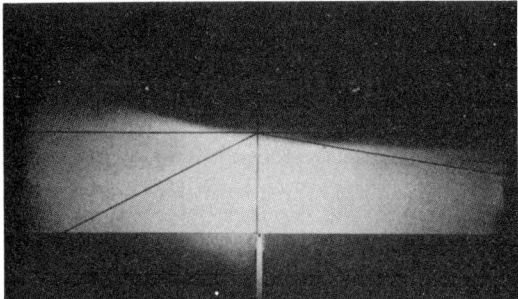

European headlight

Figure 5.4 Typical beam patterns

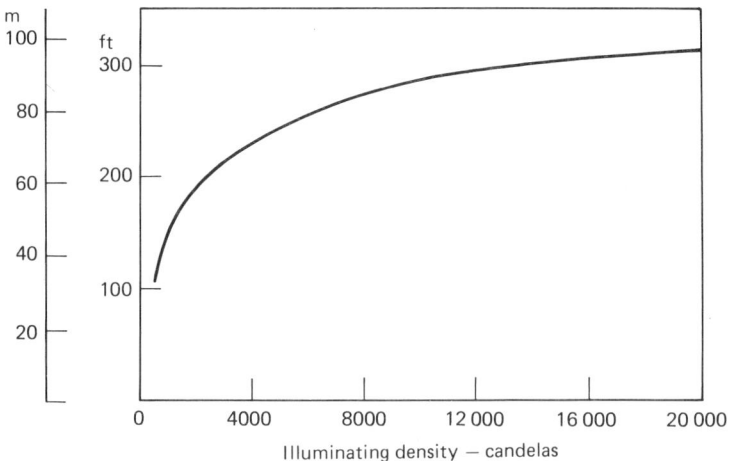

Figure 5.5 Relation between seeing distance and beam intensity for a grey object

provided the intensities are the same, but yellow lights look less glaring than white lights of equal intensity (brightness) (Jehu, 1954).

A useful review of the whole subject of vehicle headlights is given in the previously quoted paper by Yerrell (1976).

Street lighting (see also Section 4.5 in Chapter 4)

Street lights brighten the road surface so that objects are seen in silhouette, i.e. as dark objects against a light background (Figure 4.13). Research shows how increasing the brightness of the road surface decreases the risk of accidents (TTRL LF 929, 1980). Since objects are seen in the light of headlights as bright against a dark background, if both headlights and streetlights are in use at the same time the result may be worse for the driver than if sidelights were used instead of headlights. If poor street lighting is encountered on residential roads or on traffic routes, headlights should be used to enable the driver to see and other road users to see the vehicle.

In streets with good lighting designed for main traffic routes, the use of neither dipped headlights nor side lights is wholly satisfactory, because sidelights by themselves are often insufficient to mark a vehicle and signal its movements to other road users and dipped headlights cause disability glare and impair the ability to see objects beyond approaching cars (Falkner and Older, 1967). A promising solution is the dim-dip system, which will be made mandatory for new cars in 1986. In this system dipped headlights are switched on at reduced intensity whenever the sidelights and ignition are switched on (Jehu, 1963). Until the dim-dip system becomes common the recommended practice is to use dipped headlights in all lighted streets.

General visibility

Reduced visibility increases the risk of accidents. The risk is greater by night by a factor of about 1.3 (Table 5.2), while rain and fog further increase the risk (TRRL Leaflet LF 266, 1971). The effect of rain at night is that nearly twice as many accidents occur on wet roads as would be expected from daytime accident experience (Road Accidents Great Britain, 1981).

Table 5.2 Accidents in different light conditions and rates per vehicle km (1969)

Light condition (defined by hour of day)	*Accidents*		*Traffic flow 10^9 vehicle km*	*Accident rate*	
	Number	*per cent*		*per 10^6 vehicle km*	*relative to daylight*
Dark	62 636	24.1	38.1	1.64	1.33
Dawn	7215	2.8	3.9	1.85	1.50
Dusk	14 010	5.4	11.0	1.27	1.03
Daylight	172 621	66.3	140.2	1.23	1.00

Fog at night is the most difficult weather condition to combat by vehicle lighting, although specially designed fog lamps do help. Unfortunately, the distance at which an object may be detected in thick fog increases only very slowly as the intensity of the light is increased. This is illustrated in Figure 5.6.

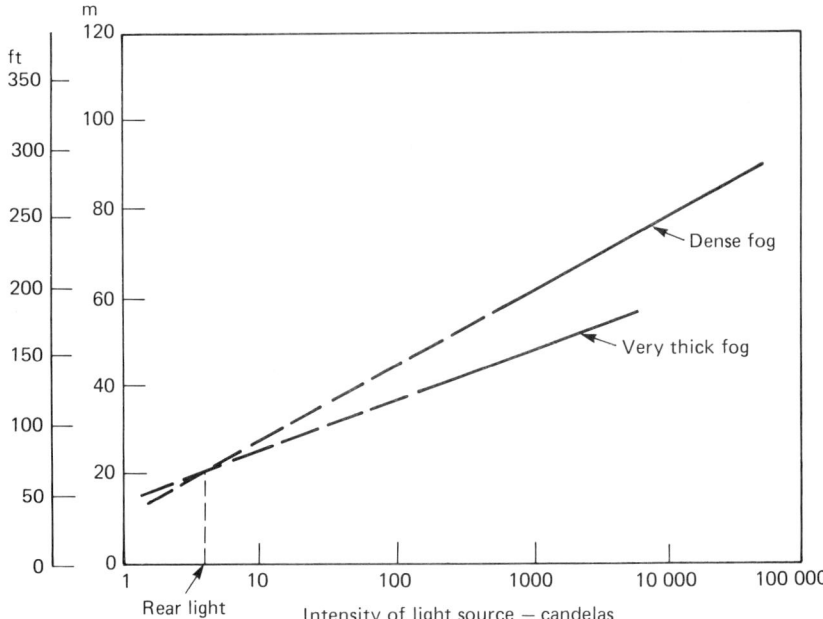

Figure 5.6 Relation between intensity (brightness) of light source and visibility distance in daylight fog

The most important requirements in a fog lamp are that the light from it should have a wide spread to illuminate the side of the road and a sharp upper edge to the beam to minimise annoying back glare. To produce such a wide beam with satisfactory intensity requires a high wattage bulb, although, as previously mentioned, intensity is less important than spread. Colour does not affect seeing distance for equal intensity, although, as with headlights, glare from yellow beams may appear to be less annoying than that from white light (Research on Road Safety, Chapter 9).

The main sources of danger in thick fog are: (1) the inability of the driver to see where he is in relation to the lane markings. As a result he may slow to a crawl or stop. (2) The distances at which following drivers can detect slow or stopped vehicles are too small to allow them to stop in time.

Figure 5.6 also shows the distances at which rear lights of various intensities are detectable in thick fog. Ordinary rear lights are quite inadequate; even specially bright rear fog lights give little margin. A really useful light would need to have an intensity similar to that seen in approaching dipped headlights (Grime, 1974).

Concertina-type fog accidents on motorways produce the most frightening single accidents although they account for only about 0.5 per cent of all serious injuries and deaths to vehicle occupants. The presence of commercial vehicles greatly increases the number and severity of injuries. When thick fog occurs, commercial vehicles make up a larger proportion of all vehicles using the motorway than in clear weather. Most deaths in these circumstances involve one or more commercial vehicles, and a high proportion of the deaths are in the commercial vehicles themselves (Grime, 1974).

Cycles and motorcycles

The problems of visibility from motorcycles are, in general terms, similar to those from cars, except that the motorcyclist, being able to see the kerb or roadside very near to his machine, and in many cases having no windscreen, is able to travel in worse conditions of fog and bad visibility than the driver of an enclosed vehicle. However, he has the same limitations on the distances at which objects can be detected ahead of him at night and in fog.

Cyclists have the same or even greater advantages than motorcyclists in their ability to move in fog, since they can easily keep going within their range of visibility. They are particularly vulnerable from the rear at night, however, since their rear lights are totally inadequate in fog. Red rear reflectors do little to improve the situation.

Yellow reflectors on pedals, yellow reflecting armbands and Sam Brown belts improve visibility from the rear at night. A flag or yellow reflecting disc at the end of an arm on the right side of the cycle has been found effective in keeping overtaking traffic at a distance.

Since motorcycles are small and often fast moving, they are less easily seen than cars and commercial vehicles. Failure to see them results in many accidents. The two most common situations are when a car or commercial vehicle turns across the path of an oncoming or overtaking motorcyclist, and when a car or commercial vehicle emerges from a side road into the path of a motorcycle on a main road without noticing the motorcycle.

In both situations the practice recommended for motorcyclists of using their headlights in daylight to increase their conspicuousness should help to reduce the number of such incidents. In the overtaking situation an outside mirror on the overtaken vehicle giving at least at 15° wide view to the rear and placed close to the line of sight of the driver is essential.

Single vehicle accidents account for at least 22 per cent of motorcycle accidents (Whitaker, 1976 and Downing, 1985). A quarter of such accidents were collisions with parked unattended vehicles. Most of the others involved loss of control, either on bends or corners, or on bumpy or slippery roads, or by hitting kerbs or animals.

Seeing and perceiving

It is often assumed that, if an object or vehicle is seen clearly, there is no excuse for the driver of a vehicle who collides with this object, since he should be continuously concentrating on the task of driving. This does assume an ideal population of drivers, to whom to see is to perceive. In reality, a driver's concentration fluctuates and the image which falls on the retina of the eye is not always registered in the brain. It has been observed, for example, that vehicles, stationary at the roadside, on straight roads, in full daylight, are frequently struck from the rear. In one study (Grime, 1961), it was found that nearly one-third of all such collisions with vehicles on rural roads in daylight occurred in those circumstances. When, therefore, figures are given in the earlier parts of this section for distances at which objects can be detected, they assume full concentration on the driving task, and take no account of any other factor such as the one just mentioned.

5.2 Stability and control of vehicles

General vehicle characteristics

The most important factors which influence steering behaviour and therefore stability are:

(1) The stiffness of the tyres in the sideways direction, and therefore the sideways 'creep' of the wheel when a side force is applied.
(2) The position of the centre of gravity.
(3) The moment of inertia of the vehicle about the vertical axis through the centre of gravity (the moment in yaw).
(4) The role moment of inertia (Grime and Jones, 1969–70).

The moments of inertia are measures of the inertial resistance of the vehicle to spinning and to rolling respectively, and are defined in Appendix 2.

Oversteer

Stiff tyres at the front and soft ones at the rear or a centre of gravity too far to the rear result in 'oversteer', so that the rear tends to swing round in cornering, with possible instability in cornering or manoeuvring. The effect of oversteer in producing instability increases with speed. An oversteering car, although stable at low speed, becomes increasingly responsive to steering wheel movement as speed increases, until, at a critical speed, the vehicle becomes uncontrollable.

Understeer

Soft tyres at the front, combined with stiff ones at the rear, produce 'understeer', when the front tyres creep sideways more than the rear ones in cornering. As speed around corners increases, the steering wheel has to be rotated further and further to get around a particular corner, until, finally, if understeering is very pronounced, the vehicle refuses to take the corner at all, and, if the wheel is rotated still further, the front wheels skid and the vehicle goes straight on (Grime and Giles, 1954–55).

Most modern vehicles with properly chosen and inflated tyres are designed with slight understeering characteristics and do not normally exhibit any of the alarming behaviour mentioned above. However, there are several ways in which oversteering, the more alarming of the two extreme modes of behaviour, may be generated. When a small car carrying two front-seat occupants has understeering characteristics it may oversteer, when loaded with two rear-seat passengers and luggage, to such an extent that it becomes uncontrollable at high speeds, say, at 60 mile/h (97 km/h). Underinflated rear tyres or radial tyres on front wheels and crossply tyres on the rear wheels can produce the same result on any car. Worn steering gear accentuates the difficulty of controlling the vehicle.

It will be clear that understeering characteristics, although unlikely to be increased by changes in loading, can, however, be increased by underinflated front tyres, or by combining radial tyres on the rear with crossply tyres on the front wheels, although this change in steering characteristics should be more readily detectable and less likely to cause difficulty than increased oversteering.

Tyre/road adhesion

In the previous discussion, attention has been confined to circumstances in which the vehicle has not begun to skid out of control, although this may well be the end result of cornering or manoeuvring at too high a speed, whether the vehicle oversteers or understeers, or indeed has neutral steering (that is, the front wheels and rear wheels have the same cornering stiffness).

Tyre/road adhesion, as measured by the coefficient of friction μ between tyre and road surface at the relevant speed, has an even greater influence on whether control is lost than the steering characteristics of the vehicle. When driver age and other characteristics are considered, the national statistics of car accidents reveal very little evidence of differences in the risk of having accidents attributable to differences in the steering characteristics of cars but large differences attributable to differences in tyre/road adhesion (Table 5.3) (Road Accidents Great Britain, 1984)

Table 5.3 Skidding in personal injury accidents (1984)

Road conditions	Accidents in 1984		
	Number involving skidding	Total number	Percentage skidding rate
Dry	27 413	274 881	10.0
Wet	25 501	145 495	17.5
Icy	4976	9136	54.5

(Jones, 1976). The coefficient of friction μ is equal to the maximum force in the plane of the road which the tyre can exert divided by the vertical load at the tyre/road interface $\mu = F/W$ where F is tyre force and W the load (Appendix 1).

Friction coefficient on dry roads

On dry roads μ for car tyres is always high and does not vary appreciably with speed, except when a locked wheel skids along a road at high speed and melting of the rubber or of the road surface takes place in the tyre track, when the coefficient may decrease below the normal value of 0.8 to 1.0. The coefficient is independent of tread pattern; indeed, smooth treads give better adhesion on dry roads than patterned ones. Even with such high coefficients, loss of control and skidding can occur although the probability of it occurring is much less than on wet roads. (See Table 5.3.) For heavy goods vehicles the coefficient of friction on dry surfaces has been found to decrease with increased load (see Section 5.6), from a value at low speeds rather less than that of car tyres.

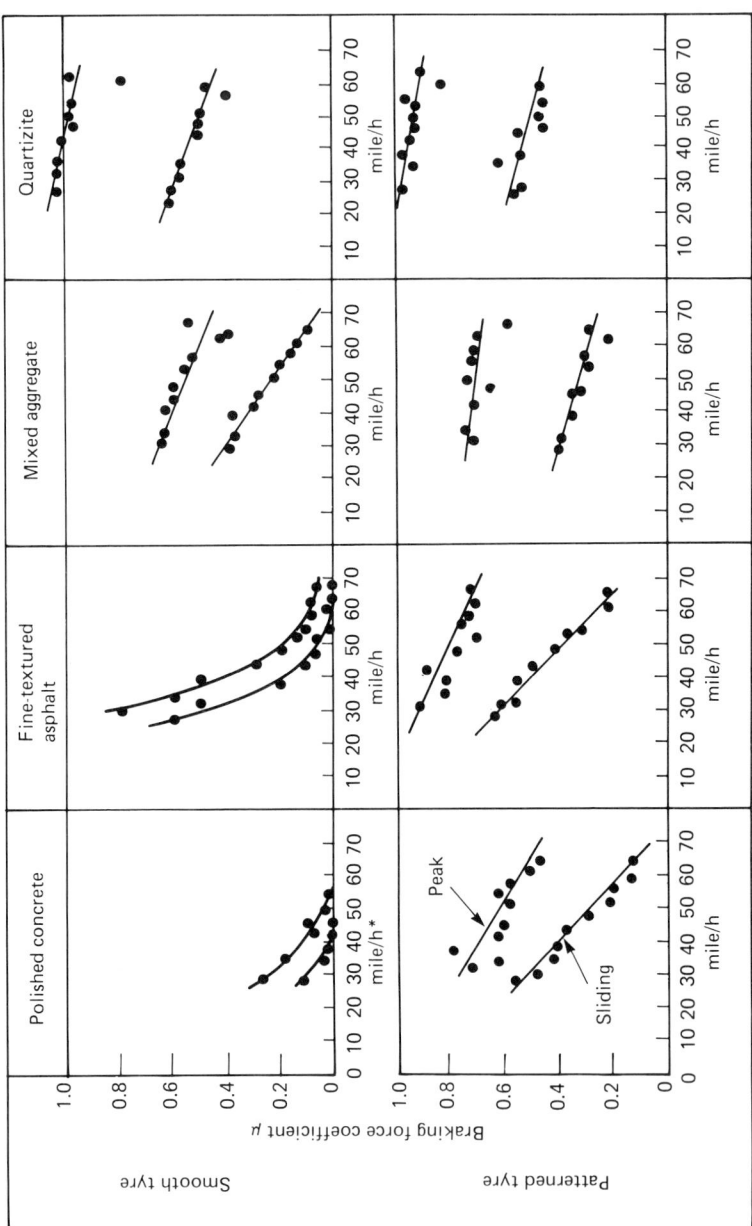

Figure 5.7 The influence of tread pattern on braking force coefficient on four surfaces, for tyre in new condition

* To convert to km/h multiply by 1.61

Wet roads

Wet roads may have coefficients of friction between 0.05 and 0.8 depending upon the texture of the road surface, the tyre tread pattern, the thickness of the layer of water on the road, the speed of the vehicle and whether its wheels are rolling or skidding (Grime and Giles, 1954–55) (Giles, 1963) (Sabey, Williams and Lupton, 1970).

A road may be considered wet when it has more than a thickness of approximately one-fiftieth of an inch of water on it – a very small thickness. An important property of all wet roads is that the coefficients of friction between tyre and road decrease with increased speed. The main reason is that as speed increases there is less time to displace the water which acts as a lubricant between tyre and road, and so to establish the intimate contact between tyre and road which is necessary for good adhesion.

Figure 5.7 gives general guidance on what may be expected from good modern tyres, in new condition, and from smooth tyres on road surfaces of four different types at speeds up to 65 mile/h (105 km/h) when the depth of water on the surface is between 0.04 and 0.08 in (1 to 2 mm) (Maycock, 1965–66). Photographs of the test surfaces referred to in Figure 5.7 are included (see Figure 5.8) for general guidance. Seven surfaces, laid on the TRRL track, were included in Maycock's tests; but the four selected for

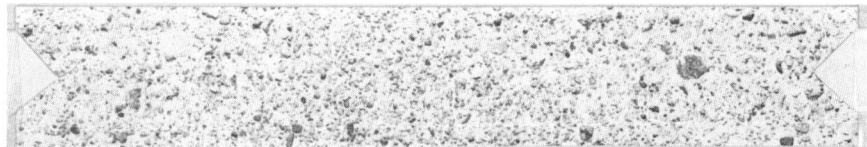

Polished concrete

Fine-textured asphalt

Mixed aggregate

Quartzite

Figure 5.8 Surfaces used in tests

illustration here are sufficient for our purposes since they cover the range of surface texture likely to be met on roads. The polished concrete surface has a smooth macro-texture and a polished micro-texture (for the meaning of these terms see Figure 4.9); fine textured asphalt has very little macro-texture but a fairly harsh micro-texture; the mixed aggregate carpet has a rough macro-texture but a polished micro-texture; quartzite has a very rough macro-texture accompanied by a harsh micro-texture. Figure 5.9 shows the patterned tyre.

Figure 5.9 Patterned tyre used in tests

Similar results were obtained, up to 80 mile/h (128 km/h), by the same method on a test surface of asphalt, laid to motorway specification, using two different cars and four brands of tyre (Williams, Davies, Riley, and Wilkins, 1981).

Peak and sliding coefficients

On wet roads there are two coefficients of friction (see Figure 5.7); the first comes into operation when the vehicle is actually skidding, either forwards with locked wheels, or sideways; the second, when the wheels are rolling and pointing in the direction of travel, is a higher coefficient, sometimes twice as great as the sliding coefficient, and is produced (a) in the direction of travel, when the brakes are applied progressively until the wheel is almost skidding, and (b) approximately at right angles to the direction of travel to oppose the outward centrifugal force in cornering, and to prevent sideways sliding.

This peak force is therefore available for both steering and braking and is probably the reason why comparatively few vehicles lose control on wet slippery roads. Once the vehicle starts to skid, the much lower skidding coefficient makes the recovery of control difficult even at moderate speeds, and almost impossible at high speeds. One should also recognise that it is almost impossible to use the peak coefficient in forward braking unless the vehicle is fitted with automatically operated nonlocking brakes.

Factors influencing skidding coefficients – road and tyre

The most important factors influencing the values of both the peak and the skidding coefficients on wet roads are the following.

(1) The texture of the road surface. This may vary from a very open texture (rough macro-texture) consisting of closely packed stones (the aggregate) projecting from the matrix which holds them in place, to a very smooth surface with no projecting stones (smooth macro-texture).
(2) The shape of the stones, if they project. The aggregate may consist of stones with sharp edges (harsh micro-texture), or those edges may be more or less smooth, usually because they have been worn smooth by tyres (polished micro-texture). Sharp edges give best penetration of the water film, and greatest grip when the film has been penetrated. Figure 4.9 illustrates combinations of texture and stone shape found on roads.
(3) The tread pattern on the tyre. This is designed with as many channels as possible to get the water away from beneath the tyre.
(4) Tyre tread material. Best results are obtained with materials having low elasticity.

Unfortunately, economic and other difficulties have prevented full use of (3) and (4) in the design of large tyres for commercial vehicles, so that the best commercial vehicle tyres provide somewhat poorer adhesion on wet roads than the best car tyres.

These are broad general statements. In practice interactions between factors occur. The principal ones are as follows.

(1) Tread pattern has little beneficial effect on surfaces with a rough macro-texture up to 30 mile/h (48 km/h) or more when the road texture alone provides adequate drainage. But at high speeds, adequate drainage can only be provided by both tyre and road channels.
(2) The sharp edges of stones can only come into operation if they can make contact with the tyre, that is, if drainage is adequate. Thus for town use, where speeds are low, fairly close-textured surfaces, i.e. smooth surfaces with harsh micro-texture consisting of small sharp stones, may give good results, but for high speed roads, sharpness of stones (harsh micro-texture) needs to be accompanied by open texture and angularity.
(3) Tyre tread material has its greatest effect on surfaces with rough macro-texture but has little effect on smooth roads (Grime and Giles, 1954–55) (Sabey, Williams and Lupton, 1970).

The operation of these factors and of their interactions may be traced in Figure 5.7. On the mixed aggregate surface, which has a rough macro-texture, the smooth and the patterned tyre produced similar results; the fine textured asphalt has a fairly harsh micro-texture but little macro-texture, so that, while at 30 mile/h (48 km/h) the coefficients were similar, at higher speeds the patterned tyre was greatly superior; quartzite, with both a rough macro-texture and harsh micro-texture, produced results with smooth and patterned tyres which were not very different.

Road surface wear

It is not surprising that wear of both road surface and tyre reduces performance in wet weather. On roads which carry a large amount of heavy traffic, all road surfacing materials with a bituminous base gradually consolidate and polish, so that a surface, originally open-textured with sharp-edged stones, may change eventually into a close-textured, smooth surface, the aggregate having been pushed down into the matrix and its edges worn smooth. The effect on concrete surfaces is not quite as drastic since it is confined to polishing the aggregate.

It is not always easy to recognise that a road surface may have become slippery due to wear, when the process has not resulted in the kind of smooth surface mentioned previously. A surface may still look very open and rough and yet the stones may have worn smooth. Such surfaces feel smooth to the touch and in the absence of test machines they may be tested with the hand. In this case, the deterioration of skidding performance is not as pronounced as when the surface becomes close-textured and smooth. The result is similar to that of the mixed aggregate surface in Figure 5.7.

Tyre wear

Similarly, as the pattern on a tyre is reduced in depth, it also provides poorer drainage. When tyre patterns have been worn down to their legal limit of 0.04 in (1 mm) depth, their wet weather performance is considerably reduced. Although no single figure can be given for this reduction (RRL Leaflet LF 163, 1971), Figure 5.10 suggests that the reduction is greatest for fine-textured surfaces or high speeds or both than for coarse-textured surfaces and low speeds. On the first test surface of Figure 5.8, for example, the reduction at 30 mile/h (48 km/h) might be small, but much greater at 60 mile/h (97 km/h).

Water depth

Increasing the depth of water on the road also reduces coefficients of friction, although with good tyre treads this only becomes marked at speeds over 30 mile/h (48 km/h); and the smoother the road the greater the effect. Figure 5.10 shows how the coefficient decreases continuously as the water depth increases, that is, there is no sudden change from an adequate coefficient to a condition of 'aquaplaning'. However, for about 95 per cent of the time when the road is wet, the depth of water is less than 0.04 in

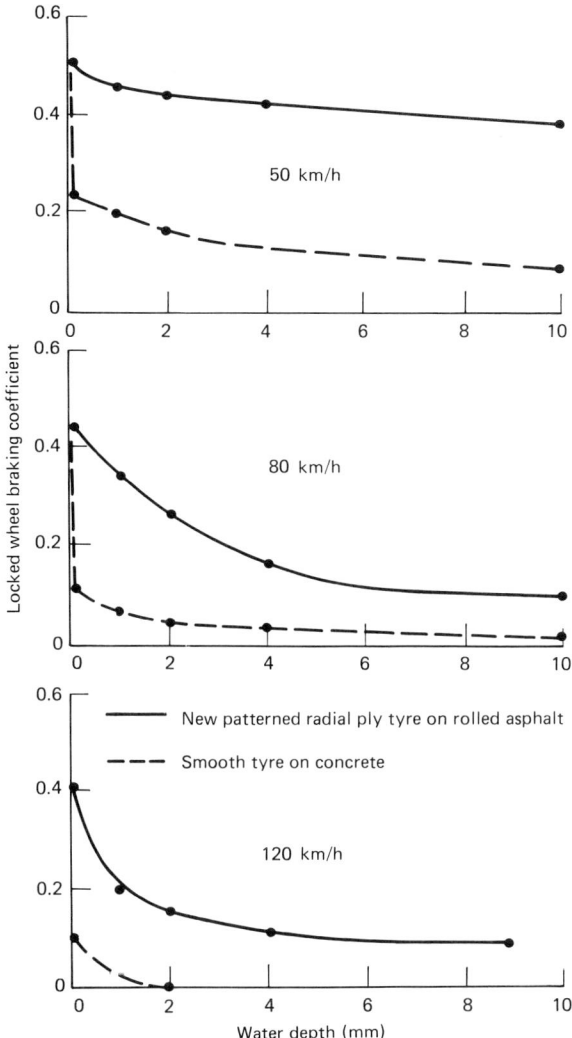

Figure 5.10 Effect of water depth, tyre tread and road surface on locked wheel braking coefficient

(1 mm), i.e. less than that represented by the first point on the figures. And except at high speed on very smooth surfaces, variation in water depth has little effect. To produce a water depth of 0.04 in (1 mm) requires heavy rainfall of about ¼ to ½ inch per hour (5 to 10 mm per hour (RRL Leaflet LF 163, 1971)).

Commercial vehicle tyres

The tyres of commercial vehicles, other than car derivatives, have a somewhat poorer performance than car tyres. In dry weather this does not matter, but on wet smooth surfaces the grip of commercial vehicle tyres

Table 5.4 Braking force coefficients for commercial vehicle tyres on a wet, smooth asphalt surface

Speed km/h	Highway service tyre		Dual-purpose tyre		Cross-country tyre	
	Peak	*Locked wheel*	*Peak*	*Locked wheel*	*Peak*	*Locked wheel*
10	–	–	0.32	0.19	0.31	–
20	0.38	0.17	0.30	0.17	0.29	0.18
30	0.35	0.15	0.28	0.15	0.26	0.12
40	0.32	0.14	0.26	0.13	0.23	0.09
50	0.32	0.13	0.24	0.11	0.20	0.08
60	0.31	0.12	0.21	0.10	0.17	0.08
70	0.30	–	0.19	0.10	0.15	–

can be very low particularly at the higher road speeds. Some figures to illustrate this are given in Table 5.4. (See also TRRL Leaflet LF 609 (1976) for results on a good skid resistant surface.)

Tread patterns

Circumferential grooving is extremely important for drainage of both car and commercial vehicle tyres. Not all tyres have patterns which include such grooves. Dual-purpose and cross-country tyres are frequently fitted to commercial vehicles used on the road, and on wet slippery roads their grip may be much less than that obtained with tyres designed for highway use with adequate circumferential grooves (see Table 5.4).

Generally both peak and locked wheel coefficients fall slowly with wear until groove depths are about ⅕ in (between 5 and 6 mm) deep, when there is a sharp fall, particularly in the peak braking force coefficient. Tyre wear leading to loss of continuity of the circumferential grooves has been found to cause a large reduction in grip even when there was an apparent tread depth of 0.5 in (14 mm).

Seasonal variation

Finally, the seasonal effect known since 1931 should be mentioned (see RRL Leaflet LF 55). In dry weather the dust held on and in the surfaces of tyres polishes away the sharp edges in the road surface, so that after a dry spell the road is more slippery when wet than before it. It is not necessary to explain this in terms of oil deposits. A period of wet weather reverses the process. The result of this reversible process is that roads gradually become more slippery when wet in the summer months and slowly recover during the winter (Figure 5.11) (RRL Leaflet LF 55, Issue 2, 1970).

Testing the frictional coefficient of wet surfaces

It is advisable to make tests of the surface(s) on which loss of control involving skidding on a wet road has occurred. This should be done as soon as possible after an accident, since the coefficients of friction may change

Stability and control of vehicles 69

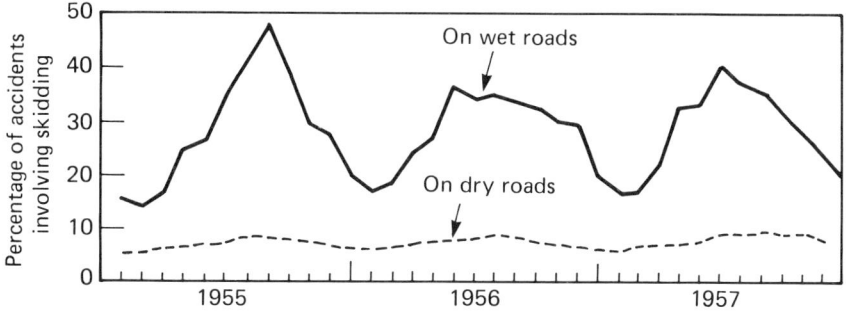

Figure 5.11 Seasonal variation in skidding accidents

with time and weather. For example, measurements made in winter will be higher than those obtained in summer. Two machines are likely to be available, the Portable Skid Resistance Tester (Figure 5.12) and SCRIM (Figure 5.13) (Sideway-force Coefficient Routine Investigation Machine) (TRRL Leaflet LF 129, 1973), the latter on hire from local authorities or the Transport and Road Research Laboratory, which also operates several other special test machines. The Portable Skid Resistance Tester (RRL Leaflet LF 39, 1971) enables spot tests to be made at any number of points along a road, and it is important to remember that its readings roughly correspond with those obtained by locking the wheels of a car fitted with good patterned tyres at 30 mile/h (48 km/h). Thus, if skidding occurred at a much higher speed, the results will only serve to provide a check on

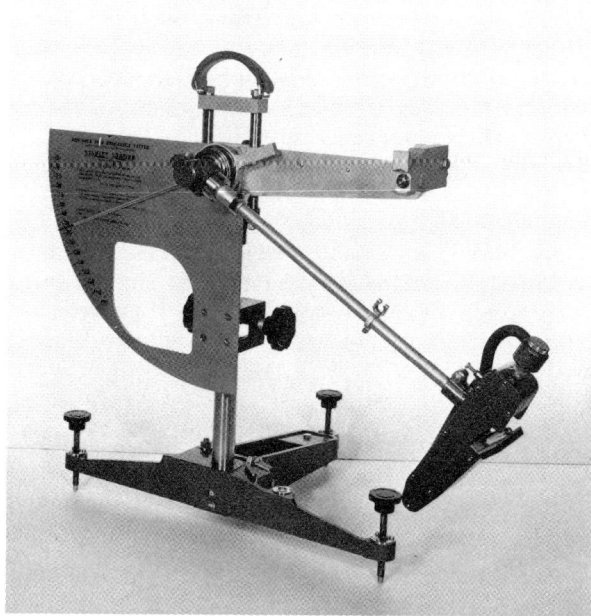

Figure 5.12 Portable skid resistance tester

Figure 5.13 SCRIM (Sideways-force coefficient routine investigation machine)

deductions based on examination of the road surface and the condition of the tyres.

If it is possible to obtain readings with the SCRIM test machine, they can be registered continuously over many miles of road at speeds up to 60 mile/h (100 km/h), and thus give a better indication of tyre road adhesion at higher speeds than can be obtained from the use of the Portable Skid Resistance Tester. Again, the results are in terms of locked wheel coefficients of treaded car tyres and must be related to those likely to be obtained with the tyres on the vehicles involved in the accidents, making use of the information given earlier in this chapter (Lupton, 1968).

Ice

The coefficient of friction of wet ice is very low, between 0.05 and 0.1, and, in contrast to wet road friction, it is constant or increases slightly with speed. Depending on conditions, dry ice or snow may provide a somewhat higher coefficient, up to about 0.2, for snow. Ice dry enough to be less slippery does not often occur in Britain.

5.3 The braking performance of vehicles and the role of braking in accidents

Braking distances

The average braking distances for cars, commercial vehicles, and motorcycles under the best conditions on dry roads are given in Figure 5.14 (TRRL Leaflet LF 537, 1975) (Watson, 1979).

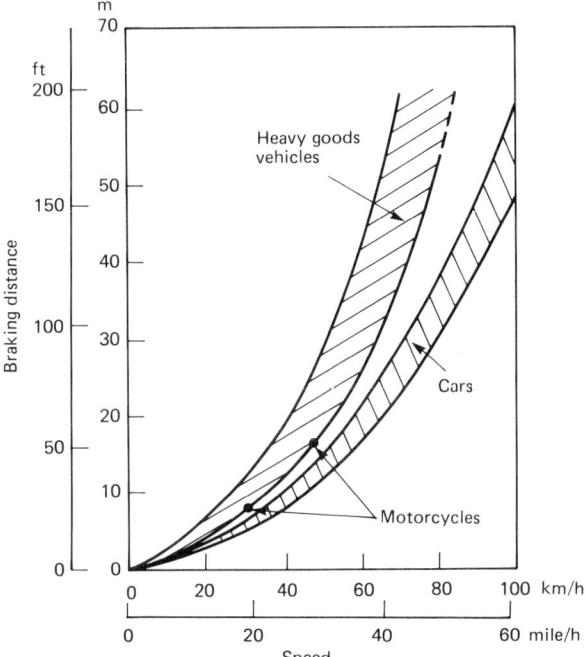

Figure 5.14 Braking distances for cars, commercial vehicles and motorcycles

These figures were obtained by skilled drivers on dry surfaces and are unlikely to be obtained in general road use. They do not include the distances travelled by the vehicles from the time the driver perceives the necessity for braking to the time when the brakes are applied. This perception time is not less than about 0.4 sec and may be as much as 2 sec.

The best distances for heavy goods vehicles were considerably worse than those for cars; motorcycles too were markedly inferior to cars, even on dry roads. Most motorcycles are fitted with disc brakes and in wet conditions water between the brake pads and the disc can result in loss of braking efficiency. By selecting disc and pad materials, however, efficient brakes can be produced which give consistent results, regardless of conditions (TRRL Leaflet LF 697, 1978). Regulations in force for machines manufactured from 1 October 1986 specify performance requirements for wet brakes and an improved standard for dry brakes and brake fade on motorcycles.

The shortest braking distances for cars are usually obtained when all four wheels of a vehicle are locked, since, even if the brakes are perfectly balanced for heavy braking, it is very difficult for a driver to keep them turning and get close enough to the point of complete locking to obtain a higher coefficient.

Loss of control after braking

When two or more wheels lock, and are kept locked, skidding occurs and may lead to loss of control. In the simplest case, when all four wheels of a car are locked, the wheels no longer function as wheels, but as four blocks of friction material. The centre of gravity of the car continues to move in the original direction but the car cannot be steered, and may rotate or slide sideways on a cambered road.

If the rear wheels lock and the front wheels do not, the motion of the car is unstable and its rear end usually swings round (Research on Road Safety, 1963). Since the front of the car can still be steered, it is sometimes possible at low speeds to correct such skids by methods taught on skid pans, but at high speeds on wet roads this can rarely be done, both because action has to be taken so quickly, and because when the car has slewed round by more than about 20° to 30°, it can no longer be steered back on to a straight course. Locking of rear wheels is a common cause of loss of control, both on wet and dry roads.

If the front wheels of a car lock and the rear ones do not, steering control is lost, and the car goes straight on. However, this is a stable motion and steering control can be regained by releasing the brakes. Although no reliable figures are available for the relative frequencies of front and rear wheel locking, the latter is probably more common because the car pitches forward, removing weight from the rear wheels to the front, when the brakes are applied.

Anti-locking brakes

Wheel locking when the brakes are applied can be prevented by using anti-locking devices. These devices detect when the wheels slow down before locking occurs and immediately release the brakes so that the wheels speed up again. The brakes are then reapplied and this cycle is repeated several times per second. Because the wheels are never allowed to lock, use is made of the peak coefficient, which is normally much higher than the skidding coefficient. As a result the overall coefficient on a slippery wet road is usually higher than the skidding coefficient; and at the same time control is retained and steering is possible.

The advantages of anti-lock braking were demonstrated in tests at the Road Research Laboratory early in the 1950s (Research on Road Safety, 1963), but they have only recently been installed on some car models since the electronic devices now being used to detect the onset of wheel locking were not available when the early tests were made. The techniques of anti-locking brake systems were discussed at a recent conference. (Conference on Anti-lock Braking Systems for Road Vehicles, 1985.)

Effect of weight transfer

The greater the tyre/road adhesion (frictional coefficient) and the more severe the brake application the greater the weight transfer from rear to front. There is therefore no single adjustment of the brakes to give correct balance on both dry and on slippery wet or icy roads. If the brakes are in correct adjustment for dry roads, with, for example, $\mu = 0.8$, so that front and rear lock simultaneously, they will provide too much braking on the front wheels on wet or icy roads with coefficients less than this and front wheel locking will result. On wet roads (but not dry ones) front to rear unbalance can be produced by having worn tyres on one axle and good ones on the other. The only way of overcoming this difficulty is by means of an anti-locking braking system which senses when a wheel is about to lock and adjusts the braking accordingly.

Rigid commercial vehicles

Rigid commercial vehicles behave in the same way as cars when front or rear wheels are locked. Variation in the loading of rear wheels due to the size of the load carried, is, however, a more important cause of trouble than is weight transfer. The load on the driving wheels may be several times greater when the vehicle is loaded and if braking is just adequate for a full load the rear wheels would immediately lock if fully applied when the vehicle was unladen. On the other hand, braking adjusted to be correct for an unladen vehicle would be inadequate for that vehicle in the fully laden state.

Articulated vehicles – trailer swing and jack-knifing

Articulated vehicles behave in a more complicated way during braking. Loss of control due to locking of some sets of wheels may take place in two ways (Wilkins, 1971):

(1) At the trailer. This is the less common mode. The trailer wheels lock and the trailer may swing out, since those wheels can exert very little sideways force. This is most likely to occur when the vehicle is braked and steered on a curved path at the same time (see Figure 5.15).

Figure 5.15 Trailer swing – tractor still moving in original direction

74 Movements of vehicles and road users before accidents

Figure 5.16 Jack-knifing – tractor turned completely around

(2) At the tractor. This is the more usual mode, and the one which may result in jack-knifing (see Figure 5.16).

In (2) the rear (driving) wheels of the tractor lock. As with cars, locking of the rear wheels produces an unstable state in which the tractor may swing round at an angle to the trailer. This can happen so quickly that the driver has no time to release the brakes and make a steering correction to bring the tractor back into line with the trailer and so regain control. Once the trailer is at such an angle to its general direction of travel that the front wheels begin to skid, all control over the subsequent motion of the vehicle may be lost. The tractor continues to turn more rapidly until it may end up folded back against the trailer, in the jack-knifed position. The whole vehicle may still continue to travel forwards in that position.

Load-sensing valves

The difference between braking in the fully laden and the unladen state, important for all commercial vehicles, is particularly so for articulated vehicles. The load on the driving wheels may be as much as four times greater when the vehicle is fully loaded. Therefore, unless provision is made to adjust braking to suit load, wheel locking is easily provoked in the unladen state, even on dry roads. Most articulated vehicles are, therefore, fitted with load-sensing brake valves, which automatically adjust the brakes on the driving wheels of the tractor to suit the load carried. They are controlled by the deflection of the road springs, and, in proper adjustment, can greatly reduce the likelihood of jack-knifing. After a jack-knifing accident they should always be checked to make sure they were working correctly.

On a wet road, if the tyre to road adhesion at the rear wheels of a tractor is less than that at the front wheels, because of differences in tyre pattern or wear, the rear wheels can lock without the front ones, even when the load-sensing valve is in correct adjustment. Load-sensing valves can also be fitted to trailer axles to reduce the risk of trailer swing, and to rigid commercial vehicles to reduce the risk of rear wheel locking in the unladen state, but in neither case is it usual to do so.

Anti-locking braking systems for commercial vehicles

Anti-locking braking systems, first developed for cars, afford the most efficient method of preventing loss of control when the brakes of an articulated vehicle are applied. In one system, an electrical signal is obtained from the propellor shaft, to detect when the rear wheels of the tractor are about to lock. When this happens, the brakes on these wheels are released until the wheels speed up again, and are then reapplied. As a result, the brakes are applied three or four times each second, and, because the peak coefficient is used during each brake application cycle, the stopping distance of the vehicle is not increased, and may even be reduced on wet slippery surfaces. An important advantage of these systems is that they work whatever the condition of the tyres (Wilkins, 1971).

King-pin friction devices

King-pin friction devices, in which friction is introduced at the joint between tractor and trailer whenever the brakes are applied, offer only a partial solution to the problem of jack-knifing, since they are only powerful enough to prevent jack-knifing when the vehicle is travelling on a straight path.

Motorcycle braking

The difficulties of controlling vehicles with locked or skidding wheels are, of course, much greater for two than for four-wheeled vehicles. If the front wheel of a motorcycle locks, the rider almost always falls off. Rear wheel locking is not as serious, but there is the same tendency for the motorcycle to swing around as is found in cars. The centre of gravity of a motorcycle is relatively much higher in relation to the wheelbase than that of a car, so there is greater weight transference from rear to front when braking, and locking of rear wheels occurs more readily. Accident records show that motorcycles are more likely to be involved in skidding accidents than other vehicles.

Anti-locking systems have been successfully tested for motorcycles, shorter braking distances being obtained with less risk of loss of control, but they have not as yet appeared on production machines (TRRL Leaflet LF 591, 1975). (See Figure 5.17.)

Figure 5.17 Anti-locking brake fitted to the front wheel of a motorcycle

5.4 Loss of control without braking

Skidding during acceleration

On icy or even on wet roads, it is possible to cause the driving wheels of a vehicle to skid during acceleration. In cars with larger engines, skidding can occur even in top gear, when accelerating at speeds of about 30 mile/h (48 km/h), if the road has a coefficient of less than 0.3; in the next lower gear, a coefficient of 0.45 may be required to prevent skidding. Such coefficients are not uncommon for wet roads. On icy roads, because coefficients even at low speeds are very low, it is often difficult to accelerate gently enough in low gear to avoid skidding (Giles, 1963).

Power jack-knifing

Skidding during acceleration can also occur at the driving wheels of the tractor of an unladen articulated vehicle, resulting in 'power jack-knifing'. This is most likely to occur at speeds of 25 mile/h (40 km/h) or more, on slippery wet roads, when accelerating to overtake, leaving a bend, or trying to maintain speed on an up gradient on wet heavily trafficked surfaces, especially when the road surface or tyres are worn sufficiently to give a low road grip in the wet (TRRL Leaflet LF 599, 1975).

Skidding due to excessive sideways acceleration

Skidding leading to loss of control can occur without braking due to excessive sideways acceleration as when bends are taken too fast or even as the result of taking violent steering action to avoid some obstacle. The relationship between the radius of curvature R of the path of the vehicle, the speed V and the minimum coefficient of friction μ necessary to prevent sideways drift on a flat surface is $\mu = v^2/gR$, where g is the acceleration due to gravity.

Figure 5.18 translates this relationship into practical terms.

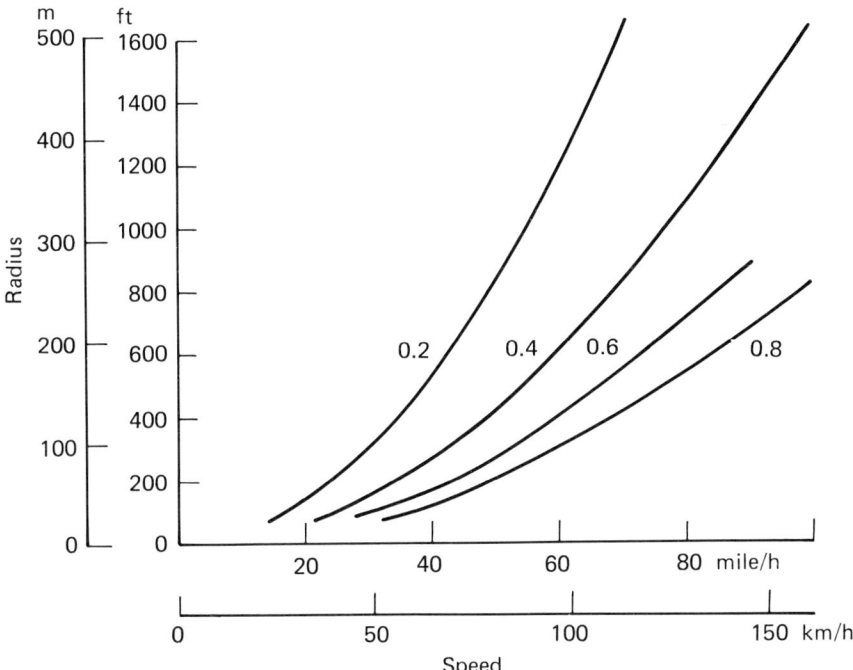

Figure 5.18 Minimum coefficients necessary to enable vehicles to negotiate bends

On wet roads, μ may be higher for the tyres on different axles of the same vehicle because of differences in tyre tread and wear. Those with the lowest coefficient will slip first, and that particular part of the vehicle will drift around. This is probably the rule rather than the exception, since there are likely to be few cases in which there is perfect balance between the front and rear wheels of a vehicle, whether it is a car, commercial vehicle, or motorcycle.

Movement after skidding

If the rear of a car breaks away first on a bend, the car may either rotate too far for control to be regained, and skid almost in a straight ahead direction, or control may be partially regained. Overcorrection of the skid may then cause the car to travel either to the left or to the right.

If the front of a car breaks away first, it will probably go straight ahead, unless it slows down sufficiently for a higher coefficient to be developed so that steering control is regained. This is only likely to happen on a wet slippery road where coefficients increase as speed is reduced.

In the same circumstances an articulated vehicle may behave in one of three ways:

(1) Trailer swing may develop if the trailer wheels lose adhesion on a curve.
(2) The vehicle may jack-knife if the driving wheels of the tractor break away first.
(3) Loss of adhesion at the front wheels results in similar behaviour to that of a car.

Loss of control due to other disturbances

Accidents sometimes occur when control is lost for no obvious reason. Omitting night accidents when reduced visibility, excessive speed, intoxication and deceptive road layout may be factors, accidents still sometimes occur when going straight ahead in daylight without cornering or braking. As might be expected, accidents of this type are most likely to occur at high speeds and on motorways. In one study, single vehicle accidents, in which no other vehicle was involved, accounted for about 40 per cent of motorway accidents away from junctions. In about one-third of such accidents tyre failure occurred but in the remainder less obvious factors operated (Grime, 1963).

Kerbs

In dry weather, a car travelling at high speed may lose control either because it strikes a kerb or runs on to a soft or very uneven verge. The central reservations of some motorways are rough, and even have potholes or ditches which can initiate loss of steering control. In such cases, loss of control is usually preceded by some kind of attention lapse by the driver. It is estimated that about 5 per cent of single vehicle accidents on rural roads can be attributed to striking kerbs, and the same percentage on motorways to rough surfaces on the central reservation.

When the road is wet and slippery, the consequent loss of control is much more difficult to correct than it is on a dry road; the vehicle may come away from the kerb, verge, or central reservation at such an angle that it immediately goes into an uncontrollable skid.

5.5 The time available for action in accidents

When studying accidents it is always useful to make rough calculations of certain times; for example, the time between the commencement of loss of control and that of impact with an obstacle. Some examples are as follows.

(1) Time available to avoid striking a pedestrian. If a vehicle is travelling at 30 mile/h (48 km/h), and the pedestrian is 30 yds (27 m) away, the driver has only about 2 seconds to take avoiding action, assuming that he does not slow down (see Figure 5.19). The times taken to strike a pedestrian (or an obstacle) from various speeds, assuming heavy braking after 0.5 sec to get the brake on, are shown in Figure 5.20. Note how short is the time usually available to the driver.

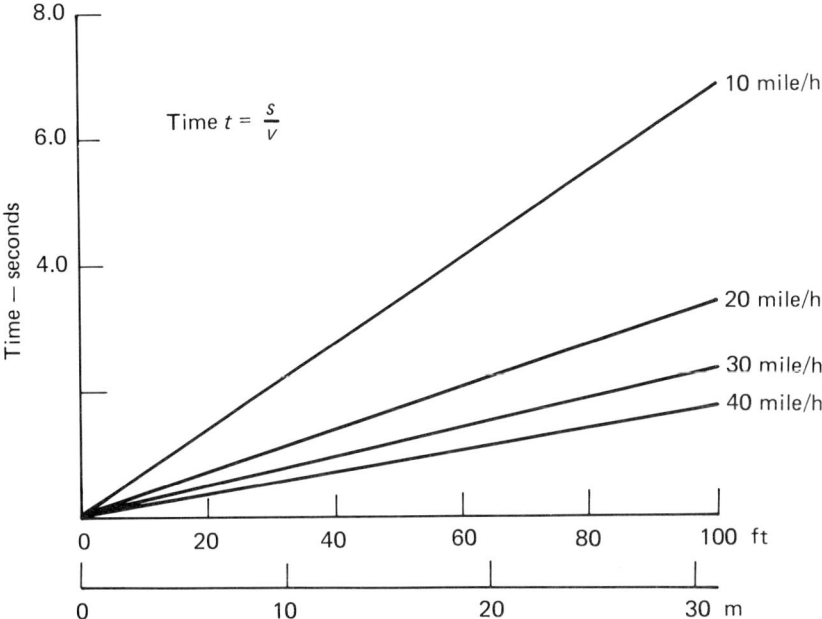

Figure 5.19 Time available to avoid an obstacle or pedestrian at various distances, at constant speed

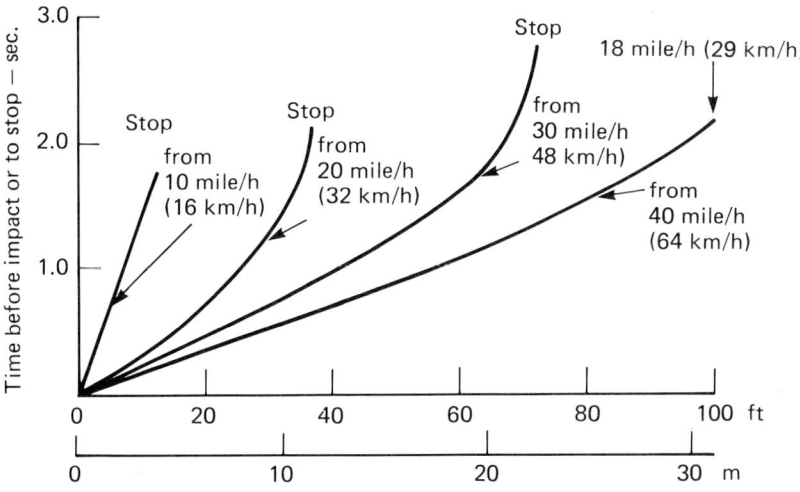

Figure 5.20 Times to reach obstacles or to stop allowing 0.5 seconds to apply brake followed by a deceleration of $0.6g$

(2) Time to avoid a head-on impact. If the closing speed is 60 mile/h (97 km/h), and if it is assumed that 5 seconds is required for sufficient avoiding action to be taken, there must be at least $5 \times 88 = 440$ ft (137 m) between the vehicles when the danger is first perceived. In a real head-on accident situation, braking nearly always takes place to lengthen the time and distance available.

80   Movements of vehicles and road users before accidents

(3) Time to cross a central reservation. The time taken for a car to cross the 15 ft (4.7 m) central reservation of a motorway from one fast lane to the opposite one, if control is lost at 60 mile/h (97 km/h) and the car changes direction by 30°, is only 0.6 sec; and even crossing from one slow lane to the opposing slow lane at that angle would take less than 2 sec.

These times emphasize the difficulties of regaining control, and of avoiding hazards of all kinds, when travelling at motorway speeds.

5.6 Skidding distances

Calculations of speeds of vehicles before accidents, particularly in accidents in which pedestrians are injured by cars, are often made from measurements of the lengths of skidmarks on the road. Such indications or their absence should be interpreted with caution. First, they rarely occur on wet roads and their absence does not prove that no heavy braking took place. Second, when they are observed on a dry road, they can only indicate the speed at the instant when the brakes had come on hard enough to cause the wheels to lock and so cause the marks; there may have been considerable slowing down before this took place, while the brakes were being applied.

If all four wheels of a car are observed to commence to skid simultaneously or nearly so, then a calculation can be made of the distance to stop and of the minimum initial speed of the car. If this speed is V then the distance s for the car to come to rest is

$$s = V^2/2a$$

where a is the deceleration and the initial speed, $V = \sqrt{2as}$. It may be noted that, while the distance to stop is inversely proportional to the deceleration, the initial speed is proportional to the square root of the deceleration. For a car skidding with four locked wheels, $a = \mu g$ where μ is the frictional coefficient between tyres and road and g the acceleration due to gravity (Appendix 1). For a dry road μ may be assumed to be about 0.8, and the expressions become

$$s = \frac{V^2}{1.6g} \text{ and } V = \sqrt{1.6gs}$$

The easiest example of the use of these expressions is one where a car strikes a pedestrian and then comes to rest, still making skidmarks with all four wheels. If the position on the road at which the pedestrian was struck can also be specified, it is also possible to estimate the speed v of the car when it struck the pedestrian. This is given by a similar equation to the last:

$$v = \sqrt{1.6g\ell}$$

where ℓ is the distance from the place where the pedestrian was struck to the rest position of the car. These relationships are illustrated in Figure 5.21 with the addition of an initial 0.5 sec of free movement at the original speed during which the brake was being applied.

To obtain the speed at which a pedestrian is struck when the distance is known, take any one of the curves in Figure 5.21, for example 30 mile/h (48 km/h), read off the distance s at which it meets the horizontal axis, subtract ℓ from that distance, and read off the speed on the curve corresponding to the distance (s − ℓ).

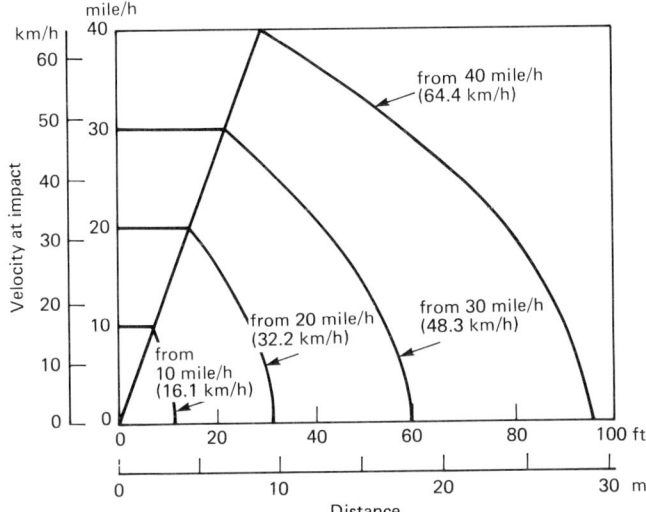

Figure 5.21 Speeds at which objects are struck from initial speeds up to 40 mile/h (64 km/h) allowing 0.5 second to apply brake followed by a deceleration of 0.8 g

The results of calculations are more uncertain if skidmarks are left by only two wheels, usually the front ones. If the front wheels leave marks, the coefficient μ for the whole car lies somewhere between, for example, 0.5 and 0.8, since the contribution of the rear brakes is unknown, but unlikely to be negligible. However, if a value of μ = 0.6 is assumed, the speed deduced from the skidding distance will not be much in error, since it is proportional to the square root of μ. For a particular skidding distance, the deduced speed with two locked wheels is 0.87 of that with all four skidding, so that in most cases of two-wheeled skids, it is reasonable to use this factor with Figure 5.21.

The above calculations are made for cars on dry roads. As mentioned in Section 5.2, for heavy goods vehicles the coefficient of friction even on dry roads may be less than that for cars; and the coefficient decreases with increased speed and load. In tests with a normal load, increasing the speed from 20 to 100 km/h (12 to 62 mile/h) produced a reduction of about one-third in the value of the coefficient (from about 0.6 to 0.4), while decreasing the load by 25 per cent increased the coefficient by 20 to 25 per cent (Wilkins and Riley, 1982).

References

Anti-lock Braking Systems for Road Vehicles (1985) Conference at the Institution of Mechanical Engineers, London, September, 1985

Braking in the rain with motorcycles fitted with disc brakes (1978) *Transport and Road Research Laboratory Leaflet*, LF 69Y

'Anti-lock braking for motorcycles' (1978) *Transport and Road Research Laboratory Leaflet* LF 591, Issue 2

DOWNING, C. S. (1985) Pedal Cycling Accidents in Great Britain. *Proc. Conf. 'Ways to Safer Cycling'*. Inst. Civil Eng. April 1985

FAULKNER, C. R. and OLDER, S. J. (1967) 'The effects of different systems of vehicle lighting on a driver's ability to see dark objects in well-lit streets'. *Road Research Laboratory Report*, LR 113

GILES, C. G. (1963) 'Factors influencing the friction between tyre and road under wet conditions'. *Proc. Symposium on Control of Vehicles During Braking and Cornering. Institution of Mechanical Engineers*

GRIME, G. (1960) 'Automobile lighting and visibility'. Crompton-Lanchester Lectures on the Private Car. Institution of Mechanical Engineers.

GRIME, G. (1961) 'Parked vehicles on rural roads'. *Traffic Engineering and Control*, April

GRIME, G. (1963) 'The importance of loss of directional control in car accidents'. *Proc. Symposium on Control of Vehicles During Braking and Cornering. Institution of Mechanical Engineers*

GRIME, G. (1974) 'Rear-end chain type accidents on motorways in Great Britain'. *12th International Study Week in Traffic Engineering and Safety, Belgrade, September*. London: OTA

GRIME, G. and GILES, C. G. (1954–55) 'The skid-resisting properties of roads and tyres. *Proc. Institution of Mechanical Engineers Automobile Division* **1**, 19–30

GRIME, G. and JONES, I. S. (1969–70) 'Car collisions – the movement of cars and their occupants in accidents'. *Proc. Institution of Mechanical Engineers*, **184**(A), (5), 87–136

JEHU, V. J. (1954) 'A comparison of yellow and white headlamp beams'. *Light and Lighting*, **47**(10), 287–291

— (1955) 'A comparison of some common headlight beams for vehicles meeting on a straight road'. *Trans. Illum. Eng. Soc.* (London), **20**(2), 69–77

— (1963) 'A dimmed headlight system'. *Bull. Mot. Ind. Res. Ass.* **1**, 4–7

JONES, I. S. (1976) *The effect of vehicle characteristics on road accidents*. Pergamon Press

LISTER, R. D. (1963) 'Some problems of emergency braking in road vehicles' *Proc. Symp. on Control of Vehicles during Braking and Cornering. Institution of Mechanical Engineers.* June

LUPTON, G. (1968) 'The field testing of skidding'. *Proc. Symp. on the Influence of the Road Surface on Skidding. Centre for Transport Studies, University of Salford*

'Machines and testing techniques used in skidding investigations' *Road Research Laboratory Leaflet*, LF 39, Issue 2, 1971

MAYCOCK, G. (1965–66) 'Studies on the skidding resistance of passenger car tyres on wet surfaces'. *Proc. Institution of Mechanical Engineers*, **180**(2A), (4)

'Measurement of skidding resistance on wet roads'. *Transport and Road Research Laboratory Leaflet*, LF 129

'Night visibility: the accident problem'. *Transport and Road Research Laboratory Leaflet*, LF 266, 1971

'Power Jack-knifing'. *Transport and Road Research Laboratory Leaflet*, LF 599, 1975

Research on Road Safety (1963) (Chapter 11)

'Road grip of commercial vehicle tyres' (1976) *Transport and Road Research Laboratory Leaflet*, LF 609

Road Accidents Great Britain (1984) HMSO

SABEY, B. E., WILLIAMS, T. and LUPTON, G. N. (1970) Factors affecting the friction of tyres on wet roads. *Proc. Society of Automotive Engineers, June*

'The minimum braking distances obtained with some cars and heavy goods vehicles (1975) *Transport and Road Research Laboratory Leaflet*, LF 537

'The relationship between road lighting quality and accident frequency' (1980) *Transport and Road Research Laboratory Digest*, LR 929

'Tyre grip on wet roads: effects of tread depth and water depth (1971) *Road Research Laboratory Leaflet*, LF 163, Issue 2

'Tyre grip on wet roads. Road Surface factors' (1970) *Road Research Laboratory Leaflet*, LF 55, Issue 2

WATSON, P. M. (1979) 'Features of the experimental motorcycle'. *Seventh Int. Technical Conference on Experimental Safety Vehicles, Paris*

WHITAKER, J. (1976) 'Motorcycle safety – accident survey and rider injuries'. *Transport and Road Research Laboratory Supplementary Report*, SR 239

WILKINS, H. A. (1971) 'The stability of articulated vehicles. *Journal of Automotive Engineering*, March

WILKINS, H. A. and RILEY, B. S. (1982) 'The road grip of commercial vehicle tyres'. *Transport and Road Research Laboratory Supplementary Report,* SR 768

WILLIAMS, A. R., DAVIES, V. E., RILEY, B. S. and WILKINS, H. A. (1981) 'Braking force coefficients of worn tyres'. *Transport and Road Research Laboratory Supplementary Report,* SR 672

YERRELL, J. S. (1971) 'Headlight intensities in Europe and Britain'. *Road Research Laboratory Report*, LR 383

— (1976) 'Vehicle headlights'. *Lighting Research and Technology,* **8**(2)

Chapter 6

What happens to vehicles during and after accidents

This chapter is concerned with the movements of vehicles and their occupants after the first contacts between vehicles or between vehicles and fixed objects have occurred. Safety in this connection is known as secondary safety. In the first instance consideration will be given to car accidents.

The most important types of accident from the point of view of injury are first, those resulting in frontal impacts, comprising frontal collisions with rigid objects in single vehicle accidents, frontal or rear-end collisions with other vehicles, and collisions with other vehicles at intersections; second, side impacts mainly at intersections; and third, overturning.

Frontal impacts may be either full or partial frontal, when only part of the front of the vehicle makes contact with a solid object or another vehicle. Frontal impacts of all types account for one-half to two-thirds of serious and fatal injuries; side impacts for rather less than one-third; overturning for about one-tenth and rear impacts for a very small remainder (2 to 3 per cent) (Grime and Jones, 1973).

6.1 General properties

The most important properties (constants) of a car or commercial vehicle are its mass, M, or its weight, W (see Appendix 2), its width a, and length b, the position of its centre of gravity (C.G.), and its moment of inertia I about a vertical axis through its centre of gravity. The position of the centre of gravity of a car can be taken without much error as at the central point, and the moment of inertia I, which is a measure of the resistance to rotation, is approximately

$$I = M \frac{a^2 + b^2}{12}.$$

This is the moment of inertia in yaw.

Together with the velocity (speed and direction of travel), or velocities of the vehicles at impact, these constants determine almost completely the motion of the vehicle(s) in collisions during and immediately after impact. This is the time interval during which most injuries occur (Grime and Jones, 1969–70).

During this impact phase, which normally lasts between one-twentieth and one-fifth of a second, the forces between tyres and ground are negligible compared with those due to the impact on the vehicle. They may be neglected in calculations concerning the impact phase.

The occupants of vehicles in collisions continue to move forward in the directions in which they were travelling before the collision occurred. Any change in direction is due to an applied force, for example at the knees in a frontal impact.

6.2 The impact phase in full frontal impacts

In full frontal impacts, whether with rigid objects or other vehicles, crushing of the front of the car lasts for about one-tenth second (range 0.05 second to 0.20 second), and the permanent deformation may be as much as 24 inches (0.6 m) at 30 mile/h (48 km/h). It is during or immediately after this time of first impact that injuries occur due to impact with the steering assembly, windscreen, or instrument panel. Unbelted front-seat passengers strike the windscreen or instrument panel with a velocity almost equal to the initial velocities of the cars, but because drivers are close to steering wheels, they make contact with them at lower velocities.

If front-seat occupants are not wearing seat belts, in most cases the manner in which the front of the car is constructed has little effect on the severity of their injuries, except insofar as high strength may prevent or reduce deformation and intrusion (Grime, 1966). This is because the crushing of the front of the car is complete or almost complete before the passenger strikes the inside of the vehicle, so that the manner of the deformation does not matter. If, however, the overlap between the two cars in a head-on collision is small, so that the deformation and duration of impact are considerably increased, the inside of the car may not have stopped when the occupant strikes it, thus reducing the severity of injury; the way in which one of the cars is constructed may in such cases influence these deformations and durations and thus affect the severity of the injuries sustained; the greater the deformation and duration the lower the probability of injury even to an unbelted occupant. If belts are worn, differences in frontal construction may have a noticeable effect in reducing the forces applied to belt wearers in full frontal impacts, and a greater effect when deformations are greater.

In frontal impacts, unbelted car occupants are subjected to lower forces if very close to the windscreen or back of the front seat than if far away; conversely, the requirement for a belted occupant is as much space as possible in front of him to allow for belt extension, slack in the belt, and folding of the body over the belt.

Mass ratio and velocity change

In a symmetrical, that is, a centre front to centre front, head-on collision, the way in which a vehicle behaves is almost completely determined by the ratio of its weight (mass) to that of the other vehicle. In almost all car-to-car collisions this ratio is less than 2, but, in collisions between cars and commercial vehicles, the ratio may be anything between about 2 and 50.

The velocity change (widely recognised as the most important injury-producing factor in collisions) of each vehicle is inversely proportional to its weight (mass), and depends only on the relative velocity at impact $V = V_1 - V_2$ and not on the individual velocities V_1 and V_2 of vehicles 1 and 2 (see Appendix 2).

The approximate velocity changes V'_1 and V'_2 in head-on and rear-end collisions are

for car 1: $\quad V'_1 = \dfrac{M_2}{M_1 + M_2} (V_1 - V_2)$, and

for car 2: $\quad V'_2 = - \dfrac{M_1}{M_1 + M_2} (V_1 - V_2)$,

where $V_1 - V_2$ is the relative velocity at impact. These expressions describe the velocity changes both in head-on and rear-end collisions. In head-on collisions the closing speed is the sum of the speeds of the two vehicles before impact; in rear-end collisions it is the difference (see Appendix 2 for a more detailed explanation).

These relationships are approximately true only because there is very little rebound; the mild steel which cars are made of is such a good energy absorber (about 95 per cent absorption) that the collision is almost inelastic, and no other material has been found to give appreciably better energy absorption. However, because in most collisions there is a small rebound velocity, a better estimate of velocity change is obtained by increasing V'_1 and V'_2 as given above by 10 per cent.

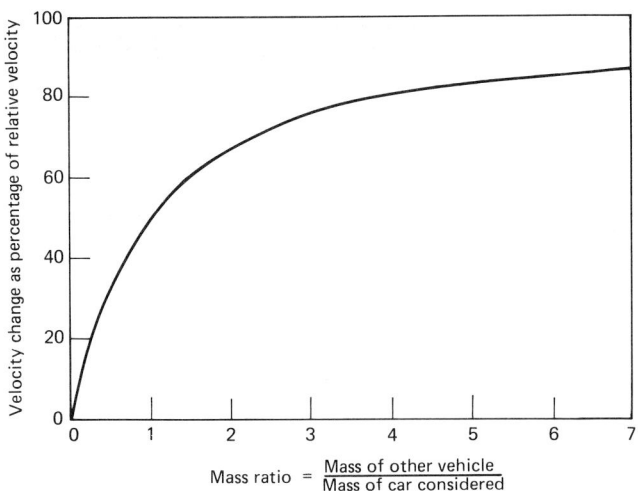

Figure 6.1 Variation of velocity change with mass ratio

Figure 6.1 shows how velocity change varies with mass ratio, defined as the mass of the other vehicle divided by the mass of the vehicle in which one is interested. Note that, when the opposing vehicle is more than four times the weight of the considered car, the velocity change is more than 80 per cent of the closing speed at impact. Mass ratio is probably the most important factor in the production of injury in frontal collisions between vehicles (see Chapter 7).

Energy absorbed in collisions

The energy absorbed in deforming the fronts of two vehicles in full frontal head-on collision is given closely by the expression

$$E = \tfrac{1}{2} \frac{M_1 M_2}{M_1 + M_2} (V_1 - V_2)^2,$$ where $V_1 - V_2$ is the closing speed.

The energy is independent of the deformation of the fronts of the vehicles and cannot be altered for the better by structural changes or use of energy absorbing materials. The way in which it is shared between the fronts of the two vehicles does, however, depend on constructional differences, the stiffer front being less deformed and absorbing less energy than the weaker one. In head-on impacts with rigid poles or walls, the energy absorbed is approximately $E = \tfrac{1}{2}MV^2$, that is the total energy of the car before impact.

6.3 Frontal off-centre impacts

The discussion thus far has been mainly concerned with full frontal impacts, in which the whole of the front of the car struck a rigid barrier, or was in symmetrical collision with another car. In most frontal impacts, however, contact is made only over part of the front. In head-on collisions, for example, it has been estimated that about 60 to 80 per cent are off-centre, two-thirds of these impacts being on the driver's side; in frontal impacts with lighting columns, trees, telegraph poles and walls, of the estimated 55 per cent which are off-centre, more than one-half are to the nearside (Grime, 1983).

The most simple example of an offset frontal impact is with a rigid barrier, such as a bridge abutment, in which contact is made over part of the front of the car. In practice such collisions are much less frequent than those with polelike objects or other cars, but the resulting movements of vehicles and occupants are similar to those in the other partially frontal collisions.

In all off-centre frontal impacts, some rotation occurs both during and after impact, so the greater the offset, the greater the angular velocity with which this occurs. In such impacts with rigid barriers, the deformations are only slightly greater than in full frontal impacts at the same speeds, and little rotation takes place, if the overlap is greater than about 50 per cent of the width of the car. This is also true of central pole impacts, so that in both cases there is little reduction in the severity of the impact as perceived by the occupants. When the impact with the barrier is off-centre, so that contact is made over, for example, 30 per cent of the front of the car, greater rotation occurs during the impact. This is usually only about 10 degrees and rotation alone does nothing to reduce the velocity of impact of the front-seat occupant with the windscreen on the impact side of the car, and has very little effect on the other side. More important is the much increased deformation of the car in an off-centre impact compared with that in a full frontal barrier impact at the same approach speed, since this correspondingly increases the duration of that impact and reduces the maximum deceleration. The reduction in velocity of impact of an unrestrained occupant's head with the windscreen is appreciable since the windscreen is still moving away when it is struck. The reduction in severity, as judged by loads in seat belts, is even greater for belt wearers. In a series of tests conducted by the Motor Industry Research Association, and described more fully in Section 6.8, the loads in the shoulder loops of belted dummies averaged 30 per cent less in off-centre than in full frontal impacts (Neilson, Penoyre and Petter, 1979).

Rotation due to off-centre impacts usually results in only a small lateral movement, unimportant in determining where the occupant strikes the inside of the car, unless it results in a head striking a harmful projection.

Similar behaviour is observed in off-centre collisions with poles, in impacts with the bottoms of ditches, and in offset collisions between cars.

6.4 Rear-end collisions

Rear-end collisions, in which one vehicle runs into the back of another, can be treated in the same way as head-on collisions, except that the closing speed is the difference between the two speeds, and, while the occupants of the striking car suffer a frontal impact similar to that experienced in head-on collisions and tend to travel forward with respect to the car, those in the struck car tend to travel backwards relative to the car and therefore apply forces to the back of the seat.

Chain or concertina-type accidents often involve the same vehicle, usually a car, in both rear-end and frontal impacts.

6.5 Impacts with walls

In impacts of cars with walls, at all angles of approach (the angle between long axis of vehicle and wall) more than about 40° (see Figure 6.2), the impact is effectively a head-on collision, though less severe than impacts at angles approaching 90°, and the front-seat occupants move towards the windscreen (Grime and Jones, 1969–1 0).

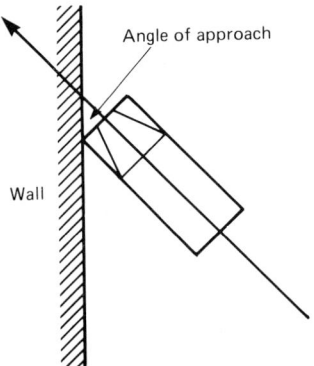

Figure 6.2 Impact with a rigid wall

The velocity of impact with the windscreen, steering assembly or instrument panel decreases as the angle of approach becomes smaller, but is greatly influenced by the coefficient of friction between the car and the wall; for example, when the coefficient changes from 0.25 to 0.5 (approximately from a wooden surface to a concrete wall), the impact velocities of the occupants on the interior of the car are approximately doubled.

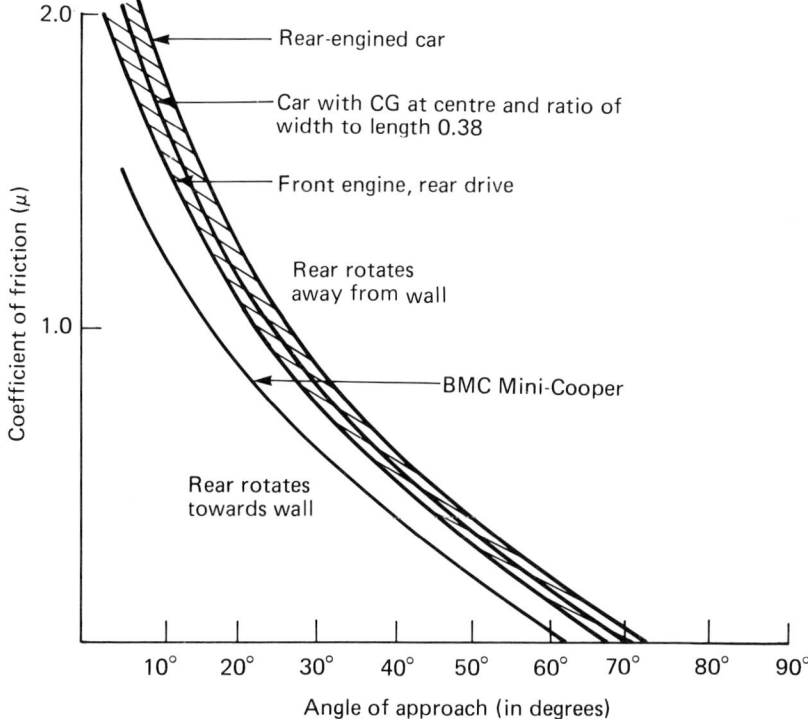

Figure 6.3 Values of μ at which no rotation takes place

After impact the car may rotate towards or away from the wall – towards the wall if friction with the wall is low, and/or the angle of approach is small, and away from it when the friction is high, and/or the angle of approach is large. Figure 6.3 shows how the sense of rotation depends upon friction and angle of approach for cars of different types under ideal conditions. In practice, the coefficients of friction may vary and centres of pressure between car and wall change during the course of the impact, so that Figure 6.3 can only be used as a rough guide to what happens.

At low coefficients of friction, or at smaller angles of approach than those resulting in impacts of occupants with the windscreen, the occupants on the side of the car nearest the wall may strike that side of the car.

The duration of impact varies from about 1/20 second at an angle of approach of 10° up to 1/7 second or more at angles of 60° and over. At high coefficients of friction the higher values of duration may be reached even at angles of approach as low as 20°.

6.6 Intersection collisions

Almost all intersection car collisions involve a striking and a struck car. The striking car suffers mainly frontal impact, and the struck car a side impact. In most such accidents the paths of the two cars are at right angles, probably at a crossroads or T-junction. The struck car is usually moving more slowly than the striking car. In one investigation about 50 per cent of the struck cars were judged to be travelling at less than 20 mile/h (32 km/h), and in about 60 per cent the angles between colliding vehicles were about 90° (Grime and Jones, 1973).

If the speeds, weights and dimensions of the two vehicles in an intersection collision at right angles are known, the velocity changes and the subsequent movements of the vehicles can be estimated (Grime and Jones, 1969–70). Conversely, if the directions of movement of the two vehicles after impact and the speed of one of them before impact are known, an estimate of the speed of the other one can be made. The calculations are rather lengthy and are best made by computer.

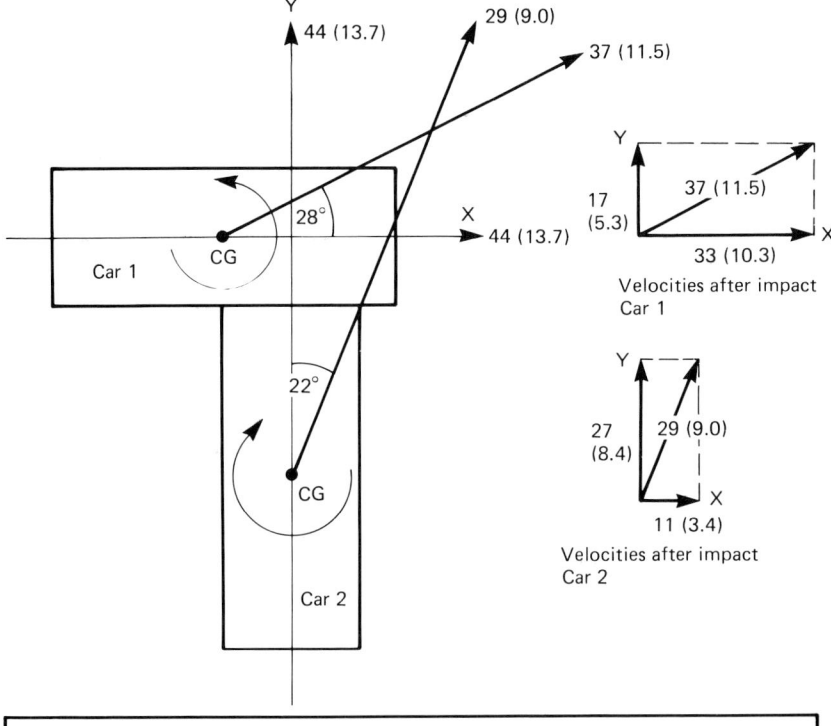

Duration of impact 0.09 sec
Velocity changes (equal) — X direction 11 ft/sec (3.4 m/s), Y direction 17 ft/sec (5.3 m/s)
Angular velocities — Car 1 136°/sec (1 revolution in 2.6 sec)
Car 2 249°/sec (1 revolution in 1.4 sec)

Figure 6.4 Front-side impact. Each car has an initial velocity of 44 ft/sec (13.7 m/sec, 30 mile/h)

Unless the struck car is stationary, both cars rotate and are slowed down after impact. The velocity change of the struck car in its original direction is usually not very great, since this is due only to friction or interlocking between the front of one car and the side of the other. As in frontal impacts, the velocity changes of the centres of gravity of the two vehicles in any particular direction are inversely proportional to their weights.

The duration of this impact phase is about 0.1 second and during that time the cars rotate and move forwards and sideways by between one and two feet at an angle to their original path. The rotations during this important impact phase are usually no more than about 10°.

It is important to have some idea of the direction in which the occupants move during the collision, in order to estimate the probable areas struck by those occupants. The front-seat occupants are particularly interesting. Occupants who are unrestrained by seat belts continue to move forward in their original direction, at very nearly the initial velocity of the car, and contact with the interior of the car generally occurs either just before or after the end of the impact phase. Rough estimates of the position at which

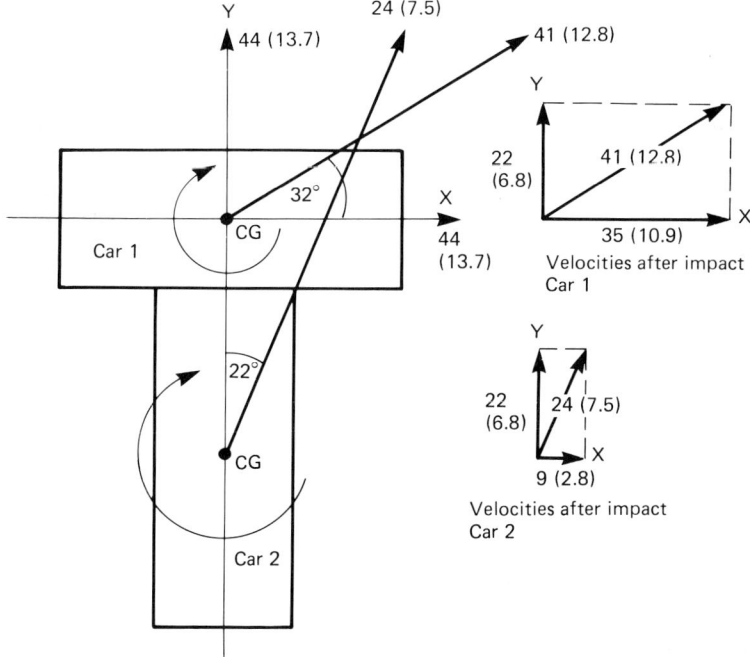

Duration of impact – 0.10 sec
Velocity changes (equal) – X direction 9 ft/sec (2.8 m/s), Y direction 22 ft/sec (6.8 m/s)
Angular velocities – Car 1 80°/sec (1 revolution in 4.5 sec)
Car 2 200°/sec (1 revolution in 1.8 sec)

Figure 6.5 Centre-side impact. Each car has an initial velocity of 44 ft/sec (13.7 m/sec, 30 mile/h)

92 What happens to vehicles during and after accidents

contact takes place can thus be made from the positions of the cars at the end of impact.

Although it is more usual for the struck car to be travelling more slowly than the striking car, the more extreme case where both are travelling equally fast will be illustrated first. As in all collisions the most common situation is for the two cars to be almost the same weight. We will use this situation as an illustration.

Figures 6.4, 6.5 and 6.6 show the positions of the cars before the impact, the directions in which the centres of gravity of the two cars move after impact, and their angular velocities, in three types of intersection collision between similar cars, of medium weight (in the range considered in Figure 6.7), each travelling at 30 mile/h (44 ft/sec or 13.6 m/sec), when the striking car emerges from a side road on the right-hand side; if the striking car comes from the left, the directions of rotation after impact are reversed.

In each of the three cases the passenger in the striking car and the driver in the struck car strike the side of the car and may be ejected if the door

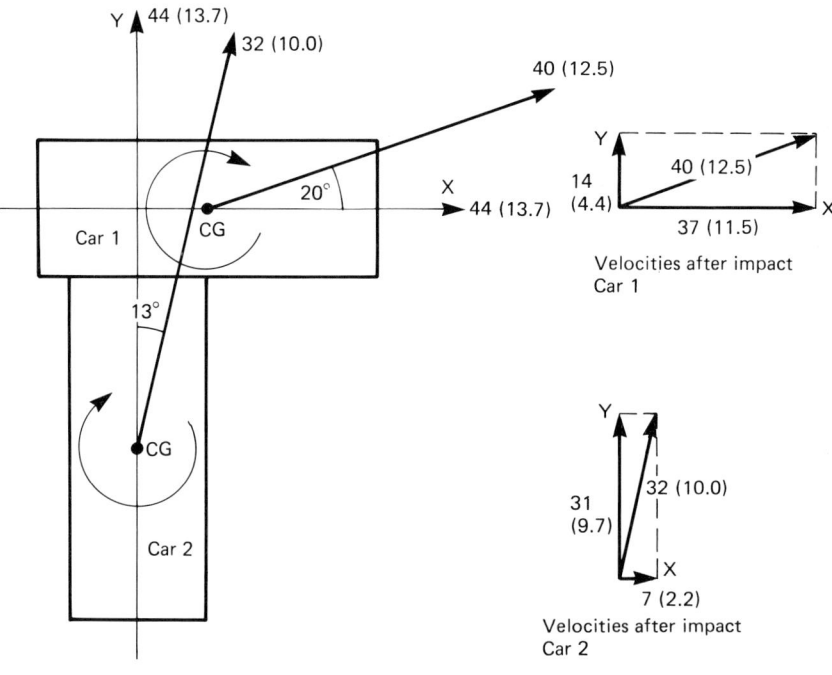

Duration of impact — 0.08 sec
Velocity changes (equal) — X direction 7 ft/sec (2.2 m/s), Y direction 14 ft/sec (4.4 m/s)
Angular velocities — Car 1 249°/sec (1 revolution in 1.4 sec)
  Car 2 161°/sec (1 revolution in 2.2 sec)

Figure 6.6 Rear-side impact. Each car has an initial velocity of 44 ft/sec (13.7 m/sec, 30 mile/h)

opens. The driver of the struck car is also likely to be injured by intrusion of the side of the car.

The driver of the striking car and the passenger in the struck car strike the windscreen, but the driver strikes the screen at a higher velocity than the passenger in the struck car, since (as previously mentioned) the velocity change of the struck car in the forward direction is not very great. The angles at which the centres of gravity of the two cars are estimated to move after impact with respect to their original directions, and their angular velocities, are shown in the figures.

When the impact is central or nearly central, the velocity changes of the centres of gravity of two similar cars in the direction of motion of the striking car are each approximately equal to one-half of the striking velocity. These velocity changes are, therefore, about the same as if the struck car had been stationary. This is the most severe type of collision, because both the velocity changes and the danger of injury from intrusion are greatest. In each case the velocity change of car 1 in its original direction is equal to the velocity of car 2 in the X direction after impact, and that of car 2 is equal to the velocity of car 1 in the Y direction. (See Figures 6.4 to 6.6 for X and Y directions.)

In the more usual case where the struck car is travelling more slowly, for example at 20 mile/h, and the striking car at 30 mile/h, the movements and rotations are similar in character to the cases illustrated, but the angles to their original paths are lower for the striking car and greater for the struck car; the angular velocities are also lower for both striking and struck cars except in a front-side impact when that of the struck car may be slightly higher.

The velocity change of the striking car in its original direction is hardly changed, but that of the struck car in its original direction is reduced. Neither of these differences is very great and both represent very severe intersection collisions.

After the impact phase ends, the cars separate and move off roughly in the directions shown in Figures 6.4 to 6.6, still rotating. On dry roads, largely because of this rotation, they soon come to rest, but on slippery wet roads they may travel much further (see Section 5.9).

6.7 Overturning (rollover)

Most overturning occurs in single vehicle accidents, that is, without contact with any other vehicle: about 50 per cent of single vehicle accidents in rural areas involve overturning and about 25 per cent in urban areas (Grime and Jones, 1973). One of the most dangerous features of overturning accidents is ejection, which occurs when a door opens as the vehicle rolls over. The ejected occupant may then be injured either by striking the road or by being crushed by the car.

In accidents which do not involve overturning, if an occupant is ejected, this almost always occurs, not because the occupant is propelled out of the vehicle, but because, while the occupant continues to move in his original direction, the vehicle rotates and perhaps moves sideways from under him so that he leaves the car through an open door.

In most cases of overturning in single vehicle accidents, even on dry roads, the wheels of the car will have struck obstacles such as kerbs, ruts and ditches. It is comparatively rare for overturning without contact with an obstacle to occur on a dry road with a high coefficient of friction. Two conditions have to be satisfied for this to occur:

(1) There must be a high coefficient of friction between tyres and road.
(2) The velocity of the car in a direction at right angles to its length must be high enough to provide enough energy to raise the centre of gravity until it is directly over the line of contact of the wheels with the ground, as well as the energy dissipated by the tyres in sliding sideways.

For an average car, the coefficient of friction necessary for overturning to occur without striking an obstacle has to be at least 0.9, and the sideways velocity greater than 20 mile/h (32 km/h); although the velocity figure is not well established.

6.8 The estimation of velocity changes from measurements of the permanent deformation of cars

The velocity change of a vehicle is the most important single factor in producing injury, and it is therefore important to be able to estimate it.

The most reliable estimates of velocity changes from damage are for head-on collisions of cars with rigid walls, the paths of the vehicles being at right angles to the walls, since many such collisions have been staged under test conditions. Although there is considerable variation in the observed permanent deformations, not only between makes of models, but also between nominally identical cars, it is found that the deformations of most European cars in the range of kerb weight between 1800 lb (820 kg) and 2500 lb (1140 kg) are clustered around the heavy central line in Figure 6.7. The deformations of most cars in this weight range fall within ±20 per cent of those given by the central line. Examples of cars tested (Neilson, Penoyre and Petty, 1979) and plotted in Figure 6.7 are the BL Marina, the Vauxhall Chevette, the VW Golf and VW Beetle, the Ford Fiesta, the Fiat 133, the Datsun Sunny, and the MGB. Six results are given for more modern cars. The Colt Lancer, Renault 5L, Ford Escort and the lighter BL Mini come near the lower limit. The deformations of much older cars such as the BMC 1100s, Ford Anglia and Hillman Minx also fall within the same limits. All deformations are measured from the front of the bumper in its original position. For the data on the six newer cars the author is indebted to Dr. I. S. Jones, Insurance Institute of Highway Safety, Washington D.C.

Particulars of 13 unnamed post-1980 European cars in the same weight range were also kindly furnished by M. Charles Thomas of Peugeot Renault, and of these, the results of twelve fell within the limits of Figure 6.7. The newer ones tended to be in the upper range of deformations.

Most of the tests on which Figure 6.7 was based were made at impact speeds between 30 and 35 mile/h (48 and 58 km/h), but the few which have been made at lower speeds suggest that the linear form of the relationship given in Figure 6.7 is sufficiently accurate for practical purposes. Figures

Estimation of velocity changes from measurements of permanent deformation of cars 95

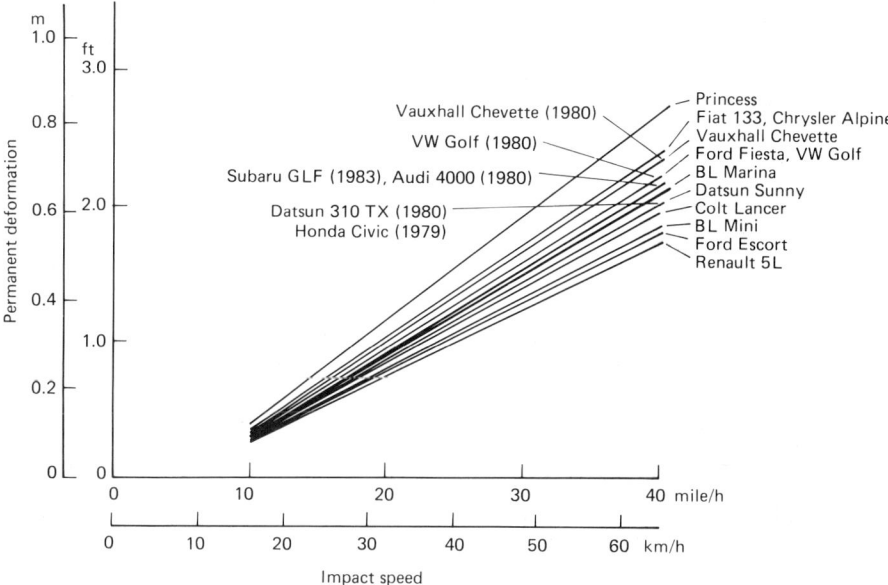

Figure 6.7 Permanent deformations of cars in full frontal impacts

6.8a, b and c are photographs of the deformations of BL Minis after tests at three different speeds of impact into a rigid barrier. Figure 6.9 shows the result of one of the full frontal impacts at 35 mile/h (58 km/h), used for Figure 6.7.

Heavier cars weighing more than 2500 lb (1140 kg) may be expected to be deformed more than those shown in the figure but information is scanty. The deformation of the Chrysler Alpine, whose weight is just over the top limit, is about 20 per cent above the line; that of the BL Princess, weighing approximately 2800 lb (1290 kg), is about 40 per cent above the line.

The deformations in centre-front to centre-front car collisions are approximately the same as those in impacts at 90° to rigid walls, at one-half of the closing speed, provided that the cars are of equal weight and crushing stiffness. This is true regardless of the individual speeds of the two vehicles. Thus, if one is stationary and the other strikes it at 60 mile/h (96 km/h), the result is the same, in terms of damage (and injury), as if both were travelling at 30 mile/h (48 km/h) or if each struck a rigid wall head-on at 30 mile/h (48 km/h). The movements of the vehicles after impact, however, are different, as will be discussed later.

If the vehicles are not identical in construction and weight, and particularly if one is larger and heavier than the other, the frontal deformations will be different. The deformations are usually greater for the lighter car. However, as mentioned in Section 6.2, the total energy E absorbed in crushing depends only on their masses (weights) and approach speed:

$$E = \tfrac{1}{2} \frac{M_1 M_2}{M_1 + M_2} (V_1 - V_2)^2$$

Figure 6.8 Damage to BMC Minis in frontal barrier tests at three different speeds (**a**) Impact speed 19.8 miles/hour (32 km/h). Deformation 0.7 ft (0.22 m)

(**b**) Impact speed 30.7 miles/hour (49.5 km/h). Deformation 1.33 ft (0.41 m)

Figure 6.8 contd.
(c) Impact speed 37.5 miles/hour (60.5 km/h). Deformation 1.72 ft (0.53 m)

Figure 6.9 Damage to Datsun Sunny after a full frontal barrier impact at 35 mile/h (56.3 km/h): deformation 1.8 ft (0.55 m)

It is independent of constructional differences. This energy is shared unequally between the two cars so that, if a direct comparison is made with impacts with rigid walls (usually referred to as barrier impacts), the velocity change of one car is usually overestimated and that of the other underestimated.

An approximate correction for this error is possible, if the deformations of the fronts of the two cars in the particular head-on collision can be measured and compared with the results of barrier impacts given in Figure 6.7, so that the equivalent test speeds (ETS) in the barrier impacts to produce the observed deformations are estimated.

Starting from the fact that the total energy absorbed in crushing the fronts of the two cars depends only on their masses (weights) and approach speed, Appendix 2 shows that, when cars 1 and 2 collide in full frontal collision, estimates can be made of the velocity changes of the two cars, if their weights are known, and their barrier test speeds, to produce the observed deformations. Appendix 2 also shows that a good approximation to the approach speed of the colliding cars is given by the sum of the equivalent barrier speeds; then knowing the ratio of the weights of the cars the individual velocity changes can be calculated since they are inversely proportional to their weights. The error in using this approximation is unlikely to be more than 5 per cent, and is always an underestimate. This procedure does not provide an estimate of individual speeds, but only of the sum of those speeds, and of the two velocity changes.

Off-centre impacts

Off-centre barrier impacts when the car overlaps the wall and contact is made only over part of the front result in greater deformations than in full frontal impacts; however, if contact is made over more than 50 per cent of the front, the difference is small. The most comprehensive series of tests to determine deformations in off-centre impacts were carried out with cars of the same models as those on which Figure 6.7 was based. All were tested at impact speeds of about 31 mile/h (50 km/h) with an overlap of about 30 per cent of the width of the car. Figure 6.10 gives the results in a form similar to that of Figure 6.7. However, in this case, although the spread of the results is about the same, individually they are less reliable. The deformations at 30 mile/h (48 km/h) are on average about 1.6 times those recorded in full frontal impacts, but this ratio varies greatly.

The results of an earlier and less extensive series of tests with varying degrees of overlap and giving very rough guidance are summarised in Figure 6.11. Figures 6.12 and 6.13 are photographs of a test impact at 31 mile/h (50 km/h) and the resulting damage. Not only the part in contact with the block but almost the whole of the front of the car was distorted by the impact. This is usually true in off-centre impacts, although, when the collision is with a rigid object, the edge of the object and therefore the overlap is not difficult to locate (see Figure 6.15).

Figures 6.14 and 6.15 illustrate the results of an impact of a small car, a Datsun, weighting 2100 lb (950 kg). This represents a very severe impact against a rigid barrier with about 30 per cent overlap and an impact velocity of 31 mile/h (13.7 m/sec). Figure 6.14 shows the position of the car when, at

Estimation of velocity changes from measurements of permanent deformation of cars   99

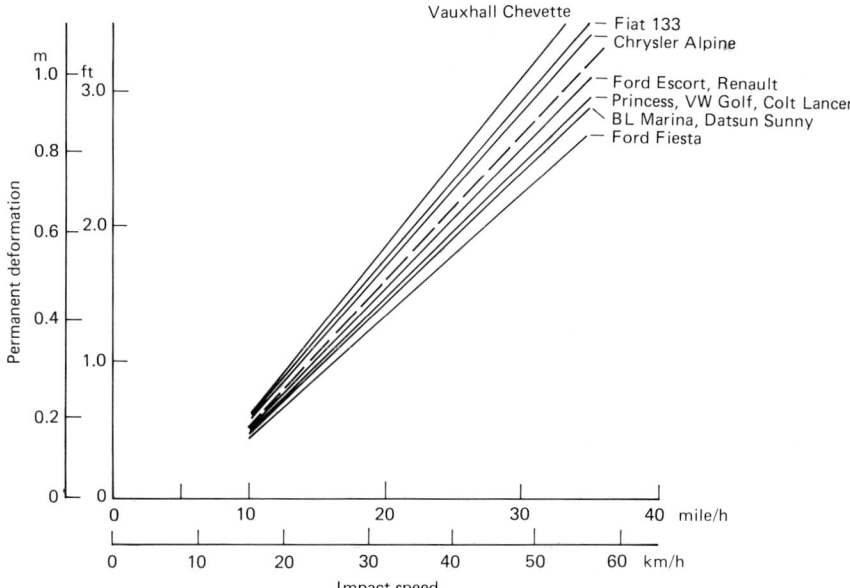

Figure 6.10 Permanent deformations of cars in partial perpendicular impacts with about 30 per cent overlap

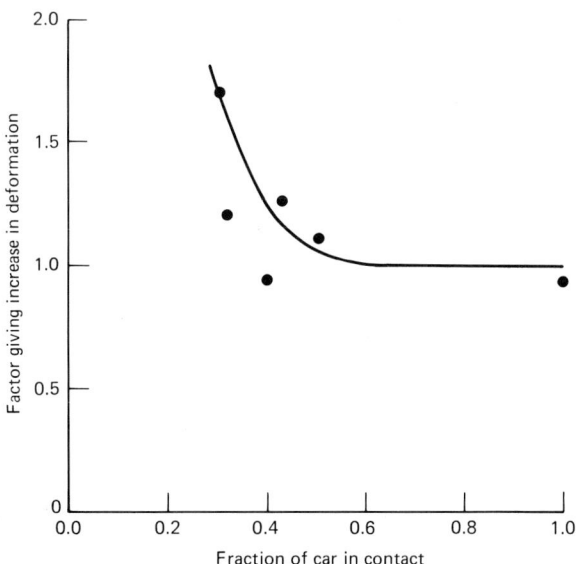

Figure 6.11 Deformation of front of car related to fraction of car in contact with rigid block

100 What happens to vehicles during and after accidents

Figure 6.12 Off-centre head-on impact of Allegro (N5) with rigid wall at 31 mile/h (50 km/h) with 25 per cent overlap

Figure 6.13 Frontal deformation of Allegro (N5)

the end of the impact phase (after 180 msec), the right-hand side of the car is about to rebound from the barrier, and therefore all impact forces have ceased. By the end of the impact the car has rotated by about 13°, and its rate of rotation is then about 1 revolution in 2.5 seconds. It comes to rest at an angle of about 45° to its original direction of movement (Brennan and Grime, 1982). Mainly because of the greater deformation of the car, about 2.5 ft (0.8 m), and consequent increase in duration of impact, a partial frontal impact of this type may be less severe in causing injury to front-seat occupants than the equivalent full frontal impact in which the deformation would have been only about 1.6 ft (0.5 m). This reduced severity is appreciable even for unrestrained occupants and is much greater if belts are worn. This is true only if the deformation on the impact side is not so great that the occupant on that side is crushed or otherwise injured by the intrusion. The measured contour of the front of the car after impact is

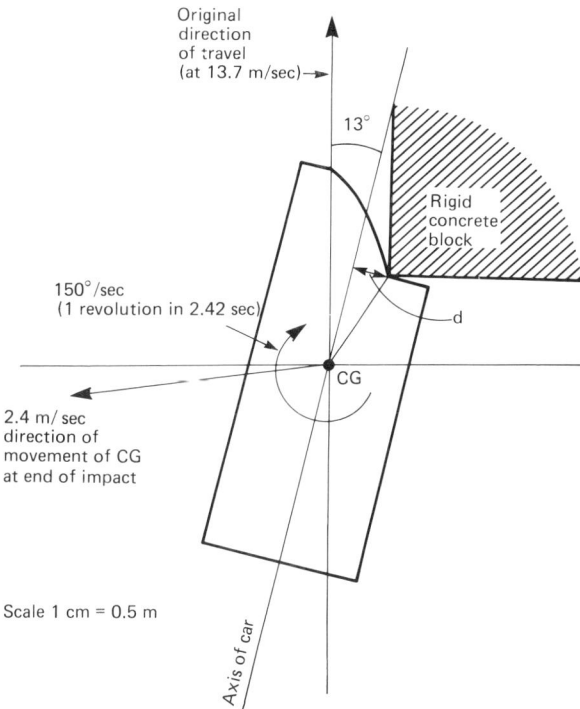

Figure 6.14 Position of movement of car at end of impact (180 msec)

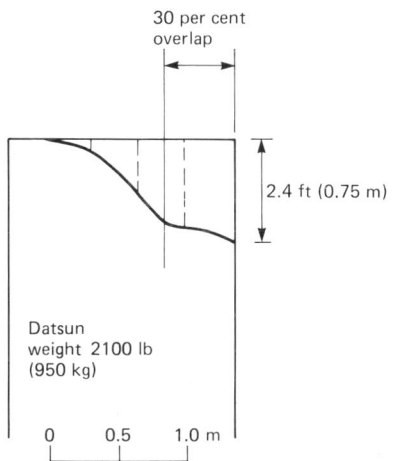

Figure 6.15 Deformation of Datsun Sunny striking a rigid concrete block at 31 mile/h (50 km/h) with 30 per cent overlap

shown in Figure 6.15. The energy of rotation is about 10 per cent of the kinetic energy at impact.

Most off-centre (offset) impacts occur when two cars collide head-on. The general behaviour is similar to that described for partial impact with a rigid block, combined with that of symmetrical head-on collisions. For example, in offset head-on collisions between identical cars, as in full frontal impacts, the behaviour of the two cars during the impact is also identical, although their movements after impact may be different if their speeds are different. Their centres of gravity suffer equal velocity changes and their rotational velocities at the end of impact are also the same. As in full frontal impacts, when two unequal cars collide the velocity changes of their centres of gravity are inversely proportional to their respective weights. Their rotational velocities, however, depend on their relative moments of inertia in a manner which is not easily calculated, although it will be obvious that the larger and heavier car will have a lower velocity of rotation than the lighter one. The energy absorbed in the impact, about 90 per cent of the initial kinetic energy of the two cars, will be shared unequally, the lighter and weaker absorbing more than the heavier car.

Offset head-on collisions, even between identical cars, differ in one important respect from offset collisions with rigid blocks: the struck surfaces are not rigid. Different parts of the front of a car have different stiffnesses, and therefore the deformations of the surfaces in contact vary very substantially across the overlapping parts. Unless the overlap is very small, i.e. wing to wing, the stronger part towards the centre of each car deforms the wing of the other. As a result, the deformations increase towards each wing. Even for collisions of equal cars it is difficult to give simple approximate rules for deriving velocity changes from damage. The best that can be done at present is to illustrate with diagrams and photographs the general levels of deformation to be expected in collisions between cars of approximately equal weight at different closing speeds, and to give some idea of what happens when cars of different weights collide. These illustrations should help to avoid gross errors in estimating velocity changes from frontal damage.

The following figures illustrate the results of six offset head-on collisions.

Figure 6.16 BL Marina v. BL Marina. Each travelling at 32 mile/h (52 km/h) – 40 per cent overlap – damage to the two cars

Estimation of velocity changes from measurements of permanent deformation of cars   103

The first five are between cars of approximately equal weights and sizes, all in the weight range 1800 to 2500 lb (820 to 1140 kg).

(1) An offset head-on collision with about 40 per cent contact between two BL Marinas each travelling at 32 mile/h (52 km/h). Figure 6.16 is a photograph of the damaged vehicles, and Figure 6.17 gives the average of the measured deformations of their fronts. The dashed part of the outline was estimated, not measured.

(2) An offset head-on collision with about 40 per cent contact between a Ford Cortina and a BL Marina, each travelling at 29 mile/h (47 km/h):

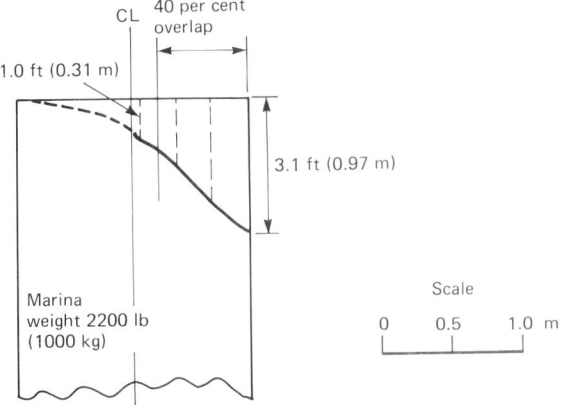

Figure 6.17 BL Marina v. BL Marina. Each travelling at 30 mile/h (48 km/h) – 40 per cent overlap – average deformation to two cars

Figure 6.18 Offset head-on test – Marina (P1) v. Ford Cortina (P2), each travelling at 29 mile/h (47 km/h)

Figure 6.19 Frontal deformations of Marina (P1) (left) and Ford Cortina (P2) (right)

Figure 6.20 Frontal deformations of Ford Cortina (P2) left and Marina (P1) (right)

Estimation of velocity changes from measurements of permanent deformation of cars   105

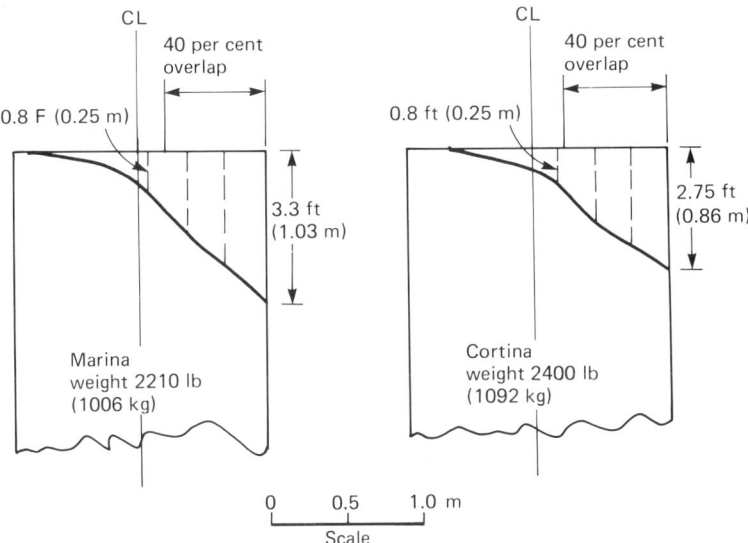

Figure 6.21 BL Marina *v*. Ford Cortina, each travelling at 29 mile/h (47 km/h) – 40 per cent overlap – estimated velocity changes Marina about 30 mile/h (48 km/h), Cortina about 28 mile/h (45 km/h)

Figure 6.22 Offset head-on collision – BL Marina *v*. Ford Escort. Damage to Marina – velocity change about 28 mile/h (45 km/h)

106 What happens to vehicles during and after accidents

Figure 6.23 Damage to Ford Escort – velocity change about 30 mile/h (48 km/h)

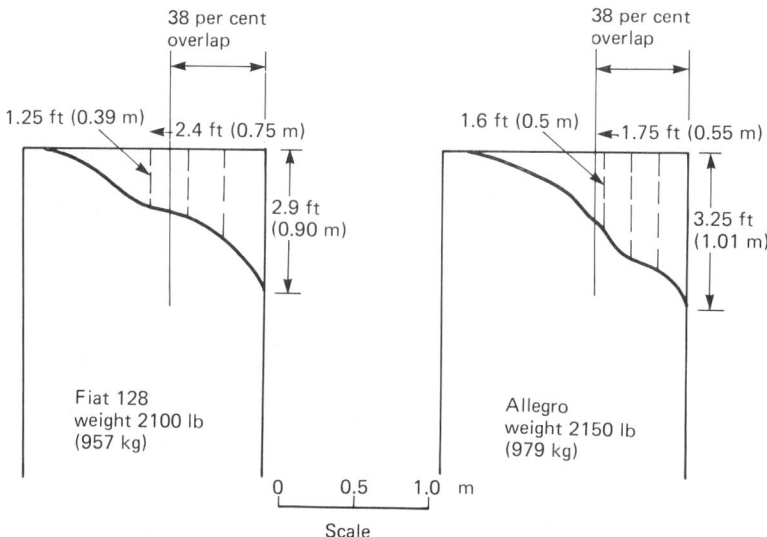

Figure 6.24 Fiat 128 v. Austin Allegro, each travelling at 32 mile/h (51 km/h) – 38 per cent overlap

Figures 6.18, 6.19, 6.20 and 6.21. Figure 6.18 is an overhead view of the vehicles after impact, showing that they have rotated by about 30 degrees, behaving in a similar manner to that observed in offset impacts with rigid blocks. Rotation was less than the 45° recorded in the test described in Figure 6.14. This is in accordance with expectation since there was contact over about 40 per cent of the front in this collision, compared with about 30 per cent in the barrier test impact.

Estimation of velocity changes from measurements of permanent deformation of cars 107

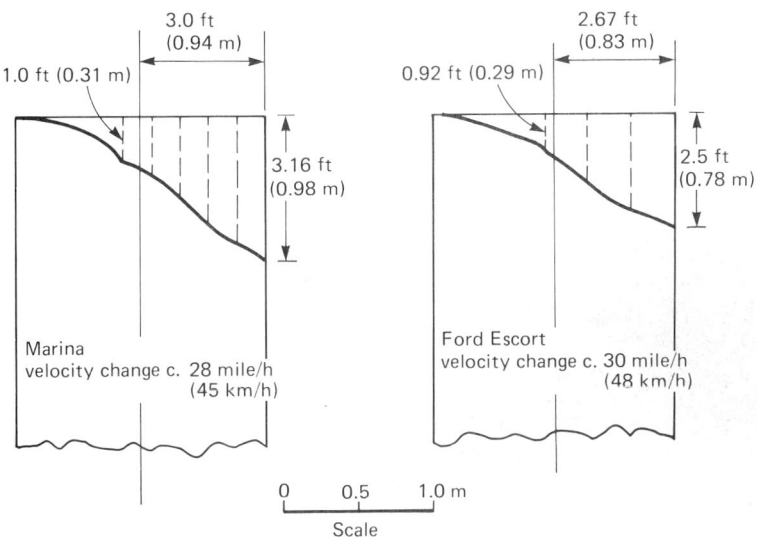

Figure 6.25 Offset head-on collision of BL Marina and Ford Escort with estimated velocity changes

Figure 6.26 Offset head-on collision – Lancia v. Marina – damage to Lancia

The deformations are difficult to estimate from the overhead view since the fronts of both cars were hidden by the displaced bonnet covers. Figures 6.22 and 6.23 are photographs of the damaged vehicles.

(3) An offset head-on collision between a Fiat 128 and an Austin Allegro each travelling at 32 mile/h (51 km/h). The resulting frontal deformations are shown in Figure 6.24.

108   What happens to vehicles during and after accidents

Figure 6.27 Damage to BL Marina

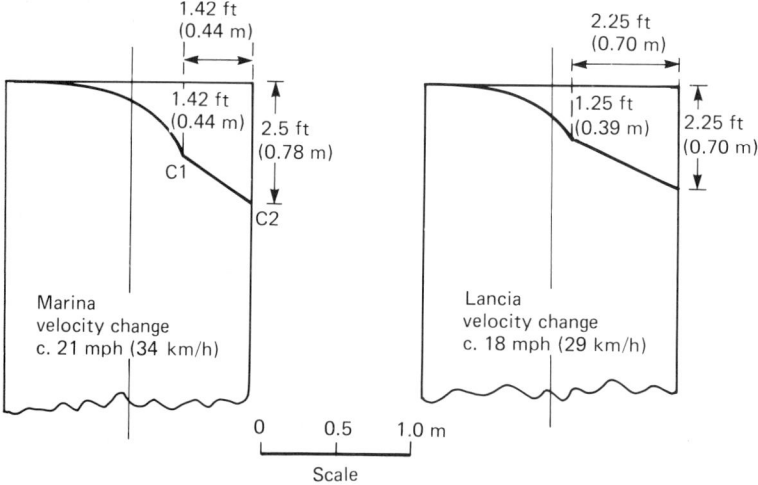

Figure 6.28 Offset head-on collision of BL Marina and Lancia with estimated velocity changes

(4) An offset head-on collision between a BL Marina and a Ford Escort at an estimated closing speed of about 58 mile/h (9.35 km/h). As before the damage is shown in Figures 6.22 and 6.23, and the deformations in Figure 6.25. The estimated offset was about 50 per cent.
(5) An offset head-on collision between a Lancia and a BL Marina at an estimated closing speed of 40 mile/h (64.5 km/h), and an offset of 40 per cent: Figures 6.26, 6.27 and 6.28.
(6) An offset head-on collision between a Volvo 244 and a BL Marina, each travelling at 32 mile/h (52 km/h): Figures 6.29, 6.30, 6.31, 6.32

Estimation of velocity changes from measurements of permanent deformation of cars 109

Figure 6.29 Offset head-on test. Volvo 244 (P19) *v*. BL Marina (P18), each travelling at 32 mile/h (52 km/h): the moment of impact

Figure 6.30 As Figure 6.29. Positions of cars after impact

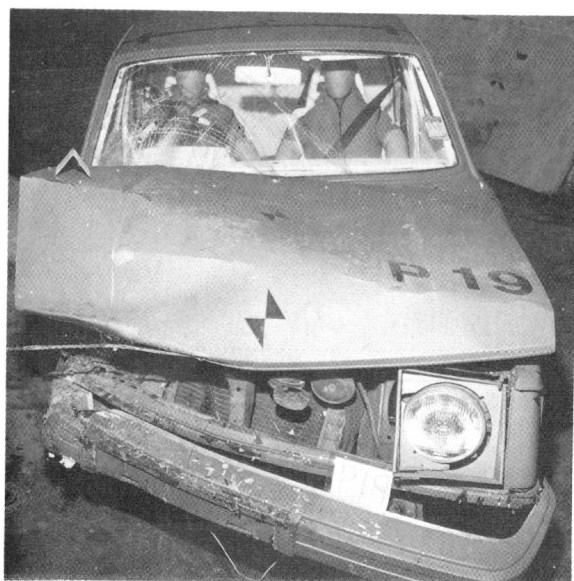

Figure 6.31 Damage to Volvo (P19)

Figure 6.32 Damage to Marina (P18)

and 6.33. These Figures describe a collision between a heavy car, the Volvo, weighing 3045 lb (1384 kg), and a car of medium weight, 2213 lb (1006 kg), giving a mass ratio of about 1.4. Figure 6.29 shows the debris flying at the instant of impact, Figure 6.30 is an overhead view after the impact, and Figures 6.31 and 6.32 are photographs of the damaged vehicles. The deformations are given in Figure 6.33.

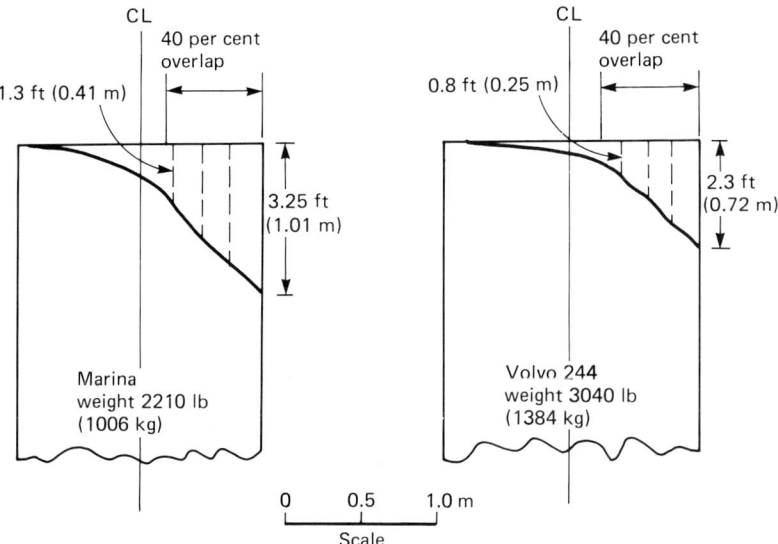

Figure 6.33 BL Marina v. Volvo 244, each travelling at 32 mile/h (52 km/h) – 40 per cent overlap, velocity changes – Marina about 37 mile/h (60 km/h), Volvo about 27 mile/h (44 km/h)

The first three collisions and the last were tests carried out by the Transport and Road Research Laboratory (Neilson, Penoyre and Petty, 1979); the third and fourth collisions were observed in road accidents and are reproduced by courtesy of the Oxford Road Accident Group and the Transport and Road Research Laboratory. While the separate speeds at impact can be given for the test collisions, only the closing speeds can be given for the road accidents. However, since the weights of the cars are known, the velocity changes of their centres of gravity can be estimated as being inversely proportional to their weights. This has also been done for the two test collisions carried out by the TRRL in which the weights of the cars were different. In offset collisions there is very little rebound velocity at the centre of gravity so that such calculations are good enough for practical purposes.

The figures of offset head-on collisions illustrate clearly the difficulty of making close estimates of the velocity changes of cars in frontal collisions but they should enable gross errors to be avoided. In particular the greatly increased deformations in offset compared with full frontal collisions should be noted since there may be a tendency to overestimate velocity changes in offset collisions.

There are no generally available records of tests of offset collisions at speeds lower than about 30 mile/h (48 km/h), so that no direct evidence can be quoted (data given in Figures 6.25 and 6.28 were calculated by computer). However, since one would expect the behaviour in impact of part of the front of a car to be similar to that of the whole, a rough guide to the estimation of the velocity change of the centre of gravity at lower speeds, down to about 15 mile/h (24 km/h), would be to reduce the velocity change in proportion to the damage, starting from the known deformation at 30 mile/h (48 km/h). An assessment of the reliability of computer calculations has been made by Nilsson-Ehle, Norin and Gustafsson (1982).

Collisions with poles

There is little information about head-on collisions with poles and similar objects, but the few test impacts for which results are available suggest that, for central impacts with rigid poles such as concrete lamp columns, the deformations may be from 0 to about 40 per cent greater than those given in Figure 6.7, and for off-centre impacts they are similar to but rather greater than those observed for central impacts, with even greater variability. The behaviour during off-centre impacts may be expected to resemble that described in Figure 6.14. If the object struck is flexible, as may be the case with a tree of small diameter, the resulting duration of impact would be greater, and both the deformation and the severity of the impact would be less.

Collisions with commercial vehicles

When cars collide head-on with medium and heavy commercial vehicles, the mass ratio is likely to be at least 4, so that the velocity change of the car is at least 80 per cent of the approach speed, and the stiffness of the front of the commercial vehicle is much greater than that of the car. In such cases almost all the energy of crushing

(nearly $\frac{1}{2} \frac{M_1 M_2}{M_1 + M_2} (V_1 - V_2)^2$) goes into crushing the front of the car.

For a full frontal impact the velocity change of the car is therefore very nearly equal to the Equivalent Test Speed, that is, the barrier impact speed needed to produce the same damage. In an offset collision the damage would have to be compared in the same way with that sustained in an offset impact with a rigid barrier, since the front of the commercial vehicle would be almost rigid compared with that of the car. Such comparisons could only be made if the car did not underrun the front of the commercial vehicle.

Collisions with walls

The general behaviour of cars in collisions with walls has been described in Section 6.5. Only when the angle of approach (see Figure 6.2) is large can velocity changes be estimated from simple considerations. This is mainly because the coefficient of friction between car and wall is a very important factor. This coefficient can vary from a very low value, when the obstacle is a steel fence, to a very high one when it is strong earth and stone hedge. The flexibility of the obstacle is also a factor since a flexible object increases the stopping distance and duration of impact. At approach angles of 60° and more, one may expect the average deformations to be similar to those experienced in full frontal impacts, and the velocity changes to be those estimated from Figure 6.7, if the obstacle is rigid and has such a high coefficient of friction that no sliding occurs. Since the durations of impact are probably similar, the severities in terms of injuries to occupants are also likely to be similar. If, on the other hand, the hedge yields on impact, so that the stopping distance of the car is increased and the duration of impact becomes greater, the severity of the impact is lessened. This is also true if the car slides along the hedge or wall.

Side impacts

Side impacts most commonly occur at intersections, and, in the struck vehicles, cause serious injuries at lower velocity changes than is the case with frontal impacts.

For cars of normal construction, the stiffness of the side of the struck car is much less than that of the front of the striking car, so the deformation and energy absorption of the struck car are greater than those of the striking car. This difference is particularly marked when that part of the front of the striking car which makes contact with the weak middle of the driver's door is relatively strong. There is little information on the deformations to be expected in such impacts. The existing information mainly refers to impacts of cars travelling at right angles (or nearly so) in which the impact occurs near the centre of the length of the struck car. The few results available suggest that, for production cars of equal weight, about 1000 kg (2200 lb), the maximum deformation of the struck car is likely to be about 14 in (0.36 m) when the striking car is travelling at 30 mile/h (48 km/h) (Finch, 1974), and proportionately less at lower speeds. The velocity changes of the two cars are each equal to about one-half of the velocity of the striking car. This result gives a rough idea of what to expect for European cars in the 1000 kg (2200 lb) weight class. More accurate estimates of deformation require a detailed knowledge of test results for the cars concerned. Results for collisions at other angles and other relative positions can be made by computer (McHenry, Baum and Neff, 1977).

In certain special cases it may be more accurate to estimate the speed of the striking vehicle from the subsequent paths and positions of rest of the two vehicles. The calculation is given in Section 6.9.

Rear impact

The velocity changes in rear impacts cannot readily be estimated since very few test data have been recorded.

Overturning

A similar situation exists for overturning. Clearly the greater the speed before overturning occurs the greater the risk of injury, but this only appears to be true when a large number of accidents is considered, since the variability in the risk of injury is so great.

Hopefully, this chapter will enable accident investigators to make rough estimates of velocity changes from measurements of damage in the most important types of vehicle collisions, or at least to avoid gross errors in such estimates. Test data for more modern cars than those for which results are given here are available only for frontal barrier tests, but the behaviour of later models in other collisions is unlikely to be very different from those given here.

6.9 Movement after impact

Injuries to the occupants of cars in road accidents occur either during the impact phase, or immediately after it, for example within the first one-fifth second, except in overturning accidents or when there is a second impact, so that, in relation to injury, the movements of the cars after impact are not usually very important. However, this movement as indicated by the final positions of the vehicles, may provide clues as to the speed of the vehicle or vehicles at impact. Although velocity changes of the centres of gravity depend only on mass ratios and closing velocities, the direction and speed of movement after impact also depend on the individual speeds before impact; and, while tyre forces may be neglected during the impact phase, in the subsequent motion they are often the only forces acting on a car to bring it to rest.

The speed of a car before a full frontal impact with a post or wall can be estimated from frontal damage since it is approximately equal to its velocity change. In a centre-front impact with a pole, or a 90° barrier impact, this is the only information available from the accident. In off-centre frontal impacts the car rotates after impact and, unless another object is struck, it is brought to rest mainly by the forces between the rear wheels and the road. If the energy of rotation is known, it should therefore be relatively simple to calculate how far the car will rotate after impact, at least on dry surfaces, where the coefficient of friction μ may be assumed to be about 0.8. In practice, however, the back of the car may rise and the rear wheels leave the ground at about the end of the impact phase, reducing or eliminating the tyre forces for part of the rotation. Any calculations based on distance rotated will therefore tend to overestimate the speed at impact, unless continuous skidmarks indicate contact; they may, however, indicate upper limits for the speed.

Appendix 2 shows that in an off-centre impact with a rigid object the velocity V of the car before impact is approximately given by $V = \sqrt{8\mu g D}$, where g is the acceleration of gravity and D the distance moved by the rear tyres in stopping the car. For an impact at 30 mile/h (48 km/h) and a typical medium-sized car on a dry surface, the calculated rotation with an offset of about 30 per cent is about 45°, a figure which is in approximate agreement with the results of test impacts. The velocity is proportional to the square root of the distance. Thus on a dry surface, for an initial velocity of 40 mph (65 km/h), one would expect a rotation of about 80°, and for 20 mile/h (32 km/h) a rotation of about 20°.

The information required in head-on collisions is the position on the road at which the fronts of the two cars met and the final positions of the two vehicles. The position of first impact can often be determined from deposits of dust or mud on the road from the undersides of the wings of the vehicles, from scratch marks if the metal of a car is sufficiently distorted, or on dry roads from skidmarks made either before or after impact.

The following useful general statements can be made if this information is available.

(1) Because of slight elasticity in the fronts of vehicles, they usually separate after impact. If it can be established that after impact they

both rebound and reverse direction away from the impact site, then their speeds at impact were approximately inversely proportional to their weights. For example, if both vehicles were of about equal weight, their speeds before impact were about equal; if one was twice the weight of the other, then the speed of the lighter vehicle was about twice that of the heavier one.

(2) If, after impact, both cars come to rest at some distance past the point of impact in the direction of original motion of the lighter car, then the lighter car was moving faster than the speed given by the inverse ratio of the weights. In the 2 to 1 weight ratio example, the lighter car would have been moving at more than twice the speed of the heavier car. Conversely if both cars came to rest at some distance beyond the point at which the fronts of the vehicles made contact, in the direction of the original motion of the heavier car, the lighter car would have been moving at less than twice the speed of the heavier car. These conclusions apply whether rotation occurs or does not occur after impact.

On dry roads, unless the initial speeds or the weights of the two vehicles are very different, the general movement of the two vehicles away from the point of impact may be quite small and it may be difficult to be sure of what has happened. For example, if the two vehicles in an offset head-on collision are of equal weight, and before impact one is travelling at 25 mile/h (40 km/h) and the other at 35 mile/h (56 km/h), since the velocity change of each vehicle is about 30 mile/h (48 km/h) the common velocity after impact is only about 5 mile/h (8 km/h) in the direction of travel of the faster car, and the movement after impact would probably be only about 2 to 3 ft (0.6 to 0.9 m). If the road was wet and slippery, these distances might be doubled and the indications might be clearer. If the closing speed cannot be estimated from the damage, it is not feasible to deduce velocity changes and speeds from final positions.

In the most simple type of intersection collision, where a vehicle moving slowly across an intersection on a dry road is struck at the centre of its side by another, an estimate of the speed of the striking vehicle can be made provided that no obstruction is encountered after the collision.

After impact both vehicles move in the original direction of the striking car, probably at a small angle to its original path. This movement is retarded only by friction between the tyres of the struck vehicle and the road, unless the front wheels of the striking car are locked in some way. (It is assumed that there was no braking by the striking car.)

The distance moved by the two vehicles after impact (see Appendix 2) is

$$D_1 = \frac{M_1^2 V_1^2}{2\mu g M_2 (M_1 + M_2)}$$

where M_1 and M_2 are the masses (weights) of the striking and struck vehicles, V_1 is the velocity of the striking vehicle, and μ and g have their previous meanings. Table 6.1 gives the estimated distances moved by the two vehicles after impact on a dry unobstructed road for three values of M_2/M_1.

On dry roads one would expect to see skidmarks from the tyres of the struck vehicle. If the tyres of the striking vehicle also leave these marks, the results shown in Table 6.1 will underestimate the speed of the striking vehicle.

Table 6.1 Distances moved by two cars after an intersection collision at right angles ($\mu = 0.8$)

Speed of car 1 before impact (in mile/h)	$\dfrac{M_2}{M_1}$	Distance moved	
		feet	metres
30 (48 km/h)	1.0	18.8	5.3
	0.67	33.6	10.3
	1.5	10.1	3.1
20 (32 km/h)	1.0	8.4	2.6
	0.67	14.9	4.6
	1.5	4.5	1.4

In intersection collisions, similar to those just considered, except that the struck car is moving at a higher speed, both vehicles rotate after the impact, and their centres of gravity again both move in the general direction of initial motion of the striking vehicle but at an angle to that direction. The angle is determined mainly by the mass ratio and by the two speeds before impact. The velocity changes of the centres of gravity are again inversely proportional to the masses of the vehicles.

As discussed in Section 6.6, the calculations of the movements, speeds of rotation (angular velocities) and velocity changes cannot be simply carried out, although the direction of movement of the struck car after impact when the impact is central or forward of centre gives a rough indication of the relative speeds of the cars before impact. The faster the struck car is moving, the smaller the angle of its deflection from the original direction of motion; for equal cars and equal speeds this angle is about 30°.

On slippery wet roads the centres of gravity of the rotating cars may travel some distance before coming to rest, and the vehicles may make more than one complete rotation. In these cases, estimating the angle at which the struck car has deviated is often easy since it is sufficiently accurate to assume that the centres of gravity travel in straight lines after impact. Care must be taken, however, that the calculation has not been made impossible by the car rolling to its final position or being deflected by some obstacle or slope.

6.10 Movements of riders of motorcycles during and after accidents

Accidents to motorcycles are similar in character to those of other mechanically propelled vehicles. The main difference is that motorcyclists are almost always injured by striking another vehicle, fixed object or the road surface, rather than the inside of a vehicle.

In one investigation (TRRL Internal Note, INO 284/78, 1978) it was found that about 25 per cent of the casualties occurred in single vehicle accidents and about 25 per cent of these were caused by collisions with parked unattended vehicles and another 33 per cent occurred when the motorcycle was negotiating a bend or corner. This proportion of single vehicle accidents is lower than that for cars (Grime and Jones, 1973).

About two-thirds of multi-vehicle collisions occurred at junctions or roundabouts, and in about three-quarters of such collisions the motorcyclist was moving ahead and the other vehicle manoeuvring. Nearly 80 per cent of accidents occurred on roads with speed limits of 40 mile/h (65 km/h) or less; thus motorcycle accidents are mainly an urban problem. In 1977 about one-half of the casualties were aged 16 to 19. Learner drivers figure largely in accidents.

In a head-on impact with a wall, if the motorcyclist is projected forward from his cycle, the speed with which the motorcyclist strikes the wall is very roughly that of his speed at impact; this is also his velocity change.

In collisions with mechanically propelled vehicles other than motorcycles the weight of the other vehicle is almost always several times that of the motorcycle, so that in a head-on collision where the motorcyclist is thrown over his handle bars and strikes the other vehicles, he may do so at a relative velocity approaching that of the sum of the speeds of the two vehicles. Therefore, even when both vehicles are travelling at quite modest speeds, the consequences for the motorcyclist may be very serious. In exceptional circumstances where a very heavy motorcycle collides with a very light car, the mass ratio may be no more than 2 to 1, and then the impact of the rider with car would not be at more than two-thirds of the closing speed.

In intersection collisions where the motorcyclist strikes a car or commercial vehicle on its side, the impact speed of his body with the car could be approximately equal to his approach speed. If the vehicle were struck in the rear by the motorcycle, the motorcyclist could strike the vehicle at a speed equal to the difference between the speeds of the two vehicles.

6.11 Accidents involving commercial vehicles

Table 6.2 gives the proportion of accidents involving commercial vehicles and cars and other commercial vehicles in one administrative area of the country. About 30 per cent were collisions with cars, but in those accidents only about 6 per cent of the fatal and serious injuries occurred in the commercial vehicles, and if light commercial vehicles were excluded (mainly car derivatives) the figure is only 2 per cent. Injuries to occupants of commercial vehicles are therefore almost entirely the result of collisions with other commercial vehicles or occur in single vehicle accidents. If collisions with cars are excluded, the pattern of accidents classified by type of impact is as shown in Table 6.3 (Jones, 1972).

The behaviour of commercial vehicles in collisions with fixed objects and other vehicles is similar to that of cars, and the same collision theory can be used to predict results. However, the moments of inertia in yaw (that is about a vertical axis through the centre of gravity (CG)) are not easily

Table 6.2 Accident sample from one administrative area 1965 to 1967

Type of accident	Number	Percentage of total
Car – single vehicle accident	177	20.9
Car v. car	349	41.2
Car v. commercial vehicle	242	28.5
Commercial vehicle v. commercial vehicle	30	5.9
Commercial vehicle – single vehicle accident	30	3.5
All accidents	848	100

Table 6.3 Percentages of impacts to commercial vehicles by type of impact (in injury accidents)

Type of impact	Light goods	Medium and heavy goods	All goods
Frontal	49.5	50.0	49.7
Side	8.0	12.4	9.9
Rear	2.7	5.9	4.1
Single vehicle – overturning	26.6	19.8	23.6
Other single vehicle	13.3	11.9	12.7
Total	100	100	100

calculable, since they depend upon the loads carried, which vary considerably. This is of little importance in collisions between cars and medium and heavy commercial vehicles, because the moments of inertia of the commercial vehicles are so much greater than those of the cars that angular movement of the commercial vehicles may be assumed to be negligible.

No information is currently available similar to that for cars in relation to the crushing of the front and side in collisions with other commercial vehicles. Similar conclusions to those for cars can, however, be derived from the final positions of commercial vehicles involved in head-on collisions.

Table 6.4 gives fatal and serious injuries as a percentage of all injuries which occurred in each type of impact. Note that in light commercial vehicles frontal impacts (which include 'single vehicle others') have the

Table 6.4 Fatal and serious injuries in commercial vehicles as a percentage of all injuries in each type of impact

Type of impact	Type of vehicle	
	Light	Medium or heavy
Frontal	49.3	32.6
Side	34.5	42.1
Rear end	25.0	13.3
Single vehicle – overturning	27.1	41.1
Single vehicle – other	39.3	38.9
All types	40.1	35.4

highest proportions of such injuries, but, in medium and heavy vehicles, side impacts and overturning accidents produce the highest proportions of fatal and serious injuries. A comparison of the whole commercial vehicle sample with car–car collisions in the same study (Jones, 1972), in terms of proportions of each type of accident, showed that commercial vehicles were involved in relatively fewer intersection accidents and more single vehicle accidents.

Although the data indicate that medium and heavy vehicles are no more likely to overturn than light commercial vehicles, when they do so serious injuries and deaths are more likely to result than in the lighter vehicles. Overturning is a more serious problem for commercial vehicles than it is for cars, especially for medium and heavy vehicles, both because such accidents form a higher proportion of the total and because the consequences are more serious. The reasons for the higher proportions of overturning accidents are 1) the CGs of commercial vehicles are relatively higher than those of cars, mainly because their heavy loads are carried relatively higher and 2) in articulated vehicles the 'fifth wheel' suspension point, which allows rotation of the trailer relative to the tractor, has very little stiffness against roll. In tests, articulated vehicles have been found to roll over at lateral accelerations of about $0.2\,g$ (equals 15 mile/h (24 km/h) on a level 65 ft (20 m) radius curve). Such accidents are therefore particularly likely at roundabouts, and statistics show that articulated vehicles are four times as likely to roll over on roundabouts as rigid commercial vehicles (see Figure 4.7).

References

'An analysis of motor cycle accidents' (1978) *Transport and Road Research Laboratory Internal Note,* INO 284/78

BRENNAN, M. and GRIME, G. (1982) 'Three frontal barrier impact tests on a medium saloon car'. Report from the Transport Studies Group, University College London (unpublished)

FINCH, P. M. (1974) 'Vehicle compatibility in car-to-car side impacts and pedestrian-to-car frontal impacts'. *Fifth Int. Tech. Conf. on Experimental Safety Vehicles*

GRIME, G. (1966) 'Safety cars – principles governing the design of cars and safety devices'. *Road Research Laboratory Report,* LR 8

— (1983) 'Car design and occupant safety'. Lecture to course on the Biomechanics of Impact Trauma, International Center for Transportation Studies, Italy

GRIME, G. and JONES, I. S. (1969–70) 'Car collisions – the movement of cars and their occupants in accidents'. *Proc. Institution of Mechanical Engineers,* **184**(2A), No. 5, 87–136

— (1973) 'The frequency and severity of injuries to the occupants of cars subjected to different types of impact in accidents: an investigation of British road accidents from police records'. *Int. Conf. on the Biokinetics of Impacts, Amsterdam*

JONES, I.S. (1972) 'Accidents involving injuries to the occupants of commercial vehicles'. *14th Int. Automobile Technology Congress of FISITA, London, June 1972. Institution of Mechanical Engineers*

McHENRY, R. R., BAUM, A. S. and NEFF, D. O. (1977) 'Yielding-barrier test data base – a study of side impact cases in the multi-disciplinary accident investigation (MDAI) file', *Report* No. ZR-5954-V-2, Calspan Corporation, New York

NEILSON, I. D., PENOYRE, S. and PETTY, S. P. F. (1979) 'Improved test procedures for frontal impact. *Seventh Int. Tech. Conf. on Experimental Safety Vehicles*

NILSSON-EHLE, ANNA., NORIN, H. and GUSTAFSSON, C. (1982) 'Evaluation of a method for determining the velocity change in traffic accidents'. *Ninth Int. Tech. Conf. on Experimental Safety Vehicles*

Chapter 7

Injuries to road users

7.1 Injuries to occupants or riders of motor vehicles

Cars and commercial vehicles

Injuries are caused by forces applied to some part(s) of the body. The main agencies for applying these forces in cars and commercial vehicles are:

(1) Impacts with the interior of the vehicle, including the steering assembly, which account for a large proportion of drivers' injuries.
(2) Crushing due to intrusion of the bodywork of the vehicle or of external objects including parts of other vehicles.
(3) Crushing due to the loads imposed by rear-seat passengers or luggage in cars or by loads carried in commercial vehicles. In cars this can occur regardless of whether seat belts are worn or not.
(4) Forces imposed by seat belts during the process of restraining the wearer.
(5) Injuries due to other inertia loads, when one part of the body is held and another is not, as in 'whiplash' injuries to the neck in rear-end impacts, when the shoulder and chest are restrained by the seat back and the head and neck are not.
(6) Ejection, when forces are set up by contact with the road, or sometimes by striking other vehicles.

In all impacts the first important factor in injury production is the velocity change of the vehicle; the second is the duration of the impact.

All these mechanisms of injury may operate in frontal impacts involving cars, whether the impacts occur in single vehicle accidents, head-on collisions, rear-end or intersection collisions. If the velocity changes of cars in frontal impacts are less than 30 to 35 mile/h (48 to 56 km/h), the main cause of injury for unrestrained occupants (that is, those not wearing seat belts) is that of impacts with the insides of the cars; for front-seat occupants the impact is almost always with the windscreen, instrument panel or steering assembly; for rear-seat occupants, usually the backs of the front seats, but sometimes the side of the car; in exceptional cases, the rear-seat occupant may be projected forward, against or through the windscreen. Head, chest and abdominal injuries produce the injuries most dangerous to life; deaths can occur at velocity changes as low as 15 mile/h (24 km/h), if seat belts are not worn (Grime, 1982).

Mass ratio, that is, the ratio of the weights of the two vehicles in a collision, has a very great influence on injuries. The effect is greatest for deaths; in a head-on collision between two vehicles in which the ratio of weights is two to one, the driver of the lighter car is on average about seven times as likely to be killed as the driver of the heavier car, and even a small difference in weights influences the risk of injury significantly. The effect is similar for intersection collisions. Both serious and slight injuries similarly depend on mass ratio though not so dramatically (Grime and Hutchinson, 1982).

Injuries can still occur even when seat belts are worn, but the risk of injury is considerably reduced. Table 27.1 compares the injuries to the occupants of the front seats of cars wearing and not wearing seat belts (Hobbs, 1978). When all types of accident are included, seat belts reduce the probability of serious injury by about 42 per cent, depending on circumstances and road environment, and the probability of death by about 39 per cent (see Chapter 3). Head injuries are reduced more than leg injuries and there is evidence that the reduction is greater for the most serious head injuries than for the less serious ones.

Table 7.1 Injuries more severe than minor (AIS 2–6) based on 1163 unbelted and 490 belted front-seat occupants of cars – percentages injured

Region	Unbelted	Belted
Head	23.7	10.6
Neck	1.2	1.6
Shoulders	2.1	1.4
Chest	5.2	3.9
Spine	1.5	0.6
Abdomen	2.0	1.2
Pelvis	0.7	0.4
Hip joints	0.6	0
Thighs	2.1	0.6
Knees	2.2	1.8
Lower legs	1.5	0.6
Feet/ankles	1.5	2.4
Arms	3.7	2.0

Head injuries to belt wearers are almost without exception caused by impact of the head against the inside of the car (Grime, 1975). In frontal impacts the driver's head usually strikes the steering assembly and the passenger's head strikes the instrument panel (see Section 6.3). This occurs not only because the belt stretches, fails or is worn too loosely, but also because the head bends forward from the neck and the trunk from the waist. Unless intrusion occurs it is rare for such injuries to be fatal. In side impacts, belts do not prevent heads from striking the sides of cars, sometimes with fatal results, but they do reduce the risk of being thrown from one side of the car to the other, and almost eliminate ejection.

Chest injuries can be caused by the belt forces set up in frontal impacts. This is not surprising when one realises that in a frontal impact with a velocity change of 30 mile/h (48 km/h) the diagonal part of the belt may impose a force of as much as 2000 lbs weight (910 kg force) on the wearer. Chest injuries due to belts rarely prove fatal, however, unless the wearer is loaded from from behind by an unbelted rear-seat passenger. As with head injuries, serious and fatal chest injuries to belt wearers can occur in side impacts in which belts offer little or no protection, at least on the struck side of the car.

Seat belts cause very few abdominal injuries but, in rare cases, in which the seat belt has been incorrectly worn over the abdomen or has slipped up over the abdomen during a frontal impact, fatalities have resulted from the forces applied by the belts (Grime, 1979).

Therefore, fatal injuries to seat belt wearers occur almost entirely in side impacts and in a few frontal impacts when there is loading from the rear or where the seat belt is incorrectly worn over the abdomen, provided that the passenger compartment remains substantially undistorted. However, in frontal impacts at velocity changes of more than 30 to 35 mile/h (48 to 56 km/h), deformation of the passenger compartment and consequent intrusion into the passenger space becomes increasingly important, particularly when the overlap with the front of the other vehicle or obstacle is small. First, it reduces the space available in front of the occupants of the front seats. This, in itself, is not very important for unbelted front-seat occupants; indeed, it may actually help by increasing their 'ride-down' distance but, since it usually produces contact surfaces with sharp edges and broken glass, it is more likely to be detrimental. For front-seat belt wearers, it is always detrimental since, as the intrusions increase, they progressively reduce the distances available for the seat-belts to operate, in addition to providing sharp objects to be struck; intrusion of the steering column presents a special hazard for the driver, even if it is of the collapsible type. Finally, when massive intrusion occurs, front-seat occupants may be crushed, regardless of whether they are wearing belts and, if the disintegration of the passenger compartment is greater still, all occupants of the car may be killed. These fatal accidents are probably one of the main influences which limit the protection given by seat belts.

At the higher velocity changes, when a frontal impact is accompanied by rotation, as in intersection accidents, unrestrained occupants are sometimes ejected and killed or seriously injured, but wearing seat belts practically eliminates this risk.

In frontal impacts, injuries due to inertial loads without contact with the inside of the car can occur to belt wearers, but are rarely serious. They usually consist of slight rib fractures, fractured collar bones, neck injuries, stiff necks and slight back injuries caused by the flexure of the body over the shoulder component of a lap and diagonal belt. As previously mentioned, if the car has no head rests, injuries due to inertial loads can also occur when a car is struck from the rear. The shoulders and trunk are supported by the back of the seat, so that the body moves forward, leaving the head behind which then has to be accelerated to the same velocity as the body by forces thus supplied by the neck. The resulting 'Whiplash' injuries, though occasionally painful for some time, are rarely serious, probably because the velocity change of the struck car is usually low.

In rare cases there may be long-term effects and in very severe accidents occupants may sustain neck fractures, or the rear end of the car may be crushed to the extent that injuries may result from intrusion as well as from inertial forces. The risk of serious injury is on average about 6 times greater to the unbelted occupants of front seats in the striking car.

Overturning is a feature of an appreciable proportion of accidents (about 10 to 15 per cent) and, as speeds increase, is likely to become more important. Injuries occur in three ways: first, unrestrained occupants of a car which rolls over completely one or more times fall around inside the car; second, the roof may collapse, crushing one or more occupants; and third, doors may open, allowing occupants to fall out and be crushed by the car or injured during ejection. Ejection is the most important factor which causes serious injuries and deaths and is almost completely eliminated by wearing seat belts. Belts also protect wearers by holding them in their seats even if there is no risk of ejection.

There is no established relationship between the speed of a car at the instant when overturning commences and the risk of injury to its occupants.

Motorcyclists

As with all road casualties, head injuries are an important cause of motorcycle deaths. When a motorcyclist's head strikes a solid object in a head-on collision with a wall or another vehicle, injuries can be expected to be serious or fatal even at comparatively low closing speeds and even when helmets are worn. Fortunately, in a large proportion of accidents, the motorcyclist's head strikes a road surface at a glancing angle. His velocity in a direction perpendicular to the road is approximately equal to that due to free fall from a height of perhaps 5 ft (1.6 m), that is, it is about 12 mile/h (19 km/h), and, although he may be travelling at a much greater velocity parallel with the road surface, the vertical velocity is probably the most influential in producing serious injury.

Another frequent source of serious though not fatal injury, is leg injury. The most severe injuries of this kind, sometimes requiring amputation, can occur when the impact to the motorcycle occurs to the leg area alone, the worst case being a near head-on collision. At a closing speed of 60 mile/h with a car or commercial vehicle, the approaching vehicle strikes the leg area at that relative speed and no available leg shields can afford much protection (see Section 7.3 for the results of research).

7.2 Injuries to pedestrians

One investigation (Harris, 1977) found that about 70 per cent of the serious and fatal pedestrian casualties were the result of impacts from cars and taxis. The car bumper, bonnet and headlamps, windscreen surround and the ground were the leading sources of injury. About 50 per cent of those killed were aged 60 and over, and children of 14 years and under accounted for about 50 per cent of those seriously injured.

Head injury was the most frequent cause of death, the rest being due to multiple injuries or injury to chest or abdomen. Impact with the ground or being run over caused most deaths, but contact with the windscreen pillar or frame or the facia were almost as important.

The greatest number of serious injuries, not resulting in death, were to the legs (including the pelvis) and these were predominantly due to contact with the bumper.

It has been estimated that about 80 per cent of the casualties were involved in accidents where the impact speed was 31 mile/h (50 km/h) or less; and about 40 per cent of the casualties were struck by vehicles travelling at estimated speeds below 20 mile/h (30 km/h or less). These low speeds are not surprising when you consider that pedestrian injury is largely an urban problem: about 90 per cent of all serious casualties occur in urban areas.

7.3 Protective measures

Seat belts

Most of the engineering effort which has gone into designing protective measures has been for the benefit of car occupants. Such measures are designed to minimise injury when an accident has occurred and do not include devices such as anti-locking brakes which are intended to reduce the risk of having an accident.

Protective measures for car occupants are of two kinds: (1) devices which restrain and control the movement of the occupant, bringing his body to rest by applying as little force as possible and preventing impacts with the interior of the car, and (2) alterations to the construction of the car. The protective device most often used is the seat belt, which, as already described, considerably reduces the risk of injury and death.

The most important function of seat belts is to protect the heads and bodies of wearers in frontal impacts, since the majority (about 60 per cent) of serious and fatal injuries occur in such accidents. Belts also reduce the severity of injury in other circumstances, but they are designed primarily to protect against injury in head-on collisions and frontal impacts.

When in the 1950s seat belts were first seriously considered as an important safety device for use in cars in Europe, they were either full harnesses with two shoulder straps and a waist belt, lap belts, or simple diagonal belts. The lap belt was little used in Europe, since it was obvious that it could not prevent head impact with European steering wheels or instrument panels. The full harness, though effective, was soon discarded as too cumbersome to put on and adjust, and was replaced by the static lap and diagonal belt, which was much easier both to install and use. The single diagonal belt, though extremely convenient in use and effective in reducing injury, was also gradually ousted by the lap and diagonal belt, mainly because, when doors open, it is less effective in preventing ejection. Today, therefore, the vast majority of seat belts in use are lap and diagonal belts, often called three-point belts. The two lower ends of these belts, comprising the ends of the lap strap and the lower end of the diagonal shoulder strap, are attached to the floor, and the upper end of the shoulder strap to the door pillar.

Lap and diagonal belts are of two types: static and emergency locking (inertia reel) belts. Static belts are adjustable to fit the wearer and when properly worn do not allow forward movement of the body, except that due to stretching, in an accident. The emergency locking belt, however, introduced in the early 1960s, does allow the wearer to lean forward. In this type of belt, the shoulder strap is not permanently anchored to the door pillar at its upper end as in static three-point belt, but runs through a metal loop attached to the pillar, and down to a spring-loaded reel, fixed low on the central door pillar. In normal driving the shoulder straps unroll freely from the reel, under light tension from the spring, allowing the wearer to lean forward to reach the controls or glove compartment. When the car strikes an object or another vehicle, or rolls over, a sensing mechanism operated either by car deceleration, or webbing acceleration, or both, locks the reel, and the belt then restrains the wearer in the normal way. The main advantages of these belts are:

(1) the spring retracts the webbing on to the reel when the belt is not in use, so that it is automatically stowed away neatly;
(2) no adjustment for length is required for wearers of different sizes, since only the correct length is withdrawn from the reel;
(3) the wearer is free to lean forwards or sideways to reach objects in the car;
(4) the shoulder strap, which is retracted by the spring, always lies closely against the wearer.

The first three advantages encourage the use of the belts; the fourth should make for greater safety since even a little slackness in belts can reduce their efficiency in frontal impacts. However, as discussed later (p.126), there are other sources of slackness in present day belts of this type, which tend to neutralise this advantage.

To understand how a seat belt, or indeed any restraint system, gives protection in frontal impacts, consider what happens to an unbelted person in the front seat of a car when the car collides with a rigid object such as a concrete lamp standard at 30 mile/h (48 km/h). If the impact is to the centre front of the car, the car is brought to rest in a very short time, usually little more than one-tenth of a second, which is the time taken for the front to crush by perhaps as much as 2 ft (60 cm). During this crushing time, the passenger's head and body continue to move forward at very nearly the full speed of the car before the impact. But the internal dimensions of cars are such that, by the time the passenger strikes whatever is in front of him inside the car (generally the windscreen or instrument panel), the car has almost come to a standstill, so that the injury-producing impact takes place at something approaching the speed of the car before the collision. This is the so-called 'second impact'; and, in spite of what car advertisements sometimes say, no alteration to the crushing properties of the front of the car can make any considerable reduction in the severity of this second impact. Similar considerations apply to the impact of the driver's head with the windscreen, although the impact to his chest is somewhat lessened by the nearness of the steering wheel, which gives a considerable measure of protection to the driver at low impact speeds.

Most head-on collisions, whether with other vehicles or fixed objects, are not fully frontal, but offset, that is, only part of the front of the car makes contact with the other vehicle or fixed object. In these cases (see Chapter 6) both the deformation of the front of the car and the duration of the impact are usually much greater than in fully frontal collisions. As a result, an unrestrained front-seat passenger strikes the car interior while it is still moving forward, so that his velocity relative to the car is less than in full frontal impact, with a corresponding reduction in injury.

Obviously, the first object of using a seat belt is to tie the occupant to the car so that his head and body do not strike anything which may cause high localised forces. A seat belt does more than this: it greatly reduces the forces which act on the whole body to bring it to rest. With no seat belt, the head and body are brought to rest by striking comparatively hard and unyielding objects, causing very large forces acting over very short distances. The seat belt, usually a lap and diagonal belt, acts in two ways to slow down the body over a much greater distance, and therefore with much lower forces on the body: first, the belt itself stretches, to allow forward movement of the body by about 8 in (20 cm) or more, and, second, because the occupant is tied to the car, some of the crushing distance of the car is also added to the stretch of the belt; this is popularly known as 'ride-down' distance. So instead of the occupant being stopped in a distance of perhaps 1 in (2.5 cm), an ideal seat belt might be expected to provide a stopping distance of 12 to 16 in (30 to 40 cm) in a typical frontal impact at 30 mile/h (48 km/h), with corresponding reduction of the forces applied to the body (Grime, 1966). There should be no impact of the head with any hard object since the head is stopped by forces exerted by the neck, which is well able to do this without incurring serious injury (Grime, 1975; Mackay et al., 1975). Another important function of seat-belts is to hold occupants in their seats in accidents of other types, particularly when overturning occurs.

However, as mentioned earlier, belted front-seat occupants do suffer injuries to head and face by impact with hard objects, usually the steering wheel or facia. Stretching of the belt is one factor in allowing the excessive forward movement from which injury results. Other important factors are, first, the slack in the belt, whether due to looseness in wearing the belt, compression of the clothing, or, in the case of inertia reel belts, wind-up of the belt on its reel, and, second, folding of the body from the waist. Various methods of pretensioning the belt immediately on impact have been developed, but none has been widely used and these shortcomings of belts remain to be rectified (Grime, 1979).

The two types of belt so far described may either be worn or allowed to lie unused in the car according to the wishes of the car occupant. However, belts can be designed to be placed automatically in position across drivers' or passengers' bodies, so that they have no choice but to wear them. An example of an automatically placed belt is shown in Figure 7.1, in which the upper and lower outer anchorage points are attached to the door. When the door is opened the outer ends of the belt are moved away from the seat, allowing entry into the car. For extra convenience, one of the lower ends of the belt, in this case the inner one, may be moved forwards by a motor when the door is opened and returned to the operating position when the door is closed. Such belts are classed as passive restraints – devices which require no action on the part of the user.

All belts fitted in British vehicles have to satisfy the requirements of the British Standard Institution and carry either their mark of approval (the Kitemark) or the European E mark; all passenger cars and car derivatives must have belts fitted in the two front seating positions.

Protective measures 127

Figure 7.1 An automatically placed seat belt

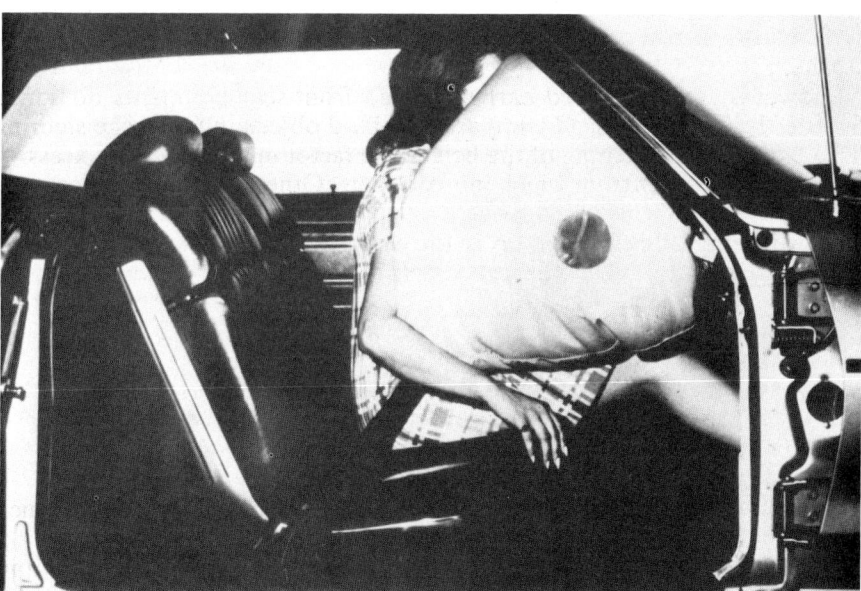

Figure 7.2 An airbag after inflation in a frontal impact

Two other main types of passive restraint will be described to complete the discussion. The first is the airbag, the original American concept of a passive restraint. The airbag is normally stored in collapsed form in the dashboard or steering column, and is explosively inflated in a few hundredths of a second when an accident occurs, forming an air cushion filling the space in front of the car occupant as shown in Figure 7.2.

128   Injuries to road users

Figure 7.3 Automatic cushion restraints

The third passive restraint, a purely mechanical system, is the Automatic Cushion Restraint. It comprises an arm, hinged from the central tunnel or console, supporting a chest pad, which is held by light spring pressure against the chest of the car occupant, and a knee restraint (see Figure 7.3). The chest pad behaves like an emergency locking belt, allowing free movement in normal travel, but locking on impact to allow forward movement of the chest only when a predetermined load is exceeded. The knee restraint is designed to decelerate the lower part of the body without serious injury to the legs (Grime, 1979).

Passive restraints offer an alternative to compulsion as a method of giving protection to a very high proportion of car occupants. They are all considerably more expensive than ordinary seat belts.

Lap and diagonal belts are standard fittings in cars, and are suitable for adults and older children over 8 years of age, according to height. For younger children three types of protective device are available; for infants, cots may be bought which can be anchored in the rear seating position; for young children, starting from the age when they are able to sit up until about the age of four, a range of safety seats is available, while for older children under 8 years of age small versions of adult seat belts can be fitted. These are usually full harnesses, with two shoulder straps.

All restraint devices for small children should be fitted in the rear seating positions of cars. Their anchorages should be capable of withstanding large forces at least 20 times the weight of the child. If only one safety seat is fitted, it should be placed at the centre of the rear seat, since this position provides greatest protection in side impacts. Figure 7.4 shows one example of these safety seats.

The seat belt law, which came into operation in January 1983, applies not only to adults but also to children occupying the front seat – it is against

Figure 7.4 Child safety seat

the law to have an unrestrained child in the front seat of a car. If the car is fitted with adult seat belts only, they can still be used by older children by using a specially designed booster cushion, fitted with hooks or straps to hold it in place. Approved seat belts and safety seats for children have been shown to be at least as effective as adult seat belts in minimising injury.

Although the effectiveness of seat belts is almost universally acknowledged, improvements to increase their efficiency are known to be possible (Grime, 1979), and will probably be introduced gradually, in much the same way that alterations have continuously been made in past years.

Car alterations

Alterations to the car itself are primarily designed to be effective in the two main types of impact, frontal and side impact.

As shown in Chapter 6, greater frontal deformation decreases the risk of injury in frontal impacts both to restrained and unrestrained occupants. Unfortunately, the deformations in partial frontal impacts are already as great as can be tolerated and there is a case for increasing the stiffnesses of the fronts of cars, particularly on the driver's side; this is more important for small than for large cars. An advantage in reduced intrusion would result, and there would be little penalty in increased risk of injury.

However, the requirement to reduce the risk of intrusion in side impacts is that the fronts of impacting cars should be made less stiff so that they absorb a greater share of the energy of impact. Tests have shown that it is possible to reconcile the two conflicting requirements by stiffening the sides of cars, strengthening and raising the sills and making alterations to the fronts of cars so that their strongest members make contact with the sills of struck cars. Tests showed that these measures resulted in dramatic reductions in penetration of the side of the struck car (Finch, 1974). At the same time the door has to be filled with padding designed to spread the load over the occupant's hip and pelvis if penetration occurs. Some of these changes are being introduced into production cars. These alterations do not radically affect the risk of head injury caused by impact with the side window glass or its frame or with the side pillars.

Seat belts are unlikely to be of any assistance in reducing injury to the occupant on the struck side of the car, but they have some effect in preventing an occupant on the other side from moving across the car to strike the side of the car with his head.

The design of the steering assembly is of considerable importance for the driver, since it can provide a considerable measure of protection in frontal impacts. The design objective is to construct the steering column in such a way that, even when the front of the car is heavily deformed, the steering wheel is not forced back on the driver; furthermore, when the driver strikes the steering wheel, it should yield at a constant load, less than that likely to cause serious injury. This objective has not yet been completely realised.

Minor leg injuries are common occurrences in frontal impacts, whether or not occupants are restrained, and very serious and disabling injuries sometimes occur. Well-designed padding, sometimes called a 'knee bolster', should be an essential feature of every car, and designed, as are steering assemblies, to yield at approximately constant load for a considerable distance, since the whole of the lower part of the body of an unrestrained occupant has to be brought to rest by forces which are low enough not to cause serious injury to the knees and bony structure of the thigh.

Padding all hard surfaces is also a requirement, even for the roof, since this may be struck by occupants' heads when a car overturns and rolls. Padding should be stiff since soft padding 'bottoms out' and does not cushion the hard surface beneath it adequately.

The design of 'safety cars' incorporating radical changes in structure has for many years engaged the attention of vehicle engineers and has resulted in useful changes in production cars. The main difficulties which occur are the penalties which have to be incurred for greatly increased safety, in weight and dimensions, reduced interior space, petrol consumption, increased constructional complication, and overall cost. In the highly competitive world of the car industry, this means that a 'trade-off' has to be made between safety and attractiveness to the buyer. Similar 'trade-offs', unfortunately, apply in all fields of safety.

Protection for motorcyclists and cyclists

In common with all other road users, the motorcyclist is most likely to be killed by injury to the head, so a great deal of effort has been put into making motorcycle helmets as efficient as possible.

The helmet is designed to minimise the force applied by making it act over as great a distance as possible. In the helmet this is achieved by a cradle around the head together with stiff padding material, the whole helmet being enclosed in a hard shell which spreads the blow over an area and also prevents penetration by sharp objects. Early research showed that most impacts occurred to the sides rather than to the top of the helmet, and the most effective modern helmets provide protection not only to the top and sides of the head but also to the face by enclosing the lower part of the face with a padded ring and a visor. Ventilation of these enclosed helmets is essential.

Limitations on the extent of possible head protection are imposed by the space available in a helmet to decelerate the head. At most this cannot be more than about 1 in (2.5 cm) since the weight and dimensions of the helmet have to be kept as low as possible, both for comfort and to prevent excessive rotation of the head in an accident. When a seat belt is used in a car, unless contact is made with the car interior, the head is decelerated by the neck over a distance greater than the stretch of the belt plus the 'ride down' distance provided by the crushing of the car – a distance of about 20 in (50 cm). There is no 'ride down' distance for the helmet, and all its protection has to be provided by compression of the layer between the shell and the head. Thus it cannot be expected to prevent serious or even fatal injury when a motorcycle rider is projected forward and strikes a wall, a post or a rigid part of a vehicle, even at speeds common in built-up areas.

In many accidents, the impact of the head is with the ground; in such cases helmets provide a large measure of protection since the blow is usually a glancing one and the relevant striking velocity is not very high. Helmets with visors also reduce the incidence of facial injuries compared with those without facial enclosure. All British-made helmets have to meet British Standard Institution requirements.

Much of the difficulty of providing protection against severe head injuries arises from the fact that, in frontal impacts, the rider is projected forward from his machine, probably with serious consequences if he then strikes another vehicle or a rigid object. Efforts have been made in two directions either to retain the rider on the machine or to reduce the velocity with which he is projected forwards.

(1) Totally enclosed motorcycles have been designed and constructed, mainly with improved weather protection in view, which may give the kind of protection afforded by a very small car. None appears to be commercially successful yet.
(2) At the Transport and Road Research Laboratory, a chest pad at the end of an arm projecting upwards from the tank of the motorcycle, has been shown, by tests with dummies, to reduce the forward velocity with which the rider leaves his cycle. This device has not yet been adopted commercially (TRRL Leaflet LF873, 1979).

Although motorcyclists' deaths are mainly due to head injuries and less frequently to injuries to the chest or abdomen, legs are by far the most commonly injured part of the body (TRRL Leaflet LF 620, 1977), and many such injuries are severe. Providing leg protection is, therefore, a matter of urgency, but because of the very large forces set up when a leg shield comes into contact with an obstacle or another vehicle, the problem is a difficult one to solve.

Research continues, and an experimental motorcycle has been described having leg guards which, in a frontal impact, absorb an appreciable proportion of the kinetic energy of the rider. An airbag, inflated on impact, was also installed and this further reduced the rider's kinetic energy and therefore his forward velocity (Chinn, Donne and Hopes, 1985).

Some form of helmet would be of great benefit to cyclists, since helmets are at their most effective when the speeds of the vehicles involved are low. However, apart from some research by the Transport and Road Research Laboratory, no serious attempts have yet been made to put this suggestion into practice on the road.

Protection for the pedestrian

A considerable research effort, using dummy pedestrians, has been directed towards making the fronts of cars less dangerous for pedestrians. The principal findings are that both the front of the car and the top surface of the bonnet should be covered with compressible energy absorbing materials, giving a considerable depth of crush, greater at the front than on the bonnet. The front of the car should extend from about 12 in (30 cm) to about 28 in (73 cm) above ground level and there should be no rigid bumper. No production car has yet incorporated such drastic suggestions, although the research has probably influenced frontal design (TRRL Leaflet LF 871, 1979). More recent research at the Transport and Road Research Laboratory has produced a car, which is almost indistinguishable from a conventional European car, and this appears to have greater potential than any previous design (Hobbs, Lawrence and Clarke, 1985).

Alterations to commercial vehicles

Collisions with commercial vehicles constitute hazards to cars, which, because of the disparity in mass, are greater than those in collisions with cars. There also exist hazards in rear-end collisions when cars underrun the structures of the commercial vehicles. In frontal collisions the disparity of mass is made more lethal by the much greater stiffness of the front of the commercial vehicle compared with that of the car. Almost all of the energy of the collision therefore goes to deform the front of the car, with the result that massive intrusion may occur into the passenger compartment. Methods of softening the fronts of commercial vehicles have been designed and tested at the Transport and Road Research Laboratory (Penoyce, S., B. S. Riley and T. M. Burgess, 1985); to prevent underrun of the rear of heavy vehicles, special bumpers are now being fitted to many such vehicles.

References

FINCH, P. M. (1974) 'Vehicle compatibility in car-to-car side impacts and pedestrian-to-car frontal impacts'. *Fifth Int. Tech. Conf. on Experimental Safety Vehicles*

GRIME, G. (1966) 'Safety cars – principles governing the design of cars and safety devices'. *Road Research Laboratory Report*, LR 8.

— (1975) 'Head and neck injuries to car occupants wearing safety belts in frontal collisions'. *Proc. Int. Conf. on Biomechanics of Serious Trauma, Birmingham, November*

— (1979) 'The protection afforded by seat belts'. *Transport and Road Research Laboratory Supplementary Report*, SR 449

— (1979) 'A review of research on the protection afforded to occupants of cars by seat belts which provide upper torso restraint'. *Acc. Anal. & Prev.*, **11**(4), December

— (1982) 'Probabilities of injury to car occupants in accidents, with a practical example. *Proc. Inst. of Mech. Engineers,* **196,** No. 35

GRIME, G. and HUTCHINSON, T. P. (1982) 'The influence of vehicle weight on the risk of injury to drivers'. *Ninth Int. Tech. Conf. on Experimental Safety Vehicles, Kyoto, Japan*

HARRIS, J. (1977) 'Research and development towards improved protection for pedestrians struck by cars'. *Transport and Road Research Laboratory Digest,* SR 238

HOBBS, C. A. (1978) 'The effectiveness of seat belts in reducing injuries to car occupants'. *Transport and Road Research Laboratory Report,* LR 811

HOBBS, C. A., LAWRENCE, G. T. L. and CLARKE, C. S. (1985) P.S. C.I. – A demonstration car with improvements for pedestrian protection. *Tenth Int. Tech. Conf. on Experimental Safety Vehicles* Oxford, July 1985

MACKAY, G. M., GLOYNS, P. F., HAYES, H. R. M., GRIFFITHS, D. K. and RATTENBURY, S. J. (1975) 'Serious trauma to car occupants wearing seat-belts'. *Proc. 2nd Int. Conf. on Biomechanics of Serious Trauma, Birmingham, November*

'Motorcycle accident survey 1974' (1977) *Transport and Road Research Laboratory Leaflet,* LF 620, Issue 2

'Protection of pedestrians struck by cars' (1979) *Transport and Road Research Laboratory Leaflet,* LF 871

'The experimental safety motorcycle – ESMI' (1979) *Transport and Road Research Laboratory Leaflet,* LF 873

CHINN, B. P., DOWNE, O. L. and HOPES, P. D. (1985) 'Motorcycle rider protection in frontal impacts'. *Tenth Int. Tech. Conf. on Experimental Safety Vehicles,* Oxford, July

Chapter 8

The potential for savings in accidents involving injury

As previously mentioned in Chapter 2, the most effective remedy is not necessarily related directly to the main factor. Studies of accident 'causation' indicate that the greatest potential for accident reduction lies in influencing human behaviour, but to change the pattern of behaviour by persuasion or training has proved to be more difficult than other measures, such as enforcement and engineering measures, which remove hazards or improve vehicles. Such measures therefore figure largely in those listed in the summary of safety measures which follows.

The estimated effect of introducing a number of measures for reducing accidents involving injury are summarised in Table 8.1, based on a table given by Sabey and Taylor (1980). Such estimates may be revised occasionally, but the alterations are unlikely to change the general picture of the relative effects of the different measures provided by the table.

Table 8.1 Summary of methods to reduce road accidents involving injury

Method	Estimated reduction in total accidents (per cent savings)
Road engineering (low-cost measures)	
Geometrical design, especially junction design and control	10
Road surface texture – rougher textures	5
Road lighting	3
Urban areas – changes in land use, road design and traffic management	5–10
Vehicle safety measures	
Vehicle maintenance, especially tyres and brakes	2
Anti-lock brakes and safety tyres	7
Conspicuity of motorcycles	3
Seat belts	7
Other occupant protection measures	5–10
Road users	
Restrictions on drinking and driving	10
More appropriate use of speed limits	5
Propaganda and information	up to 5
Enforcement and police presence	up to 5
Education and training	up to 5
Other legislation (e.g. restrictions on parking)	up to 5

The savings listed cannot simply be added to obtain an overall figure, since many of the safety measures interact. Sabey and Taylor put the potential savings at three-fifths or 60 per cent of all accidents. (For details of the calculation refer to the original paper.)

References

SABEY, B. E. and TAYLOR, H. (1980) The known risks we run: the highway. *Transport and Road Research Laboratory Supplementary Report*, SR 567

Chapter 9
General remarks on accident investigation

9.1 Probabilities of accidents and probabilities of injury

It is well known that accidents to vehicles which result only in damage far outnumber those which result in injury to a vehicle occupant. The main reason is the very large number of impacts which occur at speeds below the threshold at which injuries occur. However, it is not so obvious that accidents resulting in no injury can also occur at much higher speeds. To take a simple example, if a large number of cars of the same model, each having a driver alone and unbelted, were to run into the same massive concrete block at 15 mile/h (24 km/h), a very small number would be killed, a larger number would be seriously injured, a still larger number slightly injured, and a very considerable number would escape without injury. In real life, it is impossible to control all the conditions of an accident so perfectly as always to obtain the same result. There are obvious reasons for this: the differences between people's sizes, physical characteristics, seated position at impact, age, and tolerance to injury. As a result, in any accident of the simple kind which we have considered, there are probabilities of fatal, serious and slight injury, and of no injury, and these probabilities depend upon the speed at which the car strikes the concrete block, the probabilities of serious injury and death obviously increasing with speed.

One consequence of this idea of probability is that the probability of an accident resulting in injury (and therefore of it being included in the national statistics) increases with the number of people involved. Thus a smaller proportion of single vehicle accidents with driver alone are likely to appear in the national statistics than when two or more cars are involved in collisions, even when other circumstances of the accidents, such as the velocity changes, are similar. Another consequence is that accidents of types least likely to result in injury, such as rear-end collisions, and all urban as opposed to rural accidents, are numerically under-represented in the national statistics.

A less obvious consequence of considering probabilities of injury is the explanation it provides of why two people in apparently identical accident circumstances may sustain injuries of very different degrees of severity. The most puzzling example is when there are two front-seat occupants, one wearing a seat belt and the other unbelted, and the belted occupant is seriously injured while the unbelted one is uninjured. Suppose that this occurs when a car strikes a rigid object such as a bridge abutment at

20 mile/h (32 km/h). Accurate measures of probabilities are not yet available, but rough calculations can be made. The probability of no injury for an unbelted person at that velocity is estimated to be about 0.2, and that of serious injury for a belted occupant about 0.1. This means that in a large number of such accidents at 20 mile/h one would expect about 20 per cent of unbelted persons to be uninjured and about 10 per cent of belted occupants to be seriously injured. The probability of both happening simultaneously is, however, much less, being given by $0.2 \times 0.1 = 0.02$, i.e. once in 50 accidents. This calculation therefore indicates that such a result is to be expected, though not very often, and, when it is observed, it does not necessarily result from any failure of the seat belt to do its job. It should be noted that the figure of 1 in 50 only applies to one particular impact speed; the overall frequency may well be less than this.

The discussion of probabilities has been confined to car accidents, but clearly there exist similar probabilities of injury in accidents to other road users, although, in these cases, useful deductions are more difficult to make.

9.2 Information required in accident investigations

Examples will now be given of the actions which should be taken and the kind of information which should always be sought in an accident investigation. Experienced workers in this field will, of course, already be familiar with most of what follows, but, even for them, a summary may be useful.

Information required in every case

(1) Date, time and place.
(2) Class of road and speed limit.
(3) State of light and weather and road condition; class of street lighting (if any).
(4) A plan, drawn to scale, of the scene of the accident showing gradients, hedges and obstructions and final positions of vehicles and road users involved in the accident, and, in vehicle accidents, any marks or deposits of dust or debris on the road or its kerbs and verges, and damage to fences, hedges or other objects.
(5) Photographs of the accident scene, and the approaches to it, from appropriate viewpoints, and, in vehicle accidents, of marks on kerbs or verges and damage to fences.
(6) If rain was falling at the time, or if the surface of the road was still wet after rain, close up photographs to show the texture of the road surface.
(7) If the road was dry, close up photographs of skidmarks and other relevant marks or objects on the road surface.
(8) Statements of witnesses.
(9) Particulars of all injuries.

Additional information in single vehicle, two vehicle or multi-vehicle accidents involving cars or commercial vehicles

(1) Particulars of the make and model and year of registration of each vehicle, and its weight at the time of the accident. The weights are

most important since in two vehicle collisions the mass ratio is one of the most influential factors in injury production.
(2) The results of the examination of the condition of the vehicle or vehicles by a qualified vehicle examiner. Tyres, brakes and steering are particularly important. In wet road accidents the amount of tread remaining on the tyres of each axle is an important fact to note. In night accidents on unlit roads the intensity and aim of the headlights in use should also be recorded.
(3) Photographs and measurements of the external damage to each vehicle involved in the accident. To help reconstruction of angles of impact, and extent of damage, it is helpful to photograph the damage from above. This may often be done from a second floor window after the vehicle has been removed from the scene of the accident.
(4) Photographs of the inside of any vehicle in which injury has occurred, preferably from both sides of the vehicle.
(5) Evidence as to whether seat belts were worn. Ambulance men, police, or whoever was first at the scene of the accident should be questioned; or the seat belt webbing may have been cut to remove the wearer. A broken belt indicates that it had been worn, and marks on the webbing where it passed through a metal fitting can also provide evidence that the belt had experienced large forces. (These forces can be as much as 2000 lbf (909 kgf) and therefore are likely to leave traces on the webbing.) Other places to inspect are the metal around the anchorages of the belt where signs of distortion also indicate large forces.
(6) From statements of witnesses, marks on the road and verges and central reservations, and from all the other relevant information, it is always important in single and two vehicle accidents to establish the paths and the approximate speeds of the vehicles before and after impact, so as to obtain an estimate of the closing speed of the vehicle or vehicles at impact, and of their attitudes, i.e. their angles to their directions of travel at impact. Such estimates can be compared with those deduced from damage to the vehicles.

Information in cycle and motorcycle accidents

(1) The relevant points listed in earlier parts of this chapter.
(2) In single vehicle accidents where a cycle or motorcycle went out of control, special attention needs to be paid to the possible part played by kerbs, rough roads, or in wet weather by even short stretches of slippery road.

Additional information in pedestrian accidents

(1) The actions of the pedestrian, whether hidden by a parked vehicle or obstacle.
(2) If the accident occurred on a wet night in street lighting, photographs of the pattern of illumination of the road surface.

For detailed information relating to many of these requirements reference should be made to appropriate chapters in this manual. Since no publication can be expected to contain all the most up-to-date findings of research, it may sometimes be desirable to address enquiries for further information to the Transport and Road Research Laboratory, Crowthorne, Berks.

Appendix 1

Nomenclature and conversion table

Nomenclature

- a = width of vehicle
- b = length of vehicle
- M_1 = mass of vehicle 1
- M_2 = mass of vehicle 2
- W_1 = weight of vehicle 1
- W_2 = weight of vehicle 2
- I = moment of inertia of a vehicle about a vertical axis through its centre of gravity
- V'_1 = velocity change of vehicle 1
- V'_2 = velocity change of vehicle 2
- $V = V_1 - V_2$ = relative velocity at impact of two vehicles in frontal or rear end collisions; also referred to as the closing speed, to which it is numerically equal
- E = energy absorbed in deforming the fronts of the two vehicles in a frontal collision or the front of a vehicle in collision with an obstacle
- g = acceleration due to gravity, i.e. the rate of change of velocity of an object due to the earth's pull = 32.2 feet per second per second (9.81 metres per second per second)
- F = frictional force exerted by a tyre
- W = the load on a tyre
- μ = coefficient of friction between tyre and road or car and wall
- R = radius of curvature of path of vehicle
- v = speed of vehicle round a bend
- d = in an off-centre impact with a rigid obstacle, the distance from the long axis of a car through its centre of gravity to the point about which the car rotates at the end of the impact
- D = in an off-centre impact with a rigid obstacle, the distance through which the rear tyres move in bringing the car to rest
- D_1 = the distance moved by the two vehicles after an intersection collision at 90 degrees with the struck vehicle stationary

Conversion table

1 mile	= 1.61 kilometres (km)
1 metre	= 3.28 feet (ft)
1 mile/h	= 1.47 ft/sec = 1.61 km/h = 0.45 m/sec
1 kilogram (kg)	= 2.20 pound (lb)

Appendix 2

Measurements and calculations

A2.1 Mass and weight

Mass (M) is the quantity of matter in an object. Weight (W) is the force on a mass due to the pull of the earth's gravity (g). So $W = Mg$. However, for practical purposes, both mass and weight are measured in pounds, grams or kilograms, so that in everyday usage weight is always used; the difference between mass and weight has to be remembered when calculations are made.

A2.2 Moments of inertia

A moment of inertia is a measure of the resistance of a body (e.g. a car) to rotation about a straight line (an axis) through a particular point. The only important moment of inertia referred to in the text is that about a vertical axis through the centre of gravity. If the centre of gravity is taken to be at the geometrical centre of a car, then this moment of inertia

$$I_1 = M \frac{a^2 + b^2}{12}$$ to a satisfactory degree of accuracy.

This is the moment of inertia in yaw. Two other moments of inertia are used in calculations of the stability of vehicles, that about a longitudinal axis, the roll moment of inertia, and that about a transverse axis, the moment of inertia in pitch.

A2.3 Speed, velocity change and angular velocity

The speed and velocity of an object are numerically equal; while speed is the same regardless of the direction in which the object is travelling, the velocity has an indicated direction. In the cases considered in the text, velocity may be positive or negative. For example, in a two car head-on collision the velocity of one car is positive and the other negative; in a rear-end collision the velocity of each car is positive. Hence in the approximate equations for velocity change given on p.86, the closing speed in a head-on collision is the sum of the two separate speeds and in a rear-end collision it is the difference.

In collisions with obstacles or other vehicles, the velocity change of a vehicle in a particular direction is equal to the velocity before impact in that direction minus the velocity in the same direction after impact. The velocity change may be either greater or less than the velocity at impact. If the velocities before and after impact are of opposite sign, then the velocity change is greater than the velocity before impact; if both velocities are of the same sign, it is less than or equal to the velocity before impact; thus in the partial perpendicular impact illustrated in Figure 6.14, because rebound occurs, the velocity change on the impact side in the original direction of travel is greater than the velocity at impact, while on the other side of the car it is less. This manual has been mainly concerned with frontal impacts.

In two vehicle collisions of all types the velocity changes of the centres of gravity in any particular direction are inversely proportional to their respective weights. The angular velocity is the rate at which a vehicle rotates about an axis, such as the vertical line through the centre of gravity. It is expressed in degrees per second.

A2.4 Energy dissipated in crushing the fronts of cars

Calculations based on established physical principles show that when two vehicles meet in full frontal or rear-end collisions the energy which goes into crushing the fronts of the vehicles is closely given (within 5 per cent) by

$$E = \tfrac{1}{2} \frac{M_1 M_2}{M_1 + M_2} (V_1 - V_2)^2$$

The energy loss E is independent of the way in which the fronts of the two vehicles are constructed, and is shared between the two vehicles in a manner determined by their relative stiffness.

A2.5 The equivalent test speed (ETS)

The equivalent test speed (ETS) is the speed in a full frontal impact with a rigid barrier necessary to produce the same damage as that observed in a head-on collision, either with a rigid object or with another vehicle.

When two identical cars collide head-on in a full frontal impact, the ETS of each car is very approximately equal to one-half of the closing speed (irrespective of the individual speeds of the two cars before impact). In most head-on collisions the two vehicles are not identical, differing in mass or in frontal stiffness, or in both respects. In these cases, there are two separate ETSs, which in general are not good approximations to the respective velocity changes. However, estimates of velocity change can be made when the two values of ETS are known, either from tests of the cars involved, or, less accurately, by using average values for the weight and type of car. The derivation of the appropriate expressions is as follows. Let the two values of the equivalent test speeds be ETS_1 and ETS_2. The energy dissipated in crushing

$$E = \tfrac{1}{2} \frac{M_1 M_2}{M_1 + M_2} (V_1 - V_2)^2.$$

This is equal to the energy dissipated in the two separate barrier tests at speeds of ETS_1 and ETS_2.

$$\tfrac{1}{2} \frac{M_1 M_2}{M_1 + M_2} (V_1 - V_2)^2 = \tfrac{1}{2} M_1 (ETS_1)^2 + \tfrac{1}{2} M_2 (ETS_2)^2$$

$$(V_1 - V_2)^2 = \frac{\{M_1 (ETS_1)^2 + M_2 (ETS_2)^2\}(M_1 + M_2)}{M_1 M_2}$$

If one assumes that the collision is inelastic, the velocity change

$$V_1' = \frac{M_2}{M_1 + M_2} (V_1 - V_2)$$

$$= \frac{M_2}{M_1 + M_2} \sqrt{\frac{(M_1 + M_2)\{M_1 (ETS_1)^2 + M_2 (ETS_2)^2\}}{M_1 + M_2}}$$

$$= ETS_1 \sqrt{\frac{M_1 M_2 + M_2^2 \left(\frac{ETS_2}{ETS_1}\right)^2}{M_1 (M_1 + M_2)}}$$

A similar expression is found for V_2'.

For practical purposes in collisions between cars it is generally unnecessary to use these expressions, since numerical calculations for a number of mass ratios M_2/M_1 and ratios ETS_2/ETS_1 of the ETS values show that the closing speed or relative velocity is very nearly equal to $ETS_1 + ETS_2$; and when this is known the separate values of V_1' and V_2' are given by

$$V_1' = \frac{M_1}{M_1 + M_2} (V_1 - V_2) \text{ and } V_2' = \frac{M_1}{M_2} V_1'.$$

As previously mentioned these values of V_1' and V_2', assuming inelastic collision, are about 10 per cent too low, and, to allow for the slight elasticity in the structure of cars, should be increased by that amount.

Similar estimates of velocity change cannot yet be made for off-centre (offset) collisions between vehicles, since the appropriate tests have not yet been devised.

A2.6 The calculation of the speed of a car before impact in an off-centre impact with a rigid block, from its rest position

The following calculation can only be taken as a rough guide, since it is based on the assumptions that 10 per cent of the initial energy of the car at impact goes into rotation after impact, and that 40 per cent of the weight of the car is taken by the rear tyres during rotation to rest.

Then

$$\tfrac{1}{10} \times \tfrac{1}{2} M_1 V_1^2 = \tfrac{2}{5} \mu M_1 g D$$

where the symbols have the meanings given in Appendix 1.

This equality gives the relationship $V_1 = \sqrt{8 \mu g D}$

A2.7 The calculation of the speed of a car before impact in an intersection collision in which one car strikes another at right angles

From considerations of momentum, the common velocity of the two cars after impact is

$$\frac{M_1}{M_1 + M_2} \cdot V_1$$

where V_1 is the velocity of the striking car.

The kinetic energy after impact is therefore

$$\tfrac{1}{2} \frac{M_1}{M_1 + M_2} \cdot M_1 V_1^2.$$

If there is no braking by the striking car this energy is dissipated by the tyres of the struck car skidding sideways. Therefore

$$\mu M_2 g D_1 = \tfrac{1}{2} \frac{M_1}{M_1 + M_2} \cdot M_1 V_1^2$$

which simplifies to

$$D_1 = \frac{M_1^2 V_1^2}{2\mu g M_2 (M_1 + M_2)}$$

Table 6.1 gives estimated distances moved on a dry unobstructed road ($\mu = 0.8$) for three values of M_2/M_1 and two initial speeds of the striking car.

Index

Accident investigation
  information required in accident investigations, 137
  probabilities of injury in accidents, 2, 136
  under-representation of accidents in national statistics, 21
Accident proneness, *see* Behaviour of road users
Accident statistics
  accident rates, 12
  age, influence of, 6
  AIS scales of injury, 1
  casualties, 3, 5, 8
  casualty rates, 6, 17
  classification of injury, 1
  cyclist casualties, *see* Cyclists
  international comparisons of injuries, 2
  location of accidents, 5
  national statistics, 1
  pedestrian casualties, *see* Pedestrians
  probabilities of accidents and injuries, 2, 136
  relative involvement of different types of vehicle, 7
  road conditions and light, 11
  sex, influence of, 6, 22
  temporal variations in casualties, 9
  trends in casualties over the years, 3, 13
  types of accident, 6
  urban and rural accidents, 5, 6, 10
  vehicles involved in accidents, 7, 11
  vehicle involvement rates, 12
Alcohol
  absorption and elimination of alcohol, 19
  blood alcohol concentrations in fatally injured road users, 21
  drink driving laws, 20
  drinking behaviour of men and women drivers, 16
  drugs and alcohol, 19
  effect of drink driving legislation, 20
  equivalent amounts of different alcoholic drinks, 19
  risk of accident involvement in relation to alcohol concentration in the blood, 20

Anti-lock brakes, *see* Braking of mechanically propelled vehicles
Appendices, 140

Behaviour of road users
  accident proneness, 21
  accidents to very young children, 22, 24
  age, 16
  attitudes, 21
  behavioural studies of car drivers, 28
  cyclist manoeuvres, 24
  driver errors, 25
  effect on accidents of improvements in behaviour, 27
  elderly drivers, 25
  enforcement, 20, 28
  overtaking by car drivers, 25
  pedestrian behaviour in accidents, 23
  reaction times, 19
  sex, 16
  traffic laws, reasons for breaking, 28
  walking speeds of pedestrians, 23
  young motorcyclists, 25
Braking of mechanically propelled vehicles
  anti-locking brakes for cars, 72
  anti-locking brakes for commercial vehicles, 75
  anti-locking brakes for motor cycles, 75
  articulated vehicle braking, 73
  braking distances for cars, commercial vehicles and motor cycles, 70
  locking of car wheels, 71
  locking of wheels of commercial vehicles, 73
  motor cycle braking, 70
  weight transfer, 72

Cars and car drivers
  accident proneness, 21
  accident rates for young and old drivers, 25
  age and sex, 25
  alcohol and drugs, *see* Alcohol
  attitudes, 21
  behavioural studies of car drivers, 28

146   Index

Cars and car drivers (*cont.*)
   casualties, 26
   casualty rates for male and female drivers, 17, 18
   driver errors, 25
   effect of drink driving legislation on accidents and casualties, 20
   effect of improvements in behaviour on accidents and casualties, 27
   effect of seat belt law on accidents and casualties, 28
   elderly drivers, 25
   epilepsy in accidents, 18
   influence of age on driving behaviour at junctions, 25
   heart disease, 18
   overtaking, 25
   reaction times, 25
   reasons for breaking traffic laws, 28
   seat belt law, *see* Protective measures for car occupants
   sudden illness, 18
Collisions of vehicles, full frontal impacts
   barrier impact tests and deformations of cars in collisions with cars, 94
   collisions of cars in full frontal impacts with walls, 94, 112
   collisions with commercial vehicles, 112
   collisions with poles, 112
   deformations of cars and relative velocity at impact, 86
   deformations of cars in full frontal collisions between cars of equal and unequal weights, 95
   deformations, general
   duration of impact, 85
   effect of construction of front of car, 85
   energy absorbed in full frontal collisions of cars, 87, 95
   energy absorption of mild steel, 86
   forces on vehicles during an impact, 87
   mass ratio, 85
   moments of inertia, 84
   movements of occupants, 85
   rebound velocities, 86
   velocity changes deduced from damage, 94
Collisions of vehicles, general
   durations of impact, 84
   injury producing impacts, 84
   mass ratio, 85
   moments of inertia, 84
   properties (constants), important in impacts, 84
   types of impact, 84
   velocity change, 86
Collisions of vehicles, intersection collisions
   angular velocities of cars after collision, 92, 91–93
   deformations, 113
   directions of movement of cars after collisions, 116

Collisions of vehicles (*cont.*)
   durations of impact, 91–92
   final positions of vehicles, 116
   movements of cars after collisions, 116
   movements of occupants, 91–93
   stiffnesses of fronts and sides of cars, 113
   types of intersection collision, 90
   velocity changes, 91, 116
Collisions of vehicles, partial frontal impacts
   computer calculations of velocity changes in partial frontal collisions of cars, 112
   collisions with commercial vehicles, 112, 117
   collisions with poles, 87, 112
   collisions with walls, 87, 98
   deformations in test collisions and in real life collisions, 98, 102
   energy of rotation, 101
   impacts with rigid barriers, 98
   injury to car occupants in partial frontal impacts, 100
   loads in seat belts in full frontal and partial frontal impacts, 88, 100
   partial frontal collisions between cars, 87, 98, 102
   proportions of full frontal and partial frontal collisions, 87
   rotation in partial frontal impacts with rigid walls, 100
   rotation of typical small car in partial frontal barrier impact test, 99
   rotational velocities in partial frontal collisions of cars, 100
   variation of deformations over fronts of cars in partial frontal collisions of cars, 102
   velocity changes in partial frontal collisions of cars, 102
   velocity of unrestrained occupants striking interiors of cars, 87
Collisions of vehicles, rear end collisions
   concertina type accidents, 58
   velocity changes, 86, 113
   whiplash injuries, 122
Commercial vehicles
   accident statistics, 117
   alterations to commercial vehicles to increase safety in cars, 132
   behaviour in collisions, 117, 119
   collisions with cars, *see* Collisions of vehicles, full frontal impacts *and* Collisions of vehicles, partial frontal impacts
   injuries to occupants, 118
   involvement in accidents, 121
   moments of inertia, 117
   overturning accidents, 119
Cyclists
   age and accidents, 24
   alcohol, 21
   casualties, 8

Cyclists (*cont.*)
  casualty rates, 17
  helmets, for cyclists, 132
  manoeuvres of cyclists, 24
  sex and accidents, 24
  training, 24
  young cyclists, 24

Drugs, 19

Impacts with walls
  coefficients of friction with walls, 89, 112
  collisions with flexible objects, 112
  durations of impacts with walls, 89
  full frontal impacts with rigid walls, *see* Collisions of vehicles, full frontal impacts
  movements of occupants of cars, 88
  partial frontal impacts with walls, *see* Collisions of vehicles, partial frontal impacts
  rotations of cars, 89
  velocity of impact of occupants with interiors of cars, 89
Injuries in cars, *see* Protective measures for car occupants
  abdominal injuries to wearers of seat belts, 121–122
  approval requirements for seat belts, 126
  chest injuries to wearers of seat belts, 121
  childrens seat belts and safety seats, 128
  ejection, 123
  head injuries to wearers of seat belts, 121
  injuries in overturning accidents, 123
  injuries most dangerous to life, 122
  injuries to belt wearers due to inertial loads, 122
  injuries to belt wearers in frontal impacts, 126
  injuries to belt wearers in side impacts, 121, 124
  injuries to unrestrained occupants, 120–121, 125
  intrusion and injury, 122
  leg injuries, 121, 130
  mass ratio and injury, 120
  mechanisms of injury, 120
  overall reduction in injury due to seat belts, 28
  passive restraints, 126
  safety cars, 130
  seat belt laws for adults, 28
  seat belt laws for children, 128
  structural alterations to cars to increase safety, 129
  types of seat belt, 124
  unsurvivable accidents, 122
  whiplash injuries, 122
Interactions between the main factors in accidents, 14

Loss of control
  anti-locking brakes for articulated vehicles, *see* Braking of mechanically propelled vehicles
  anti-locking brakes for cars, *see* Braking of mechanically propelled vehicles
  anti-locking brakes for motor cycles, *see* Braking of mechanically propelled vehicles
  articulated vehicles skidding behaviour, 73, 78
  braking, loss of control after, 71
  excessive sideways acceleration, 76
  jack knifing, 78
  kerbs and loss of control, 78
  king pin friction devices, 75
  load sensing valves, 74
  loss of control for no obvious reason, 78
  loss of control without braking, 76
  movements of cars and rigid commercial vehicles after skidding, 71, 73, 79
  pedestrian accidents, speeds of striking cars, 78
  power jack knifing of articulated vehicles, 76
  rigid commercial vehicles, 73
  skidding distances, 80
  skidding during acceleration, 76
  time available for action in accidents, 78
  tyre failures on motorways, 78
  weight transfer, 72

Medical factors
  epilepsy, 18
  heart disease, 18
  sudden illness, 18
Moments of inertia, 84, 141
Motor cycles
  age and injuries, 25
  anti-locking brakes for motor cycles, 75
  braking, 70
  casualties, 25
  casualty rates, 25
  chest protection, 131
  circumstances of accidents, 116
  collisions with other vehicles, 117, 131
  conspicuity, 59
  disc brakes, 71
  enclosed motor cycles, 131
  headlamps, in daylight, 59
  head-on impacts with walls, 131
  helmets, 123, 130
  injuries, 123
  leg protection, 123, 131
  movements of motorcyclists during and after accidents, 116
  sex, 25
  single vehicle accidents, 59, 117
  velocity changes in impacts, 117
  young motorcyclists, 25

Movement after impact
  calculations of velocity change from final positions of cars in impacts with fixed objects, 143
  deductions from final positions of vehicles in intersection collisions, 144
  directions of movement of centres of gravity of cars after intersection collisions, 90
  rotation in partial head-on collisions, 100, 102, 114
  speeds at impact in head-on collisions from final positions of cars, 114
  tyre forces, 84

Nomenclature, see Appendix 1, 140

Obstructions on and off the carriageway, 46
  clearways, 49
  collisions with street furniture, 46
  crash barriers, 48
  kerbs, 48
  lamp columns, breakaway columns, 46
  parked vehicles, 48
  road works, 48
Overturning (rollover)
  ejection in overturning, 94
  kerbs in overturning, 94
  overturning in single vehicle, accidents, 94
  overturning without striking an obstacle, 94
  test data, 113

Pedestrians
  accidents to very young children, 22, 24
  age of pedestrian casualties, 22
  alterations to cars to reduce severity of pedestrian accidents, 132
  bridges and underpasses, 24
  cars and taxis in pedestrian accidents, 123
  casualty rates, 17
  causes of death and injury, 123
  circumstances of pedestrian accidents, 23
  comparative safety of zebra and pelican crossings, 23
  conspicuity of zebra crossings, 23
  Green Cross code, 27
  impact speeds in pedestrian accidents, 124
  mechanisms of injury, 123
  pedestrian behaviour in accidents, 23
  pelican crossings, 23
  places where pedestrian casualties occur, 22–23
  risks on zebra crossings, 23
  sex, 22
  vehicles, involved in pedestrian accidents, 123
  walking speeds of pedestrians, 23
  zebra crossings, 23
Probabilities of injury in accidents, 136

Protective measures for car occupants
  abdominal injuries to belt wearers, 121–122
  alterations to fronts and rears of commercial vehicles, 132
  alterations to fronts and sides of cars, 129
  approval requirements for seat belts, 126
  automatically placed seat belts, 126
  belt types, 124
  chest injuries to belt wearers, 121
  compulsory wearing of seat belts, 28
  effectiveness of seat belts, 28
  head and face injuries to belt wearers, 121
  history of seat belts, 124
  how seat belts work, 125
  injuries to belt wearers due to intrusion, 122
  knee bolsters in cars, 130
  most important function of seat belts, 124
  padding in cars, 130
  passive restraints, 126
  protective devices for children, 128
  safety cars, 130
  seat belts in overturning accidents, 126
  seat belt law for children in cars, 128
  steering wheels, 125
  whiplash injuries, 122
Protective measures for motorcyclists and cyclists
  airbags on motor cycles, 131
  helmets for cyclists, 132
  helmets for motorcyclists, 130
  leg protection, 131
  totally enclosed motor cycles, 131
Protective measures for pedestrians
  alterations to the fronts of cars, 132

Road design
  anti-dazzle screens, 46
  bends, influence on accidents, 32
  breakaway lamp columns, 46
  crash barriers, 48
  crests and downgrades, 32
  deaths in collisions with street furniture, 46
  deceptive layouts, 37
  horizontal and vertical curves, 32
  junctions, see Road junctions
  kerbs, 48
  laybys, 48
  parked vehicles, 48
  road and lane widths, 31
  road delineation and marking, 38
  road works, 48
  roundabouts, 37
  safety measures, on roads, trade-off between cost and benefit, 31
  shoulders, verges and medians, 32, 43
  spray, 42
  street furniture, 46
  surfaces, see Road surfaces
  traffic signs and signals, 39
Road junctions
  accidents at junctions, 33
  alterations to junctions, 34–35

Hong Kong, Macao and Taiwan Province

6. Both English and Chinese are official languages in Hong Kong.
   英语和汉语都是香港的官方语言。
7. Hong Kong is a shopping paradise, dietary world, leisure summer resort, and culture window.
   香港是购物天堂、饮食世界、休闲胜地和文化之窗。
8. Today Hong Kong's population is 6.5 million.
   如今香港人口为 650 万。
9. Hong Kong possesses the highest bronze statue of Buddha in the open air in the world.
   香港有世界上最高的露天铜佛。
10. The Chinese mainland is the biggest market for Hong Kong's imports and exports.
    中国内地是香港最大的进口和出口市场。
11. Hong Kong maintains one of the highest economic growth rates in the world.
    香港是世界上经济增长速度最快的地区之一。
12. Tourism has been a pillar of Hong Kong's economy for decades.
    数十年来,旅游业一直是香港经济的支柱。

Wonderful Paragraph 精彩片段

Victoria Peak 太平山

High above Hong Kong Island on the b... y magnificent harbour and is Hong Kong's premier visitor attractio... to experience the dazzling city views. Arriving late afternoon ...our, Kowloon and the hills be- panorama of Hong Kong Isla... n-dotted skyline by night. What's yond. Later, you can thri... de of fantastic entertainment, dining more, The Peak offers

and shopping options.

Paragraph 2

P 凌霄阁
eak Tower

The Peak Tram pulls into the Peak Tower, the icon of Hong Kong, on its last stop. Peak Tower sits at an elevation of over 396 meters (about 1299 feet) with a commanding view of the spectacular Victoria Harbor, Kowloon and the New Territories. Commissioned in 1993 and completed in May of 1997, the tower is a center of catering and amusement. The most spectacular attraction is the wonder hall, which is called "Believe it or not". It is the unique chain museum in the world, constructed by Robert L. Ripley in 1930. Inside the hall you see exhibits portraying the adventurous events experienced by Ripley. There are primitive forest, beauty taking sun bath, frenzied car, turning tunnel, shark aquarium, ultimate cruel torture, marvelous spectacles of human race and animals, complete works of tongue twister and mass media fun station etc.

Paragraph 3

R 浅水湾
epulse Bay

Repulse Bay, located south of Stanley, is famous for its long, broad beach, its clean water, fresh sand, calm tide and gentle waves, and its popularity with locals and visitors, especially in summer. It is the most representative bay in Hong Kong, and it was named after a pirate ship that used to sail here in 19th century.

With its lush green hills, sandy beaches, the sub-tropical backdrop and breathtaking views over stars. Several open-air ... ideal place for a romantic dinner under the some barbecued food, inc... nearby specialize in the joys of wholesome seafood delicacies. All are ch... freshest prawns, squid, fish and other ... Repulse Bay also offers a ... of activity every night of the week. ... of shopping and entertainment facilities. The ornate Life Guard Club was built in a traditional Chinese style; its ceilings decorated with magnificent swirling dragons. Sea View Tower was built nearby in ancient Chinese color. Inside there are twin ten-meter-high statues of Tin Hau, the Queen of Heaven, and Avalokitesvara, the Goddess of Mercy, both of whom are protectors of fishermen.

Paragraph 4

Man Mo Temple 文武庙

One of the oldest and most famous and beautiful temples in Hong Kong is Man Mo Temple. It is located at the intersection of Hollywood Road and Ladder Street. The temple was built in the 1800s, at the beginning of the British colonial rule. A copper bell in the temple, made during the reign of Emperor Daoguang (1820-1850), proudly proclaims the temple's long history.

Although it has been remodeled several times, the temple still maintains its original appearance. Inside the temple are delicate wooden bases used for transporting deities during parades and festivals and incense burners made of copper and other metals. Huge tower-shaped incense coils are always hanging from the ceiling of the hall and over the courtyard. And the smoke of the burning incense, together with the sunbeams, adds an element of mystery to the temple and indicates happiness, health and fortune.

The temple is a perfect combination of Taoism and Buddhism. Two deities are worshiped side by side in the temple shrine. They are Wenchang and Guan Yu. Wenchang, with a brush in his hand, takes charge of literature, especially during the imperial examinations, which determined a man's official rank in feudal times. Guan Yu, holding a sword in his hand, is in charge of war. There are statues of other Chinese gods as well, like Baogong, the symbol of justice and the town god who protects the whole city.

Paragraph 5

九龙公园
Kowloon Park

Standing on a small hill in the heart of Tsim Sha Tsui, Kowloon Park, covering an area of 14 hectares, is a former site of a military barracks. It was open to public in 1989 and it is the most popular park in Kowloon, where many territory-wide functions are regularly held.

Kowloon Park is a welcome respite from the crowds of Tsim Sha Tsui. Located above street level, the park has extensive recreation and sports facilities, including Chinese style gardens, an aviary, a sculpture exhibit, an air-conditioned game hall and an indoor heated Olympic-sized swimming pool complex.

The major open-air attraction is the Sculpture Walk. Its displays include striking works by local sculptors and a magnificent bronze statue by Scotland's Sir Eduardo Paolozzi. Particularly inviting is also the bird lake crowded with beautiful pink lesser flamingos and ducks. Kowloon Park is also home to the Urban Council Health Education Exhibition and Resource Center, where you can see interactive exhibits on health and Hygiene.

Paragraph 6

海洋公园
Ocean Park

Ocean Park, lying between Aberdeen and Repulse Bay, is the largest leisure paradise in Southeast Asia, and one of the largest marine parks in the world. Covering a total area of over 200 acres, the park was built on both sides of the mountain. A cable car system links the lowland and headland sections and provides spectacular views of Hong Kong and the South China Sea.

港澳台地区
Hong Kong, Macao and Taiwan Province

H欢乐谷
Happy Valley

The low-lying area located between Wan Chai and Causeway Bay is the famous Happy Valley, where the people of Hong Kong gather to enjoy the excitement of horse racing and maybe gambling on the races.

One of the oldest and the most famous architectural sites in Hong Kong, Happy Valley Racecourse was founded in the mid 1840s. The area was formerly a piece of marsh land but following extensive reclamation, the first horse-racing was held here in 1846. Evening meetings occurred in 1973 and in 1978; Hong Kong's second racecourse was created in Sha Tin in the New Territories. Hong Kong is now recognized internationally as a racing venue and is a favorite spectator sport among Hong Kong residents, many of whom like to have a flutter on the horses. The yearly racing season runs from September to the following June, when two weekly meetings are held. One is on Wednesday evening, and the other on either Saturday or Sunday afternoon. Entrance to the public enclosure is just HK $10. For those who do not wish to make their own arrangements it is possible to join parties organized by the Hong Kong Tourism Board.

Happy Valley venue which can accommodate up to 35 000 race-goers has advanced tracks, giant computer screens and other modern facilities. Needless to say, spectators are reminded that it is forbidden to use flash photography as this has an adverse effect on the horses and their performance. Audiences can view the race card and betting information on the giant screens. Mere words cannot describe the spectacular and exciting scene at these races, something that most visitors to Hong Kong would be loath to miss.

Hong Kong's Horse-Racing Museum is also located here; this tells the interesting history and anecdotes of Hong Kong horse-racing, and there are exhibits of various harnesses.

What's more, this racecourse is also an ideal venue for large-scale activities and it also offers a high quality service for visitors. So, do not hesitate to have a visit here.

"香港"的由来

一说来自"香江"。据说早年岛上有一溪水自山间流出入海,水质甘香清甜,为附近居民与过往船只供应淡水,称为"香江"。由香江出海的港口也就称为"香港"。香江故址在今薄扶林附近,早已不存,但"香江"却成了香港的别名。

另一说香港名称来自"香姑"。香姑是传说中的女海盗,盘踞香港岛,后该岛被称为香姑岛,简称香岛,再演变成香港。

还有一说香港之名源于"红香炉"。传说很久以前从海上飘来一个红香炉,泊于天后庙前,居民以为天后显圣,便把红香炉供奉在庙中。岛上有个山也称为红香炉山。后来把这地方叫做"红香炉港",简称"香港"。

有根据的一种说法,是说香港得名与香树、香市有关。香树生长于广东沿海及越南北部,以东莞、新安等县为多,香港沙田及大屿山亦有种植。

香树长高至二十尺时,割出树液,就可制成"香",是多种香制品的原料,可作供神和上贡的佳品,"莞香"闻名全国。明神宗万历元年以前,香港一带均属东莞县。沙田、大埔一带是"莞香"的著名产地。

因香产丰盛,这里的香市贸易也十分发达。香产品多数先运送到九龙的尖沙咀,再用"大眼鸡"船运至石排湾(即今日的香港仔)集中,然后转运往中国内地、南洋以至阿拉伯国家。故尖沙咀古称"香埠头",石排湾这个转运香料的港口,也就被称为"香港",附近的村庄也被称为"香港村",后来"香港"一名被扩大应用于全岛。

港澳台地区
Hong Kong, Macao and Taiwan Province

Vocabulary 妙词连珠

One country, Two systems 一国两制	Long Harbour 大滩海
SAR's Day 香港特区成立日	Port Shelter 牛尾海
Southern Gateway to China 中国南大门	Lover's Rock 情人石
Hong Kong dollar; HK dollar 港元	Huanggang Customs/Port 皇岗海关/口岸
Hong Konger(s)/Hongkonger(s) 香港人(佬)	Kowloon (City) 九龙(城)
Hongkongite (香)港式风格	New Territories 新界
Hong Kong Tourism Board (HKTB) 香港旅游发展局	Lantau Island 大屿山(大屿岛)
	Wan Chai 湾仔
Dragon air 港龙航空公司	Yau Tsim Mog 油尖旺
Lion Rock 狮子山	Sha Tin 沙田

271

Unit 2　Macao SAR
澳门特别行政区

Key Sentences
流畅精句

1. Macao SAR Situated on west side of the estuary of the Pearl River in south China and connected with Zhuhai City of Guangdong.
   澳门特别行政区位于我国南部沿海珠江口两侧,北与广东省珠海市相连。
2. Macao is called as "an oriental gem".
   澳门被称作"东方宝石"。
3. Macao is called the Las Vegas or Monte Carlo of the east.
   澳门被称作东方的拉斯维加斯或者蒙特卡罗。
4. Portuguese and Chinese are the two official languages in Macao.
   葡萄牙语和汉语是澳门的两种官方语言。
5. Macanese cuisine is Portuguese with Indian, Malay, African and South American influences.
   澳门菜肴是葡萄牙风味的,但受印度菜、非洲菜和南美洲菜的影响。
6. The Macao Basic Law guarantees Macao's entertainment industry will not change after 1999.
   《澳门基本法》保证了澳门的娱乐业在1999年以后不会改变。
7. The Sino-Portuguese Joint Declaration was signed in 1987.
   中葡联合声明于1987年签署。
8. Known as the "Monte Carlo of the East", Macao is a famous gambling city. Gambling in Macao is legal and occupies an important position in local economy. Major attractions in Macao include St. Paul's Ruins, Casino Lisboa, A-Ma Temple, Memorial House Of Dr Sun Yat-Guia Hill, and others.

港澳台地区
Hong Kong, Macao and Taiwan Province

澳门被称为"东方的蒙特卡罗",博彩业具有合法性,在澳门经济中占有重要地位。旅游名胜有大三巴牌坊、葡京娱乐场、妈阁庙、国父纪念馆、东望洋山和西望洋山等。

Wonderful Paragraph
精彩片段

Paragraph 1

澳门历史城区
The Historic Centre of Macao

"The Historic Centre of Macao" is a living representation of the city's historic settlement, encompassing architectural legacies interwoven in the midst of the original urban fabric that includes street scapes and piazzas, such as Barra Square, Lilau Square, St. Augustine's Square, Senado Square, Cathedral Square, St. ominic's Square, Company of Jesus Square and Camoes Square. These major urban squares and street scapes provide the linkage for a succession of over twenty monuments, including A-Ma Temple, Moorish Barracks, Mandarin's House, St. Lawrence's Church, St. Joseph's Seminary and Church, Dom Pedro V Theatre, Sir Robert Ho Tung Library, St. Augustine's Church, "Leal Senado" Building, Sam Kai Vui Kun Temple, Holy House of Mercy, Cathedral, Lou Kau Mansion, St. Dominic's Church, Ruins of St. Paul's, Na Tcha Temple, Section of the Old City Walls, Mount Fortress, St. Anthony's Church, Casa Garden, the Protestant Cemetery and Guia Fortress (including Guia Chapel and Lighthouse) altogether known as "The Historic Centre of Macao".

Paragraph 2

澳门博物馆
The Museum of Macao

The Museum of Macao was inaugurated on 18th of April, 1998. It's aim is to preserve the cultural traditions, usages and habits, which specifically belong to Macao, in a place where East, and West have so peculiarly learnt how to meet and to live side by side along the centuries.

Located at the Monte Fort and facing St. Paul's Ruins, the Museum also occupies the ancient Fortress, which, dominating the Inner Harbour, was built by the Jesuits at the beginning of the 17th century.

Although the Museum does not possess a collection of a high monetary value, it includes a vast number of objects of a great historical value which have been carefully chosen and are appealingly exhibited. It is the wish of this museum to be able to show the way of life of the several communities, which have inhabited the city for ages.

Paragraph 3

R大三巴牌坊
uins of St. Paul's

The Ruins of St. Paul's (also known as Sam Ba Sing Tzik) stands adjacent to the famous Mount Fortress and Macau Museum. The front facade and the grand stone stairs are the only remains of the greatest church in Macau.

First constructed in 1580, St. Paul's Church caught fires in 1595 and 1601. However, reconstruction started in 1602 soon after the church was burnt down. Completed in 1637, the church became the biggest Catholic Church in East Asia at that time. Unfortunately, a violent typhoon hit Macau in 1 835 and the church caught fire for the third time leaving its glory a history. According to historical materials, St Paul's Church, built with white stones, had a grand vaulted roof. It had three magnificently decorated halls.

Built with granites, Sam Ba Sing Tzik has a baroque facade rich in ornamentation but with classic oriental characteristics. From the bottom up, the structure has five tiers. The first tier is comprised of ten Ionic columns with three entrances. The entrance in the middle has "MATER DEI" carved into it. The two entrances on each side are decorated with bas – reliefs in the pattern of "HIS". The second tier features ten Corinthian columns with three windows. A Catholic saint is enshrined in each of four tabernacles between columns. The two tiers as a whole is said to represent the Society of Jesus and the activities of missionaries.

The remaining three tiers are the most decorated. The statue of Madonna stands in the middle of the third tier, while the statue of Jesus stands on the fourth. The walls are covered with bas – reliefs in various patterns like devils, angels, symbols of crucifixion, a Portuguese sailing ship, etc. The triangular combination of the upper three tiers reflects the Holy Trinity (the Father, the Son and the Holy Spirit) as well as the Blessed Virgin Mary. A cross stands at the coping of the wall.

It is worth mentioning that the stone lions at the sides of the third and fourth tiers are distinctively Chinese. There are also bas-reliefs in designs of chrysanthemum and cherry, as well as Chinese inscriptions. The surviving fa?ade has long been acknowledged as a perfect fusion of western and eastern cultures.

The Ruins of St. Paul's has been restored during 1990 and 1995. The Museum of Sacred Art and Crypt was also built at that time. It has exhibitions of religions artworks including paintings, sculptures and statues.

Paragraph 4

东望洋炮台
Guia Fort

Built on the highest point of Macau between 1637 and 1638, the fortress contains a chapel and a lighthouse. The chapel inside is in the style of Portuguese heritages of the 17th century.

To the right of this chapel is a bell which was made in 1707. The lighthouse, which is the dominating feature of the Fort, was built by a local-born Portuguese. It was first lit up on September 24, 1865, and is the oldest on the China coast. Standing only 16 feet tall, its beam can be seen from 20 miles at sea under good weather conditions. To this day, it provides a guiding beacon to the passing boats.

用英语说中国——旅游亮点
Introduce China in English—Scenic Spots

> **Paragraph 5**

黑沙海滩
Hac Sa Beaches

Both located on Colone Island, Cheoc Van and Hac Sa beaches are suitable for sun bathing and swimming. Cheoc Van is a white sanded beach with a lovely swimming pool.

Hac Sa, literarily means "Black Sand", is the most popular beach amongst local residents. Wind surfers can be hired on the beach and there are barbecue pits at one end of the beach.

The Hac Sa recreation center is adjacent to the bus stop and contains a number of recreational facilities, including swimming pool, roller skating rink, a mini golf course, a children's playground and tennis courts.

There is also a horse riding center beside the recreation center. Horses are available for beginners as well as advanced riders, and horses can even be taken out on trails under certain conditions.

> **Paragraph 6**

妈祖文化村
A-Ma Cultural Village

Close to the world's tallest statue of the goddess A-Ma (also known as Tian Hou), which stands on a 170-metre high peak on a mountaintop on Macau's Colone Island, a 7 000-square meter cultural complex celebrates the beloved deity's legend.

This village, which comprises a bell tower, drum tower, carved marble altar in the Tian-Hou Palace, a dressing hall, museum and shops will attract many A-Ma devotees and interested tourists.

> **Paragraph 7**

渔人码头
Fisherman's Wharf

The first ever-the med entertainment attraction in the tourism industry of

Macau, Macau Fisherman's Wharf is centrally located at Macao's outer harbour, 5-minute walk from the Macau Ferry Terminal and Heliport. The total investment of the project is anticipated to reach HKD 1.9 billion. The project occupies an area of over 93 000m², combining entertainment, retail, food, hotel, marina, convention and exhibition facilities in one place. Be it for business or pleasure, visitors will surely find a brand new experience in this world-class entertainment complex.

Paragraph 8

澳门塔 Macao Tower

Opened officially on 19th December 2001, the Macao Tower Convention & Entertainment Centre (MTCEC) comprises of a communications and observation Tower, a 4-level Convention & Entertainment Centre and a 2-level underground basement, as well as an Outdoor Plaza.

The Macao Tower Convention & Entertainment Centre is designed by CCMBeca that has begun construe.

Cultural Links 文化链接

澳门一日三节

农历四月初八在澳门是一个很重要的日子,既是佛教的浴佛节,又是道教的谭公诞,还是澳门本土的醉龙节。

浴佛节

浴佛节原是佛教的"释迦佛祖诞",是佛教中一个非常重要的庆典。根据习俗,在这一天澳门的佛教寺庙内都要举行"浴佛"活动,包括:僧人用五香水浴佛,作龙华会,象征弥勒降生。

谭公诞

谭公诞就是庆祝谭公诞辰的节日。据说谭公幼年时为一牧童,所以现在他显灵时会化身为小孩来为渔民降福。或预测天气,或治疗疾病。他是

用英语说中国——旅游亮点
Introduce China in English—Scenic Spots

继妈祖之后,深受渔民崇拜的另一位海上之神。每到他的诞期那天,路环的谭公庙前会举行声势浩大的庆祝活动,包括上演粤剧、集体巡游、舞醉龙等节目。

醉龙节

醉龙节在澳门是一个很重要的传统节日,只在很少的地方有庆祝活动,因为它是渔业行会的一个传统节日。

据传说,数百年前,香山县(今中山市)境内瘟疫横行,乡民苦不堪言。有一日乡民们路过一条河时,河中突然跃出一条巨蛇,乡民们合力斩杀了此蛇,蛇的血将河水都染红了。而乡民们在喝了河水后身体就康复了,瘟疫也消除了,于是大家认为巨蛇是龙的化身,便创出了舞醉龙节目以志纪念。

现在每到此日,澳门有些渔业人士会举行独特的醉龙醒狮大会庆祝。他们以舞醉龙方式到全澳各区巡游。这里的舞醉龙与中国内地盛行的方式很不同,醉龙只有头和尾,用坚实木料制成,没有龙身。巡游时由两名艺人分别执拿头尾舞动,同时他们一边舞龙,一边喝酒,舞步似醉非醉,十分有趣。

Vocabulary 妙词连珠

Chief Executive of Macao SAR 澳门特首	地殿大教堂
Macao pataca 澳门币	Monte Fortress 大炮台
the Macanese 澳门人	Macao City Museum 澳门博物馆
Macao Peniusula 澳门半岛	Barra Temple 妈阁庙
Macao Tourist Attractions 澳门观光	Lin Fong Temple 莲花庙
Ruins of St. Paul 大三巴牌坊	Maritime Museum 海事博物馆
Guia Lighthouse 东望洋灯塔	Wine Museum 葡萄酒博物馆
Chapel of Our Lady of Guia 圣母雪	Lisboa Casino 葡京赌场
	theory of game 博弈

港澳台地区
Hong Kong, Macao and Taiwan Province

Unit 3 台湾省 Taiwan Province

Key Sentences 流畅精句

1. Facing the Pacific, Taiwan is located in the southeast sea area of China with Taiwan Straits between Fujian and Taiwan.
   台湾省位于我国东南海域,东临太平洋,西隔台湾海峡与福建省相望。
2. Taiwan has been part of China since time immemorial.
   台湾自古以来就是中国的领土。
3. Standing east of Jiayi County and with Datashan the main peak, Mt. Ali is 2 663 meters above sea level.
   阿里山位于嘉义县以东,主峰大塔山,海拔2 663米。是台湾著名的天然森林公园和旅游胜地。
4. Taiwan has an area of 36 000 square kilometers.
   台湾面积3.6万平方公里。
5. The widest part from east to west in Taiwan is 144 kilometers.
   台湾从东到西最宽为144公里。
6. The longest from north to south in Taiwan is 394 kilometers.
   台湾从南到北最长为394公里。
7. The entire Chinese, including compatriots in Taiwan, all look forward to the early reunification of the motherland.
   全体中国人民,包括台湾同胞在内都盼望祖国统一。
8. The most popular ones are the Sun and Moon Lake, and Ali Mountains.
   最受人们欢迎的是日月潭和阿里山。
9. Sun and Moon Pool is the largest fresh water lake in Taiwan.
   日月潭是台湾最大的淡水湖。

10. Ali Mountains is a famous natural forest park and a summer resort as well.

   阿里山是著名的天然森林公园和旅游胜地。

11. Its four most beautiful sceneries are cloud seas, private tree, sun rising and cherry blossom.

   它有最美的四大景：云海、神木、日出和樱花。

Wonderful Paragraph
精彩片段

Paragraph 1

S日月潭
un and Moon Pool

Sun and Moon Lake is situated to the north of Mt. Yushan (Jade Mountain) and to the south of Mt. Nenggao, Nantou County in Taiwan province. It is due to the physical features of the lake near Guanghau Island that it is named Sun and Moon Lake. To the northeast of the island the lake resembles the round shape of the sun while to the southwest the lake resembles a crescent moon, hence the name, Sun and Moon Lake. The sun and moon portions of the lake are linked by an islet. Originally named Zhuzi, this islet was renamed "Guang Hua (brilliance) Islet" in celebration of recovering Taiwan after victory in the Japanese war.

Originally, Sun and Moon Lake was only a small natural lake. However, during the Japanese occupation a dam was built to raise the lake's water level and generate hydroelectric power. It is now the largest natural lake in Taiwan drawing water from the Juoshuei River, which has its source on Mt. Hehuan. With an elevation of 760 meters above sea level, the lake's perimeter is 35 kilometers, the depth of the water is 30 meters on average and the lake area is over 900 hectares.

港澳台地区
Hong Kong, Macao and Taiwan Province

> Paragraph 2

阿里山风景区
Ali Mountains Scenic Area

Located in the northeast part of the Jiayi County in Taiwan Province, Ali Mountain is in fact the general name of the eighteen hills including Zhu Hill and Tower Hill. The highest peak of Ali Mountain is Tower Hill with the height of 2 663 meters (about 8 736 feet). Ali Mountain is world famous for its five rare sites including the Sunrise, the Ali Mountain Forest Railway, the famous Alishan Sacred Tree, the Grand Sea of Clouds, and the Flamboyant Cherry Blossom. It is said that one who has not been to Ali Mountain will never know its wonderful beauty.

There is a Chinese Juniper within the Ali Mountain forest area, with some 53 meters (about 174 feet) high, and 23 meters (about 75 feet) wide. This Juniper is so huge that more than ten people can surround the circumference. It has a history of more than 3 000 years, thus is called Alishan Sacred Tree. The most wondrous tree is a three-generation tree. The three generations of this tree exist in the same trunk. Now since the first and second generations have faded, the third generation is still flourishing. This tree is really a wonder of nature. The forest sea on Ali Mountain creates a relaxed and pleasant environment for the people living in the city nearby.

The sea of clouds and the cherry blossom should not be overlooked. If you want to avoid sunstroke, the comfortable climate in midsummer on Ali Mountain will be a good choice.

> Paragraph 3

阳明山
Mt. Yangming

Located in the north of Taiwan, Mt. Yangming is the largest and most beautiful natural area in the province. It boasts of volcanic sights, natural valleys, waterfalls, hot springs, and a multitude of flower and plant varieties.

The mountain can be divided into two parts: the Front Mountain Park (also called Zhongzheng Gongyuan in Pinyin) and the Back Mountain Park (also called Yangming Gongyuan in Pinyin). In the Front Mountain Park, you can see the exquisitely designed bridges crossing limpid brooks, elegant pavilions standing on the low mountains, and various flowers blossoming along the trails. All of these sights form a simple and primitive world, which can completely relax your body and mind. The most famous waterfall here is called the Grass Mountain Waterfall, from which water flows all year round. In the northeast of the park, you can see an ancient architectural site. It is the Zhongshan Lou where Taiwan politicians often hold important activities.

Yangming Gongyuan is the most beautiful and important part of Mt. Yangming. It is encircled by several mountains, which include Mt. Seven Star, Mt. Gauze Hat, Mt. Bamboo Lake, Mt. Zhongzheng, and Mt. Datun. Mt. Datun is the main group of volcanoes that is famous for its amazing geography. On Mt. Seven Star, the hot springs spout with average temperatures ranging from 60°C (140°F) to 70°C (158°F). Bathing in the hot springs will help to cure diseases like neuralgia, anemia, and diabetes. The famous Flower Season, symbolized by the Flower Clock, is also held here. There are more sights to see in the park, such as the sparkling Xiaoyin Pool, the well-rounded Seven Color Fountain, the magnificent Guangfu Lou, and various waterfalls.

Due to the warm and humid climate and the volcanic geography, the mountain is rich in animal, insect, and plant species. There are 1 224 kinds of plants, among which cress, metasequoia, and gingko are considered as very precious rare plants. For the insects, the most famous is the butterfly. There are about 133 different kinds of butterflies, which make Mt. Yangming one of the best places to see them.

港澳台地区
Hong Kong, Macao and Taiwan Province

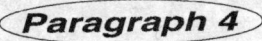
Paragraph 4

J玉山ade Mountain

In the center of Taiwan Island, Jade Mountain extends to the west of the Central Mountain. It runs approximately north-south for about 280 km (about 174 miles). Most peaks of Jade Mountain are over 2 000 meters (about 6 500 feet) high, so Jade Mountain has gained the name "Roof of Taiwan". In 1985, Jade Mountain National Park, which has Jade Mountain at the center, was opened to the public.

Jade Mountain consists of 11 peaks, including Jade Peak, South Peak, North Peak, and East Peak.

Jade Peak is the main peak of Jade Mountain. With an elevation of nearly 4 000 meters (about 13 000 feet), it is not only the highest peak in Taiwan, but also the highest one in eastern China. In the winter, Jade Peak is often capped with thick snow which makes the entire peak shine like stainless jade, hence its name. At the top of Jade Peak, one can overlook the Taiwan Strait and the Pacific Ocean. Owing to its height and steepness, Jade Peak is recognized as the most prominent of Taiwan's Ten Peaks.

One can climb the mountain on foot or drive a car to enjoy the landscape along the road. Any season of the year is fine to visit the mountain except at some times in the winter when roads are covered by snow. At this time it is too treacherous for climbers or cars.

One should also be well equipped before the climbing. Prepare clothes to resist the cold on top of the mountain and take medicine for mountain sickness. If one has any intention of rock climbing, ropes and hooks must be prepared. If it is possible, climbing with an experienced guide is a better choice. Before climbing the mountain, one must apply for permission. Make your visit an environmentally friendly one too.

Introduce China in English—Scenic Spots

Paragraph 5

神木 Mysterious Tree

Situated in eastern side of the Mysterious Tree Terminal, the red Chinese juniper is 53 metres high; the upper girth of the tree is 23 metres in perimeter. Legend relates that the tree was planted When Duke Zhou acted as a regent, it was called "Duke Zhou Juniper", and reputed as the mysterious tree in Ali Mountain. When tourists visit the Ali Mountains without seeing the tree with his or her own eyes, it is not a worthwhile trip for tourists to the mountains. On the left side of the tree is a pavilion. In the south-eastern side of the tree there is a "Guangwu Juniper（光武桧）", which was planted during the reign of Emperor Han Guangwu (Liu Xiu, 6 BC-AD 57, reigned AD 25-57), more than 1 900 years old. Beside there is a "giant sleepless night mysterious tree 眠目大神木". It is estimated that the tree has a history of over 4 000 years old and acclaimed as the "King of the Tress" in Taiwan (台湾树王).

Paragraph 6

台湾故宫博物院 Taiwan Palace Museum

The Taipei Palace Museum is located in the northwestern part of Taipei City, facing Shuangxi Park and surrounded by verdant trees and rolling hills. The palace was constructed as a replica of the Beijing Palace Museum. It has an area of more than 10 000 square meters and is grand and imposing in character. Approximately some 620 000 historical items and works of art are stored here, in a magnificent four-storied building. The construction of the Taipei Palace Museum was begun in 1962 and completed in the summer of 1965. Some 240 000 of the items that are kept here originally belonged to the Beijing Palace Museum.

A large number of calligraphies and paintings by famous painters are exhibited in the Taipei Palace Museum. The Taipei Palace Museum also contains a number of famous items of the scholar's studio. Among these the most representative is the inkstone of the Song-dynasty Su Dongpo (1037-1101), the northern Song calligrapher and literati figure, also the inkstone of Zhao Mengfu (1254-1322), the famous Yuan-dynasty calligrapher.

The permanent display of the Taipei Palace Museum contains twenty thousand objects. These are rotated once every three months. Every ten years is a full cycle, so that even rare objects can be exhibited and seen by everyone.

Cultural Links 文化链接

台湾乌龙茶的传说

据说台湾乌龙茶是一位叫林凤池的台湾人从福建武夷山把茶苗带到台湾种植而发展起来的。林凤池祖籍福建,是一个有志气的青年。一年,他听说福建要举行科举考试,一心想去参加,可是家穷没路费,怎能去呢?乡亲们得知此事后,都纷纷捐助给林凤池凑路费。临行时,乡亲们对他说:"你到了福建,可要向咱祖家的乡亲们问好呀,说咱们台湾乡亲十分怀念他们。"还交代说:"考上了,以后要再来台湾,别忘了这是你的出生故里呵。"林凤池学问好,考中了举人,住了几年后,决定要回台湾探亲,临行前考虑带什么礼物呢?觉得福建武夷山的乌龙茶有名,就要了36颗乌龙茶苗带回台湾,种在了南投县鹿谷乡的冻顶山上。经过乡亲们的精心培育繁殖,建成了一片茶园,采制的台湾乌龙茶清香可口。后来林凤池奉旨晋京,他把这种台湾乌龙茶献给了道光皇帝,皇帝饮后称赞说:"好茶,好茶。"问是什么地方的茶,林凤池说是福建茶种移至台湾冻顶山采制的。道光皇帝说:"好吧,这茶就叫冻顶茶。"从此台湾乌龙茶也叫"冻顶茶"。

用英语说中国——旅游亮点
Introduce China in English—Scenic Spots

Vocabulary
妙词连珠

Ludao Island 绿岛
Diaoyu Island 钓鱼岛
Lanyu Island 兰屿
Pengjia Island 彭佳屿
Chiwei Island 赤尾屿
Kinmen Island 金门岛
Mt. Ali; Ali Mountains 阿里山
The World of the Moon 月世界
Yehliu Cape 野柳岬
Peitou Ht Spring 地热谷

Penghu Bay 澎湖湾
Fishing Lamps around Penghu Islands 澎湖渔火
Confucius Temples at Taipei and Tainan 台北与台南孔庙
to originate 起源于
icons 偶像
flower 开花
permeate 渗透
aroma 芳香,香味;韵味

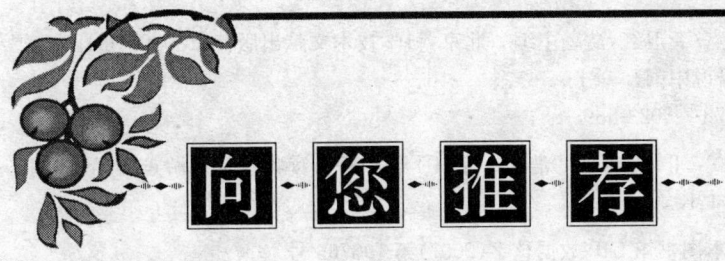

教 辅 书

一语多译英语——魅力英语	12.00
时尚旅游英语——魅力英语	12.00
婚恋情感英语——魅力英语	12.00
诙谐调侃英语——魅力英语	12.00
成功励志英语——魅力英语	12.00
谜语绕口令英语——魅力英语	12.00
箴言贺语英语——魅力英语	12.00
幽默趣味英语——魅力英语	12.00

注：邮费按书款总价另加 20%

> **图书在版编目(CIP)数据**
>
> 旅游亮点/龚卫红,浩瀚主编.-北京:科学技术文献出版社,2008.8(重印)
> (用英语说中国)
> ISBN 978-7-5023-5893-8
>
> Ⅰ.旅… Ⅱ.①龚…②浩… Ⅲ.①英语-语言读物 ②旅游点-简介-中国 Ⅳ.H319.4:K
>
> 中国版本图书馆 CIP 数据核字(2007)第 193765 号

出　版　者	科学技术文献出版社
地　　　址	北京市复兴路 15 号(中央电视台西侧)/100038
图书编务部电话	(010)51501739
图书发行部电话	(010)51501720,(010)51501722(传真)
邮购部电话	(010)51501729
网　　　址	http://www.stdph.com
E-mail:stdph@istic.ac.cn	
策　划　编　辑	李　洁　崔　岩
责　任　编　辑	崔　岩
责　任　校　对	赵文珍
责　任　出　版	王杰馨
发　行　者	科学技术文献出版社发行　全国各地新华书店经销
印　刷　者	富华印刷包装有限公司
版(印)次	2008 年 8 月第 1 版第 2 次印刷
开　　　本	880×1230　32 开
字　　　数	266 千
印　　　张	9.25
印　　　数	8001～11000 册
定　　　价	14.00 元

Ⓒ 版权所有　违法必究

购买本社图书,凡字迹不清、缺页、倒页、脱页者,本社发行部负责调换。

Road junctions (*cont.*)
  crossroads, 34–35
  delineation and marking, 38
  hazards at roundabouts, 37
  junction layout for dual carriageways, 35
  junction layout for single carriageways, 36
  overturning of articulated vehicles, 37
  principles of junction layout, 34–35
  roundabouts, 37
  splay junctions, 33
  T-junction layout, 33–34
  traffic signs and signals, 39
Road surfaces
  hazards built into surfaces, 43
  lighting, influence of, 44, 57
  macro- and micro-structure of surfaces in relation to skidding, 39
  reflectorisation, 38
  restoring skid resistance, 42
  skidding, characteristics of skid resistant surfaces, 39
  skidding coefficients and speed, 40
  skidding coefficients required for different road conditions, 41
  skidding, general, *see* Skidding
  skidding on dry roads, 39
  spray, 42
  surfaces of shoulders, verges, and central reservations, 43
  texture measurements, 42
  texture requirements for skid resistance on wet high speed roads, 42

Safety cars, 130
Safety measures, applied to whole areas of towns
  distribution of accidents in towns, 50
  remedial measures away from central areas of towns, 50
Skidding
  changes of surface with traffic and time, 66, 68
  coefficients of friction on dry roads, 61
  coefficients of friction on ice and snow, 70
  coefficients of friction on wet roads, 63
  commercial vehicle tyres on dry roads, 81
  commercial vehicle tyres on wet roads, 65, 67
  deceptive appearance of open textured surfaces, 39
  decrease of skidding coefficient on wet roads with speed, 63
  interaction between factors affecting skidding coefficients on wet roads, 65
  peak and sliding coefficients of friction, 64
  seasonal variation of skidding coefficients, 68
  skidding coefficients at high speeds on wet roads, 63
  stone shape, 39, 65
  surface texture and tyre tread material, 65

Skidding (*cont.*)
  surface texture required for high-speed traffic, 63
  texture of road surface and skidding, 39, 65
  test machines for measuring skid resistance, 69
  treating slippery road surfaces, 42
  tyre tread material, 65
  tyre tread pattern, 65
  water depth and skidding, 66
  wear of tyres, 66
Speed control measures
  engineering methods of controlling speeds, 49
  international study of speed limits, 49
  linked traffic signals, 49
  road humps, 50
  speed limits and accidents in Great Britain, 49
  speeds on British roads, 49
  yellow bars on the road, 50
Stability and control of vehicles
  braking distances for cars, motor cycles and commercial vehicles, 70
  general vehicle characteristics and steering behaviour, 60
  inflation pressures, 60
  load, 60
  oversteer, 60
  skidding coefficients, *see* Skidding
  tyre characteristics, 60
  tyre road adhesion, *see* Skidding
  understeer, 60

Visibility from vehicles
  Anglo-American headlamps, 54
  brightness of road surfaces, 57
  characteristics of headlights, 53
  collisions with parked vehicles on rural roads, 48, 59
  colour of car, 53
  colour of light, 54
  concertina type fog accidents, 58
  Continental headlamps, 54
  dim-dip system of lighting, 57
  driver's view from cars, 52
  driver's view from commercial vehicles, 52
  fog and fog lamps, 57
  headlights in street lighting, 57
  light distributions of headlamps, 54
  mirrors, 52
  reduced visibility and accidents, 57
  reflectors on cycles, 59
  seeing and perceiving, 59
  seeing distances with dipped headlamps and opposing glare, 54, 56
  seeing distances with full headlamps and no opposing glare, 54
  sources of danger in thick fog, 59
  street lighting, seeing in street lighting, 57
  visibility problems for cyclists and motorcyclists, 59